I0006092

Concord Edition

THE COMPLETE WORKS OF
RALPH WALDO EMERSON

WITH A BIOGRAPHICAL INTRODUCTION AND NOTES BY

EDWARD WALDO EMERSON AND A GENERAL INDEX

ILLUSTRATED WITH PHOTOGRAVURES

VOLUME III

1859.

Ralph Waldo Emerson in 1859

ESSAYS

BY

RALPH WALDO EMERSON

SECOND SERIES

ORD LIBRA

BOSTON AND NEW YORK
HOUGHTON, MIFFLIN AND COMPANY
The Riverside Press, Cambridge
1904
Sc

COPYRIGHT, 1876
BY RALPH WALDO EMERSON
COPYRIGHT, 1883 AND 1903, BY EDWARD W. EMERSON
ALL RIGHTS RESERVED

448379

CONTENTS

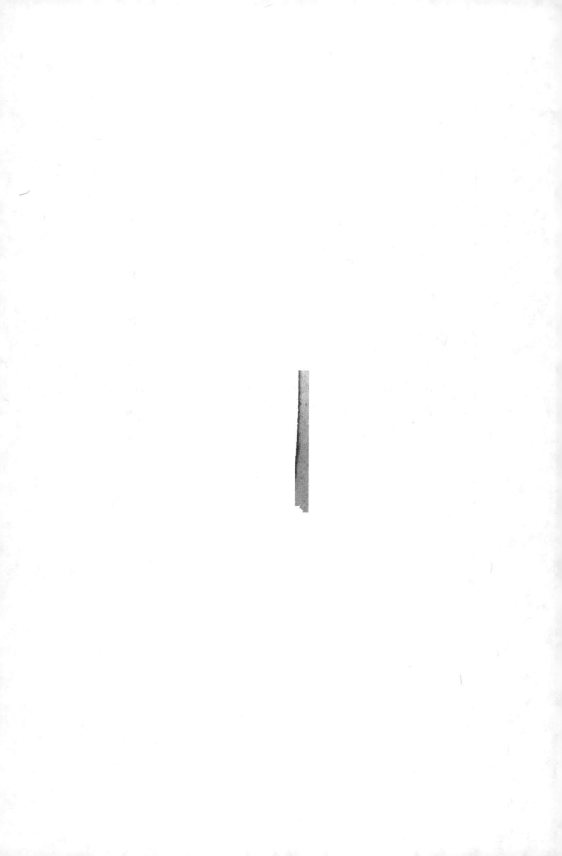

LIST OF ILLUSTRATIONS

I

THE POET

A MOODY child and wildly wise
Pursued the game with joyful eyes,
Which chose, like meteors, their way,
And rived the dark with private ray:
They overleapt the horizon's edge,
Searched with Apollo's privilege;
Through man, and woman, and sea, and star
Saw the dance of nature forward far;
Through worlds, and races, and terms, and times
Saw musical order, and pairing rhymes.

Olympian bards who sung
　　Divine ideas below,
Which always find us young,
　　And always keep us so.

THE POET

THOSE who are esteemed umpires of taste are often persons who have acquired some knowledge of admired pictures or sculptures, and have an inclination for whatever is elegant; but if you inquire whether they are beautiful souls, and whether their own acts are like fair pictures, you learn that they are selfish and sensual. Their cultivation is local, as if you should rub a log of dry wood in one spot to produce fire, all the rest remaining cold. Their knowledge of the fine arts is some study of rules and particulars, or some limited judgment of color or form, which is exercised for amusement or for show. It is a proof of the shallowness of the doctrine of beauty as it lies in the minds of our amateurs, that men seem to have lost the perception of the instant dependence of form upon soul. There is no doctrine of forms in our philosophy. We were put into our bodies, as fire is put into a pan to be carried about; but there is no accurate adjustment between the spirit and the organ, much less is the latter the germination of the former. So in regard to other forms, the intellectual men do not believe in

any essential dependence of the material world
on thought and volition. Theologians think it
a pretty air-castle to talk of the spiritual meaning of a ship or a cloud, of a city or a contract,
but they prefer to come again to the solid ground
of historical evidence ; and even the poets are
contented with a civil and conformed manner of
living, and to write poems from the fancy, at a
safe distance from their own experience.[1] But
the highest minds of the world have never
ceased to explore the double meaning, or shall
I say the quadruple or the centuple or much
more manifold meaning, of every sensuous fact;[2]
Orpheus, Empedocles, Heraclitus, Plato, Plutarch, Dante, Swedenborg, and the masters of
sculpture, picture and poetry. For we are not
pans and barrows, nor even porters of the fire
and torch-bearers, but children of the fire, made
of it, and only the same divinity transmuted
and at two or three removes, when we know
least about it.[3] And this hidden truth, that the
fountains whence all this river of Time and its
creatures floweth are intrinsically ideal and beautiful, draws us to the consideration of the nature
and functions of the Poet, or the man of Beauty ;
to the means and materials he uses, and to the
general aspect of the art in the present time.

The breadth of the problem is great, for the poet is representative. He stands among partial men for the complete man, and apprises us not of his wealth, but of the common wealth. The young man reveres men of genius, because, to speak truly, they are more\himself than he is. They receive of the soul as he also receives, but they more. Nature enhances her beauty, to the eye of loving men, from their belief that the poet is beholding her shows at the same time. He is isolated among his contemporaries by truth and by his art, but with this consolation in his pursuits, that they will draw all men sooner or later. For all men live by truth and stand in need of expression. In love, in art, in avarice, in politics, in labor, in games, we study to utter our painful secret. The man is only half himself, the other half is his expression.

Notwithstanding this necessity to be published, adequate expression is rare. I know not how it is that we need an interpreter, but the great majority of men seem to be minors, who have not yet come into possession of their own, or mutes, who cannot report the conversation they have had with nature. There is no man who does not anticipate a supersensual utility in the sun and stars, earth and water. These

stand and wait to render him a peculiar service.
But there is some obstruction or some excess
of phlegm in our constitution, which does not
suffer them to yield the due effect. Too feeble
fall the impressions of nature on us to make
us artists. Every touch should thrill.' Every
man should be so much an artist that he could
report in conversation what had befallen him.
Yet, in our experience, the rays or appulses have
sufficient force to arrive at the senses, but not
enough to reach the quick and compel the re-
production of themselves in speech. The poet
is the person in whom these powers are in balance,² the man without impediment, who sees
and handles that which others dream of, trav-
erses the whole scale of experience, and is representative of man, in virtue of being the largest
power to receive and to impart.

For the Universe has three children, born
at one time, which reappear under different
names in every system of thought, whether they
be called cause, operation and effect; or, more
poetically, Jove, Pluto, Neptune; or, theologi-
cally, the Father, the Spirit and the Son; but
which we will call here the Knower, the Doer
and the Sayer. These stand respectively for the
love of truth, for the love of good, and for

the love of beauty. These three are equal. Each is that which he is, essentially, so that he cannot be surmounted or analyzed, and each of these three has the power of the others latent in him and his own, patent.[1]

The poet is the sayer, the namer, and represents beauty. He is a sovereign, and stands on the centre. For the world is not painted or adorned, but is from the beginning beautiful; and God has not made some beautiful things, but Beauty is the creator of the universe. Therefore, the poet is not any permissive potentate, but is emperor in his own right.[2] Criticism is infested with a cant of materialism, which assumes that manual skill and activity is the first merit of all men, and disparages such as say and do not, overlooking the fact that some men, namely poets, are natural sayers, sent into the world to the end of expression, and confounds them with those whose province is action but who quit it to imitate the sayers. But Homer's words are as costly and admirable to Homer as Agamemnon's victories are to Agamemnon. The poet does not wait for the hero or the sage, but, as they act and think primarily, so he writes primarily what will and must be spoken, reckoning the others, though primaries also, yet, in respect to him, secondaries and servants ; as sitters or models in the studio of a painter, or as assistants who bring building-materials to an architect.

For poetry was all written before time was, and whenever we are so finely organized that we can penetrate into that region where the air is music,[1] we hear those primal warblings and attempt to write them down, but we lose ever and anon a word or a verse and substitute something of our own, and thus miswrite the poem.[2] The men of more delicate ear write down these cadences more faithfully, and these transcripts, though imperfect, become the songs of the nations. For nature is as truly beautiful as it is good, or as it is reasonable, and must as much appear as it must be done, or be known. Words and deeds are quite indifferent modes of the divine energy. Words are also actions, and actions are a kind of words.

The sign and credentials of the poet are that he announces that which no man foretold. He is the true and only doctor; he knows and tells; he is the only teller of news, for he was present and privy to the appearance which he describes. He is a beholder of ideas and an utterer of the necessary and causal. For we do not speak now of men of poetical talents, or of industry and skill in metre, but of the true poet. I took part in a conversation the other day concerning a recent writer of lyrics, a man of subtle mind, whose head appeared to be a music-box of delicate tunes and rhythms, and whose skill and command of language we could not sufficiently praise. But when the question arose whether he was not only a lyrist but a poet, we were obliged to confess that he is plainly a contemporary, not an eternal man.', He does not stand out of our low limitations, like a Chimborazo under the line, running up from a torrid base through all the climates of the globe, with belts of the herbage of every latitude on its high and mottled sides ; but this genius is the landscape-garden of a modern house, adorned with fountains and statues, with well-bred men and women standing and sitting in the walks and terraces. We hear, through all the varied music, the groundtone of conventional life. Our poets are men of talents who sing, and not the children of music. The argument is secondary, the finish of the verses is primary.

For it is not metres, but a metre-making argument that makes a poem, — a thought so passionate and alive that like the spirit of a plant or an animal it has an architecture of its own, and adorns nature with a new thing. The thought and the form are equal in the order of time, but in the order of genesis the thought is prior to the form.[1] The poet has a new thought; he has a whole new experience to unfold; he will tell us how it was with him, and all men will be the richer in his fortune. For the experience of each new age requires a new confession, and the world seems always waiting for its poet. I remember when I was young how much I was moved one morning by tidings that genius had appeared in a youth who sat near me at table. He had left his work and gone rambling none knew whither, and had written hundreds of lines, but could not tell whether that which was in him was therein told; he could tell nothing but that all was changed, — man, beast, heaven, earth and sea. How gladly we listened! how credulous! Society seemed to be compromised. We sat in the aurora of a sunrise which was to put out all the stars. Boston seemed to be at twice the distance it had the night before, or was much farther than that. Rome, — what was Rome? Plutarch and Shakspeare were in the yellow leaf, and Homer no more should be heard of. It is much to know that poetry has been written this

very day, under this very roof, by your side.
What! that wonderful spirit has not expired!
These stony moments are still sparkling and
animated! I had fancied that the oracles were
all silent, and nature had spent her fires; and
behold! all night, from every pore, these fine
auroras have been streaming. Every one has
some interest in the advent of the poet, and no
one knows how much it may concern him. We
know that the secret of the world is profound,
but who or what shall be our interpreter, we
know not. A mountain ramble, a new style of
face, a new person, may put the key into our
hands. Of course the value of genius to us is
in the veracity of its report. Talent may frolic
and juggle; genius realizes and adds. Mankind
in good earnest have availed so far in understanding themselves and their work, that the
foremost watchman on the peak announces his
news. It is the truest word ever spoken, and
the phrase will be the fittest, most musical, and
the unerring voice of the world for that time.

All that we call sacred history attests that the
birth of a poet is the principal event in chrono-
logy.[1] Man, never so often deceived, still watches
for the arrival of a brother who can hold him
steady to a truth until he has made it his own.

With what joy I begin to read a poem which **I**
confide in as an inspiration! And now my chains
are to be broken ; I shall mount above these
clouds and opaque airs in which I live, — opaque,
though they seem transparent, — and from the
heaven of truth I shall see and comprehend
my relations. That will reconcile me to life and
renovate nature, to see trifles animated by a
tendency, and to know what I am doing. Life
will no more be a noise ; now I shall see men
and women, and know the signs by which they
may be discerned from fools and satans. This
day shall be better than my birthday : then I
became an animal; now I am invited into the
science of the real. Such is the hope, but the
fruition is postponed. Oftener it falls that this
winged man, who will carry me into the heaven,
whirls me into mists, then leaps and frisks about
with me as it were from cloud to cloud, still
affirming that he is bound heavenward ; and I,
being myself a novice, am slow in perceiving
that he does not know the way into the heavens,
and is merely bent that I should admire his
skill to rise like a fowl or a flying fish, a little
way from the ground or the water ; but the all-
piercing, all-feeding and ocular air of heaven
that man shall never inhabit. I tumble down

again soon into my old nooks, and lead the life
of exaggerations as before, and have lost my
faith in the possibility of any guide who can lead
me thither where I would be.

But, leaving these victims of vanity, let us,
with new hope, observe how nature, by worthier
impulses, has insured the poet's fidelity to his
office of announcement and affirming, namely
by the beauty of things, which becomes a new
and higher beauty when expressed. Nature
offers all her creatures to him as a picture-lan-
guage. Being used as a type, a second wonderful value appears in the object, far better than
its old value ; as the carpenter's stretched cord,
if you hold your ear close enough, is musical in
the breeze. " Things more excellent than every
image," says Jamblichus, "are expressed through
images." Things admit of being used as symbols because nature is a symbol, in the whole,
and in every part. Every line we can draw in
the sand has expression ; and there is no body
without its spirit or genius. All form is an effect
of character ; all condition, of the quality of the
life ; all harmony, of health ; and for this reason a perception of beauty should be sympathetic, or proper only to the good. The beautiful rests on the foundations of the necessary.

The soul makes the body, as the wise **Spenser** teaches : —

> " So every spirit, as it is more pure,
>   And hath in it the more of heavenly light,
>   So it the fairer body doth procure
>   To habit in, and it more fairly dight,
>   With cheerful grace and amiable sight.
>   For, of the soul, the body form doth take,
>   For soul is form, and doth the body make." [1]

Here we find ourselves suddenly not in a critical speculation but in a holy place, and should go very warily and reverently. We stand before the secret of the world, there where Being passes into Appearance and Unity into Variety.

The Universe is the externization of the soul. Wherever the life is, that bursts into appearance around it. Our science is sensual, and therefore superficial. The earth and the heavenly bodies, physics and chemistry, we sensually treat, as if they were self-existent ; but these are the retinue of that Being we have. " The mighty heaven," said Proclus,[2] " exhibits, in its transfigurations, clear images of the splendor of intellectual perceptions ; being moved in conjunction with the unapparent periods of intellectual natures." Therefore science always goes abreast with the just elevation of the man, keeping step with religion and metaphysics ; or the state of science is an index of our self-knowledge. Since every thing in nature answers to a moral power, if any phenomenon remains brute and dark it is because the corresponding faculty in the observer is not yet active.

No wonder then, if these waters be so deep, that we hover over them with a religious regard. The beauty of the fable proves the importance of the sense ; to the poet, and to all others ; or, if you please, every man is so far a poet as to be susceptible of these enchantments of nature ; for all men have the thoughts whereof the universe is the celebration. I find that the fascination resides in the symbol. Who loves nature? Who does not? Is it only poets, and men of leisure and cultivation, who live with her? No ; but also hunters, farmers, grooms and butchers, though they express their affection in their choice of life and not in their choice of words. The writer wonders what the coachman or the hunter values in riding, in horses and dogs. It is not superficial qualities. When you talk with him he holds these at as slight a rate as you. His worship is sympathetic ; he has no definitions, but he is commanded in nature by the living power which he feels to be there present.

No imitation or playing of these things **would** content him; he loves the earnest of the **north** wind, of rain, of stone and wood and iron.[1] **A** beauty not explicable is dearer than a beauty which we can see to the end of. It is nature the symbol, nature certifying the supernatural, body overflowed by life which he worships with coarse but sincere rites.

The inwardness and mystery of this attachment drive men of every class to the use of emblems. The schools of poets and philosophers are not more intoxicated with their symbols than the populace with theirs. In our political parties, compute the power of badges and emblems. See the great ball which they roll from Baltimore to Bunker Hill![2] In the political processions, Lowell goes in a loom, and Lynn in a shoe, and Salem in a ship. Witness the cider-barrel, the log-cabin, the hickory-stick, the palmetto, and all the cognizances of party. See the power of national emblems. Some stars, lilies, leopards, a crescent, a lion, an eagle, or other figure which came into credit God knows how, on an old rag of bunting, blowing in the wind on a fort at the ends of the earth, shall make the blood tingle under the rudest or the most conventional exterior. The people fancy they hate poetry, and they are all poets and mystics!

Beyond this universality of the symbolic language, we are apprised of the divineness of this superior use of things, whereby the world is a temple whose walls are covered with emblems, pictures and commandments of the Deity, — in this, that there is no fact in nature which does not carry the whole sense of nature; and the distinctions which we make in events and in affairs, of low and high, honest and base, disappear when nature is used as a symbol. Thought makes everything fit for use. The vocabulary of an omniscient man would embrace words and images excluded from polite conversation. What would be base, or even obscene, to the obscene, becomes illustrious, spoken in a new connection of thought. The piety of the Hebrew prophets purges their grossness. The circumcision is an example of the power of poetry to raise the low and offensive. Small and mean things serve as well as great symbols. The meaner the type by which a law is expressed, the more pungent it is, and the more lasting in the memories of men; just as we choose the smallest box or case in which any needful utensil can be carried. Bare lists of words are found

suggestive to an imaginative and excited mind ;
as it is related of Lord Chatham that he was
accustomed to read in Bailey's Dictionary when
he was preparing to speak in Parliament. The
poorest experience is rich enough for all the
purposes of expressing thought. Why covet a
knowledge of new facts ? Day and night, house
and garden, a few books, a few actions, serve us
as well as would all trades and all spectacles.
We are far from having exhausted the significance of the few symbols we use. We can
come to use them yet with a terrible simplicity.
It does not need that a poem should be long.
Every word was once a poem. Every new relation is a new word. Also we use defects and de-
formities to a sacred purpose, so expressing our
sense that the evils of the world are such only
to the evil eye.¹ In the old mythology, mytho-
logists observe, defects are ascribed to divine
natures, as lameness to Vulcan, blindness to
Cupid, and the like, — to signify exuberances.

For as it is dislocation and detachment from
the life of God that makes things ugly, the poet,
who re-attaches things to nature and the Whole,
— re-attaching even artificial things and viola-
tion of nature, to nature, by a deeper insight,—
disposes very easily of the most disagreeable

facts. Readers of poetry see the factory-village and the railway, and fancy that the poetry of the landscape is broken up by these; for these works of art are not yet consecrated in their reading; but the poet sees them fall within the great Order not less than the beehive or the spider's geometrical web. Nature adopts them very fast into her vital circles, and the gliding train of cars she loves like her own.[1] Besides, in a centred mind, it signifies nothing how many mechanical inventions you exhibit. Though you add millions, and never so surprising, the fact of mechanics has not gained a grain's weight. The spiritual fact remains unalterable, by many or by few particulars; as no mountain is of any appreciable height to break the curve of the sphere. A shrewd country-boy goes to the city for the first time, and the complacent citizen is not satisfied with his little wonder. It is not that he does not see all the fine houses and know that he never saw such before, but he disposes of them as easily as the poet finds place for the railway. The chief value of the new fact is to enhance the great and constant fact of Life, which can dwarf any and every circumstance, and to which the belt of wampum and the commerce of America are alike.

The world being thus put under the mind for verb and noun, the poet is he who can articulate it. For though life is great, and fascinates and absorbs ; and though all men are intelligent of the symbols through which it is named ; yet they cannot originally use them. We are symbols and inhabit symbols ; workmen, work, and tools, words and things, birth and death, all are emblems ; but we sympathize with the symbols, and being infatuated with the economical uses of things, we do not know that they are thoughts. The poet, by an ulterior intellectual perception, gives them a power which makes their old use forgotten, and puts eyes and a tongue into every dumb and inanimate object. He perceives the independence of the thought on the symbol, the stability of the thought, the accidency and fugacity of the symbol. As the eyes of Lyncæus were said to see through the earth, so the poet turns the world to glass, and shows us all things in their right series and procession. For through that better perception he stands one step nearer to things, and sees the flowing or metamorphosis ; perceives that thought is multiform ; that within the form of every creature is a force impelling it to ascend into a higher form ; and following with his eyes the life, uses the forms

which express that life, and so his speech flows
with the flowing of nature. All the facts of the
animal economy, sex, nutriment, gestation, birth,
growth, are symbols of the passage of the world
into the soul of man, to suffer there a change
and reappear a new and higher fact. He uses
forms according to the life, and not according
to the form. This is true science. The poet
alone knows astronomy, chemistry, vegetation
and animation, for he does not stop at these
facts, but employs them as signs. He knows
why the plain or meadow of space was strown
with these flowers we call suns and moons and
stars; why the great deep is adorned with animals, with men, and gods; for in every word
he speaks he rides on them as the horses of
thought.[1]

By virtue of this science the poet is the Namer
or Language-maker, naming things sometimes
after their appearance, sometimes after their essence, and giving to every one its own name
and not another's, thereby rejoicing the intellect,
which delights in detachment or boundary. The
poets made all the words, and therefore language
is the archives of history, and, if we must say it,
a sort of tomb of the muses. For though the
origin of most of our words is forgotten, each

word was at first a stroke of genius, and **obtained**
currency because for the moment it **symbolized**
the world to the first speaker and to the **hearer.**[1]
The etymologist finds the deadest word **to have**
been once a brilliant picture. Language is **fos-**
sil poetry. As the limestone of the **continent**
consists of infinite masses of the shells **of ani-**
malcules, so language is made up of **images or**
tropes, which now, in their secondary use, **have**
long ceased to remind us of their poetic **origin.**
But the poet names the thing because he sees
it, or comes one step nearer to it than any other.
This expression or naming is not art, but a
second nature, grown out of the first, as a leaf
out of a tree. What we call nature is a certain
self-regulated motion or change ;[2] and nature
does all things by her own hands, and does not
leave another to baptize her but baptizes herself ; and this through the metamorphosis again.
I remember that a certain poet described it to
me thus : —

Genius is the activity which repairs the decays
of things, whether wholly or partly of a material
and finite kind. Nature, through all her kingdoms, insures herself. Nobody cares for planting the poor fungus ; so she shakes down from

the gills of one agaric countless spores, any one
of which, being preserved, transmits new bil-
lions of spores to-morrow or next day. The
new agaric of this hour has a chance which the
old one had not. This atom of seed is thrown
into a new place, not subject to the accidents
which destroyed its parent two rods off. She
makes a man; and having brought him to ripe
age, she will no longer run the risk of losing
this wonder at a blow, but she detaches from
him a new self, that the kind may be safe from
accidents to which the individual is exposed. So
when the soul of the poet has come to ripeness
of thought, she detaches and sends away from
it its poems or songs, — a fearless, sleepless,
deathless progeny, which is not exposed to the
accidents of the weary kingdom of time; a fearless, vivacious offspring, clad with wings (such
was the virtue of the soul out of which they
came) which carry them fast and far, and infix
them irrecoverably into the hearts of men.[1]
These wings are the beauty of the poet's soul.
The songs, thus flying immortal from their mortal parent, are pursued by clamorous flights of
censures, which swarm in far greater numbers
and threaten to devour them; but these last are
not winged. At the end of a very short leap

they fall plump down and rot, having **received**
from the souls out of which they came no **beauti-**
ful wings. But the melodies of the poet **ascend**
and leap and pierce into the deeps of infinite **time**.

So far the bard taught me, using his freer
speech. But nature has a higher end, in the
production of new individuals, than security,
namely *ascension, or the passage of the soul into
higher forms*. I knew in my younger days the
sculptor who made the statue of the youth which
stands in the public garden. He was, as I remember, unable to tell directly what made him
happy or unhappy, but by wonderful indirections
he could tell. He rose one day, according to
his habit, before the dawn, and saw the morning
break, grand as the eternity out of which it came,
and for many days after, he strove to express
this tranquillity, and lo! his chisel had fashioned
out of marble the form of a beautiful youth,
Phosphorus, whose aspect is such that it is said
all persons who look on it become silent.[1] The
poet also resigns himself to his mood, and that
thought which agitated him is expressed, but
alter idem, in a manner totally new. The expression is organic, or the new type which things
themselves take when liberated. As, in the

sun, objects paint their images on the retina of
the eye, so they, sharing the aspiration of the
whole universe, tend to paint a far more delicate copy of their essence in his mind. Like
the metamorphosis of things into higher organic forms is their change into melodies. Over
everything stands its dæmon or soul, and, as
the form of the thing is reflected by the eye,
so the soul of the thing is reflected by a melody.
The sea, the mountain-ridge, Niagara, and every
flower-bed, pre-exist, or super-exist, in pre-can-
tations, which sail like odors in the air, and
when any man goes by with an ear sufficiently
fine, he overhears them and endeavors to write
down the notes without diluting or depraving
them.¹ And herein is the legitimation of criticism, in the mind's faith that the poems are a
corrupt version of some text in nature with
which they ought to be made to tally. A rhyme
in one of our sonnets should not be less pleasing than the iterated nodes of a seashell, or the
resembling difference of a group of flowers. The
pairing of the birds is an idyl, not tedious as
our idyls are ; a tempest is a rough ode, without falsehood or rant·; a summer, with its harvest sown, reaped and stored, is an epic song,
subordinating how many admirably executed

parts. Why should not the symmetry and **truth**
that modulate these, glide into our spirits, **and**
we participate the invention of nature ?

This insight, which expresses itself by **what**
is called Imagination, is a very high sort of seeing, which does not come by study, but by the
intellect being where and what it sees; by sharing the path or circuit of things through forms,
and so making them translucid to others.[1] The
path of things is silent. Will they suffer a
speaker to go with them? A spy they will not
suffer; a lover, a poet, is the transcendency of
their own nature, — him they will suffer. The
condition of true naming, on the poet's part, is
his resigning himself to the divine *aura* which
breathes through forms, and accompanying that.

It is a secret which every intellectual man
quickly learns, that beyond the energy of his
possessed and conscious intellect he is capable
of a new energy (as of an intellect doubled on
itself), by abandonment to the nature of things;
that beside his privacy of power as an individual
man, there is a great public power on which he
can draw, by unlocking, at all risks, his human
doors, and suffering the ethereal tides to roll and
circulate through him; then he is caught up into
the life of the Universe, his speech is thunder,

his thought is law, and his words are universally intelligible as the plants and animals. The poet knows that he speaks adequately then only when he speaks somewhat wildly, or " with the flower of the mind ; " not with the intellect used as an organ, but with the intellect released from all service and suffered to take its direction from its celestial life ; or as the ancients were wont to express themselves, not with intellect alone but with the intellect inebriated by nectar. As the traveller who has lost his way throws his reins on his horse's neck and trusts to the instinct of the animal to find his road, so must we do with the divine animal who carries us through this world. For if in any manner we can stimulate this instinct, new passages are opened for us into nature ; the mind flows into and through things hardest and highest, and the metamorphosis is possible.

This is the reason why bards love wine, mead, narcotics, coffee, tea, opium; the fumes of sandalwood and tobacco, or whatever other procurers of animal exhilaration. All men avail themselves of such means as they can, to add this extraordinary power to their normal powers ; and to this end they prize conversation, music, pictures, sculpture, dancing, theatres, travelling, war, mobs,

fires, gaming, politics, or love, or science, or
animal intoxication, — which are several coarser
or finer *quasi*-mechanical substitutes for the true
nectar, which is the ravishment of the intellect
by coming nearer to the fact.' These are auxiliaries to the centrifugal tendency of a man, to
his passage out into free space, and they help
him to escape the custody of that body in which
he is pent up, and of that jail-yard of individual
relations in which he is enclosed. Hence a great
number of such as were professionally express-
ers of Beauty, as painters, poets, musicians and
actors, have been more than others wont to lead
a life of pleasure and indulgence; all but the
few who received the true nectar; and, as it was
a spurious mode of attaining freedom, as it was
an emancipation not into the heavens but into
the freedom of baser places, they were punished
for that advantage they won, by a dissipation
and deterioration. But never can any advantage
be taken of nature by a trick. The spirit of the
world, the great calm presence of the Creator,
comes not forth to the sorceries of opium or of
wine. The sublime vision comes to the pure
and simple soul in a clean and chaste body.
That is not an inspiration, which we owe to narcotics, but some counterfeit excitement and fury.

Milton says that the lyric poet may drink wine
and live generously, but the epic poet, he who
shall sing of the gods and their descent unto
men, must drink water out of a wooden bowl.[1]
For poetry is not 'Devil's wine,' but God's
wine. It is with this as it is with toys. We fill
the hands and nurseries of our children with all
manner of dolls, drums and horses; withdraw-
ing their eyes from the plain face and sufficing
objects of nature, the sun and moon, the animals,
the water and stones, which should be their toys.
So the poet's habit of living should be set on a
key so low that the common influences should
delight him. His cheerfulness should be the
gift of the sunlight; the air should suffice for
his inspiration, and he should be tipsy with
water. That spirit which suffices quiet hearts,
which seems to come forth to such from every
dry knoll of sere grass, from every pine stump
and half-imbedded stone on which the dull
March sun shines, comes forth to the poor and
hungry, and such as are of simple taste. If thou
fill thy brain with Boston and New York, with
fashion and covetousness, and wilt stimulate thy
jaded senses with wine and French coffee, thou
shalt find no radiance of wisdom in the lonely
waste of the pine woods.

If the imagination intoxicates the poet, it is not inactive in other men. The metamorphosis excites in the beholder an emotion of joy. The use of symbols has a certain power of emancipation and exhilaration for all men. We seem to be touched by a wand which makes us dance and run about happily, like children. We are like persons who come out of a cave or cellar into the open air. This is the effect on us of tropes, fables, oracles and all poetic forms. Poets are thus liberating gods.[1] Men have really got a new sense, and found within their world another world, or nest of worlds; for, the metamorphosis once seen, we divine that it does not stop. I will not now consider how much this makes the charm of algebra and the mathematics, which also have their tropes, but it is felt in every definition; as when Aristotle defines *space* to be an immovable vessel in which things are contained;—or when Plato defines a *line* to be a flowing point; or *figure* to be a bound of solid; and many the like. What a joyful sense of freedom we have when Vitruvius announces the old opinion of artists that no architect can build any house well who does not know something of anatomy. When Socrates, in Charmides, tells us that the soul is cured of its maladies by certain

incantations, and that these incantations are beautiful reasons, from which temperance is generated
in souls; when Plato calls the world an animal,
and Timæus affirms that the plants also are animals; or affirms a man to be a heavenly tree,
growing with his root, which is his head, upward;
and, as George Chapman, following him, writes,

> " So in our tree of man, whose nervie root
> Springs in his top; " — [1]

when Orpheus speaks of hoariness as " that white
flower which marks extreme old age; " when
Proclus calls the universe the statue of the intellect; when Chaucer, in his praise of ' Gentilesse,'
compares good blood in mean condition to fire,
which, though carried to the darkest house betwixt this and the mount of Caucasus, will yet
hold its natural office and burn as bright as
if twenty thousand men did it behold; [2] when
John saw, in the Apocalypse, the ruin of the
world through evil, and the stars fall from heaven
as the fig tree casteth her untimely fruit; when
Æsop reports the whole catalogue of common
daily relations through the masquerade of birds
and beasts; — we take the cheerful hint of the
immortality of our essence and its versatile habit
and escapes, as when the gypsies say of themselves " it is in vain to hang them, they cannot
die."

The poets are thus liberating gods. The ancient British bards had for the title of their order, " Those who are free throughout the world." They are free, and they make free. An imaginative book renders us much more service at first, by stimulating us through its tropes, than afterward when we arrive at the precise sense of the author.[1] I think nothing is of any value in books excepting the transcendental and extraordinary. If a man is inflamed and carried away by his thought, to that degree that he forgets the authors and the public and heeds only this one dream which holds him like an insanity, let me read his paper, and you may have all the arguments and histories and criticism. All the value which attaches to Pythagoras, Paracelsus, Cornelius Agrippa, Cardan, Kepler, Swedenborg, Schelling, Oken, or any other who introduces questionable facts into his cosmogony, as angels, devils, magic, astrology, palmistry, mesmerism, and so on, is the certificate we have of departure from routine, and that here is a new witness. That also is the best success in conversation, the magic of liberty, which puts the world like a ball in our hands. How cheap even the liberty then seems ; how mean to study, when an emotion communicates to the

intellect the power to sap and upheave nature;
how great the perspective! nations, times, sys-
tems, enter and disappear like threads in tapestry
of large figure and many colors; dream delivers
us to dream, and while the drunkenness lasts
we will sell our bed, our philosophy, our religion, in our opulence.

There is good reason why we should prize
this liberation. The fate of the poor shepherd,
who, blinded and lost in the snow-storm, perishes
in a drift within a few feet of his cottage door, is
an emblem of the state of man. On the brink
of the waters of life and truth, we are miserably
dying. The inaccessibleness of every thought
but that we are in, is wonderful. What if you
come near to it; you are as remote when you
are nearest as when you are farthest. Every
thought is also a prison; every heaven is also
a prison. Therefore we love the poet, the inventor, who in any form, whether in an ode or
in an action or in looks and behavior, has yielded
us a new thought. He unlocks our chains and
admits us to a new scene.[1]

This emancipation is dear to all men, and the
power to impart it, as it must come from greater
depth and scope of thought, is a measure of intellect. Therefore all books of the imagination

III

endure, all which ascend to that truth that the writer sees nature beneath him, and uses it as his exponent. Every verse or sentence possessing this virtue will take care of its own immortality. The religions of the world are the ejaculations of a few imaginative men.

But the quality of the imagination is to flow, and not to freeze. The poet did not stop at the color or the form, but read their meaning; neither may he rest in this meaning, but he makes the same objects exponents of his new thought. Here is the difference betwixt the poet and the mystic, that the last nails a symbol ¹ to one sense, which was a true sense for a moment, but soon becomes old and false. (For all symbols are fluxional; all language is vehicular and transitive, and is good, as ferries and horses are, for conveyance, not as farms and houses are, for homestead. Mysticism consists in the mistake of an accidental and individual symbol for an universal one.) The morning-redness happens to be the favorite meteor to the eyes of Jacob Behmen, and comes to stand to him for truth and faith; and, he believes, should stand for the same realities to every reader. But the first reader prefers as naturally the symbol of a mother and child, or a gardener

and his bulb, or a jeweller polishing a gem.
Either of these, or of a myriad more, are equally
good to the person to whom they are significant.
Only they must be held lightly, and be very
willingly translated into the equivalent terms
which others use. And the mystic must be
steadily told, — All that you say is just as true
without the tedious use of that symbol as with
it. Let us have a little algebra, instead of this
trite rhetoric, — universal signs, instead of these
village symbols, — and we shall both be gainers.
The history of hierarchies seems to show that
all religious error consisted in making the symbol too stark and solid, and was at last nothing
but an excess of the organ of language.

Swedenborg, of all men in the recent ages,
stands eminently for the translator of nature into
thought. I do not know the man in history to
whom things stood so uniformly for words.
Before him the metamorphosis continually plays.
Everything on which his eye rests, obeys the
impulses of moral nature. The figs become
grapes whilst he eats them. When some of his
angels affirmed a truth, the laurel twig which
they held blossomed in their hands. The noise
which at a distance appeared like gnashing and
thumping, on coming nearer was found to be

the voice of disputants. The men in one of his visions, seen in heavenly light, appeared like dragons, and seemed in darkness; but to each other they appeared as men, and when the light from heaven shone into their cabin, they complained of the darkness, and were compelled to shut the window that they might see.

There was this perception in him which makes the poet or seer an object of awe and terror, namely that the same man or society of men may wear one aspect to themselves and their companions, and a different aspect to higher intelligences. Certain priests, whom he describes as conversing very learnedly together, appeared to the children who were at some distance, like dead horses; and many the like misappearances. And instantly the mind inquires whether these fishes under the bridge, yonder oxen in the pasture, those dogs in the yard, are immutably fishes, oxen and dogs, or only so appear to me, and perchance to themselves appear upright men; and whether I appear as a man to all eyes. The Brahmins and Pythagoras propounded the same question, and if any poet has witnessed the transformation he doubtless found it in harmony with various experiences. We have all seen changes as considerable in wheat and caterpillars. He is the poet and shall draw us with love and terror, who sees through the flowing vest the firm nature, and can declare it.[1]

I look in vain for the poet whom I describe. We do not with sufficient plainness or sufficient profoundness address ourselves to life, nor dare we chaunt our own times and social circumstance. If we filled the day with bravery, we should not shrink from celebrating it. Time and nature yield us many gifts, but not yet the timely man, the new religion, the reconciler, whom all things await. Dante's praise is that he dared to write his autobiography in colossal cipher, or into universality. We have yet had no genius in America, with tyrannous eye, which knew the value of our incomparable materials, and saw, in the barbarism and materialism of the times, another carnival of the same gods whose picture he so much admires in Homer; then in the Middle Age; then in Calvinism. Banks and tariffs, the newspaper and caucus, Methodism and Unitarianism, are flat and dull to dull people, but rest on the same foundations of wonder as the town of Troy and the temple of Delphi, and are as swiftly passing away. Our log-rolling, our stumps and their politics, our fisheries, our Negroes and Indians, our boats and our repudiations, the wrath of rogues and the pusillanimity of honest men, the northern trade, the southern planting, the western clearing, Oregon and Texas, are yet unsung. Yet America is a poem in our eyes; its ample geography dazzles the imagination, and it will not wait long for metres. If I have not found that excellent combination of gifts in my countrymen which I seek, neither could I aid myself to fix the idea of the poet by reading now and then in Chalmers's collection of five centuries of English poets. These are wits more than poets, though there have been poets among them. But when we adhere to the ideal of the poet, we have our difficulties even with Milton and Homer. Milton is too literary, and Homer too literal and historical.

But I am not wise enough for a national criticism, and must use the old largeness a little longer, to discharge my errand from the muse to the poet concerning his art.

Art is the path of the creator to his work. The paths or methods are ideal and eternal, though few men ever see them; not the artist himself for years, or for a lifetime, unless he come into the conditions. The painter, the sculptor, the composer, the epic rhapsodist, the orator, all partake one desire, namely to express themselves symmetrically and abundantly, not dwarfishly and fragmentarily. They found or put themselves in certain conditions, as, the painter and sculptor before some impressive human figures; the orator into the assembly of the people; and the others in such scenes as each has found exciting to his intellect; and each presently feels the new desire. He hears a voice, he sees a beckoning. Then he is apprised, with wonder, what herds of dæmons hem him in. He can no more rest; he says, with the old painter, " By God it is in me and must go forth of me." He pursues a beauty, half seen, which flies before him. The poet pours out verses in every solitude. Most of the things he says are conventional, no doubt; but by and by he says something which is original and beautiful. That charms him. He would say nothing else but such things. In our way of talking we say ' That is yours, this is mine;' but the poet knows well that it is not his; that it is as strange and beautiful to him as to you; he would fain hear the like eloquence at length. Once having tasted this immortal ichor, he cannot have enough of it, and as an admirable creative power exists in these intellections, it is of the last importance that these things get spoken.' What

a little of all we know is said! What drops
of all the sea of our science are baled up! and
by what accident it is that these are exposed,
when so many secrets sleep in nature! Hence
the necessity of speech and song; hence these
throbs and heart-beatings in the orator, at the
door of the assembly, to the end namely that
thought may be ejaculated as Logos, or Word.

Doubt not, O poet, but persist. Say 'It is
in me, and shall out.' Stand there, balked and
dumb, stuttering and stammering, hissed and
hooted, stand and strive, until at last rage draw
out of thee that *dream*-power which every night
shows thee is thine own; a power transcending
all limit and privacy, and by virtue of which a
man is the conductor of the whole river of electricity. Nothing walks, or creeps, or grows, or
exists, which must not in turn arise and walk
before him as exponent of his meaning. Comes
he to that power, his genius is no longer ex-
haustible. All the creatures by pairs and by
tribes pour into his mind as into a Noah's ark,
to come forth again to people a new world.
This is like the stock of air for our respiration
or for the combustion of our fireplace; not a
measure of gallons, but the entire atmosphere
if wanted. And therefore the rich poets, as

Homer, Chaucer, Shakspeare, and Raphael,
have obviously no limits to their works except
the limits of their lifetime, and resemble a mir-
ror carried through the street, ready to render
an image of every created thing.

O poet! a new nobility is conferred in groves
and pastures, and not in castles or by the sword-
blade any longer. The conditions are hard, but
equal. Thou shalt leave the world, and know
the muse only. Thou shalt not know any longer
the times, customs, graces, politics, or opinions
of men, but shalt take all from the muse. For
the time of towns is tolled from the world by
funereal chimes, but in nature the universal
hours are counted by succeeding tribes of animals and plants, and by growth of joy on joy.
God wills also that thou abdicate a manifold
and duplex life, and that thou be content that
others speak for thee. Others shall be thy
gentlemen and shall represent all courtesy and
worldly life for thee; others shall do the great
and resounding actions also. Thou shalt lie
close hid with nature, and canst not be afforded to
the Capitol or the Exchange. The world is full
of renunciations and apprenticeships, and this is
thine; thou must pass for a fool and a churl for
a long season. This is the screen and sheath in

which Pan has protected his well-beloved **flower**, and thou shalt be known only to thine **own**, and they shall console thee with tenderest **love**. And thou shalt not be able to rehearse the names of thy friends in thy verse, for an old shame before the holy ideal.' And this is the reward; that the ideal shall be real to thee, and the impressions of the actual world shall fall like summer rain, copious, but not troublesome to thy invulnerable essence. Thou shalt have the whole land for thy park and manor, the sea for thy bath and navigation, without tax and without envy; the woods and the rivers thou shalt own, and thou shalt possess that wherein others are only tenants and boarders. Thou true land-lord! sea-lord! air-lord! Wherever snow falls or water flows or birds fly, wherever day and night meet in twilight, wherever the blue heaven is hung by clouds or sown with stars, wherever are forms with transparent boundaries, wherever are outlets into celestial space, wherever is danger, and awe, and love, — there is Beauty, plenteous as rain, shed for thee, and though thou shouldst walk the world over, thou shalt not be able to find a condition inopportune or ignoble.

II

EXPERIENCE

THE lords of life, the lords of life, —
I saw them pass,
In their own guise,
Like and unlike,
Portly and grim,
Use and Surprise,
Surface and Dream,
Succession swift, and spectral Wrong,
Temperament without a tongue,
And the inventor of the game
Omnipresent without name ; —
Some to see, some to be guessed,
They marched from east to west :
Little man, least of all,
Among the legs of his guardians tall,
Walked about with puzzled look : —
Him by the hand dear Nature took ;
Dearest Nature, strong and kind,
Whispered, ‘ Darling, never mind !
To-morrow they will wear another face,
The founder thou ! these are thy race !’

EXPERIENCE

WHERE do we find ourselves? In a series of which we do not know the extremes, and believe that it has none. We wake and find ourselves on a stair; there are stairs below us, which we seem to have ascended; there are stairs above us, many a one, which go upward and out of sight. But the Genius which according to the old belief stands at the door by which we enter, and gives us the lethe to drink, that we may tell no tales, mixed the cup too strongly, and we cannot shake off the lethargy now at noonday. Sleep lingers all our lifetime about our eyes, as night hovers all day in the boughs of the fir-tree.¹ All things swim and glitter. Our life is not so much threatened as our perception. Ghostlike we glide through nature, and should not know our place again. Did our birth fall in some fit of indigence and frugality in nature, that she was so sparing of her fire and so liberal of her earth that it appears to us that we lack the affirmative principle, and though we have health and reason, yet we have no superfluity of spirit for new creation? We have enough to live and bring the year about, but not an ounce to impart or to invest. Ah that our Genius were a little more of a genius! We are like millers on the lower levels of a stream, when the factories above them have exhausted the water. We too fancy that the upper people must have raised their dams.[1]

If any of us knew what we were doing, or where we are going, then when we think we best know! We do not know to-day whether we are busy or idle. In times when we thought ourselves indolent, we have afterwards discovered that much was accomplished and much was begun in us.[2] All our days are so unprofitable while they pass, that 't is wonderful where or when we ever got anything of this which we call wisdom, poetry, virtue. We never got it on any dated calendar day. Some heavenly days must have been intercalated somewhere, like those that Hermes won with dice of the Moon, that Osiris might be born.[3] It is said all martyrdoms looked mean when they were suffered. Every ship is a romantic object, except that we sail in. Embark, and the romance quits our vessel and hangs on every other sail in the horizon. Our life looks trivial, and we shun to record it. Men seem to have learned of the horizon the art of perpetual retreating and reference. 'Yonder uplands are rich pasturage, and my neighbor has fertile meadow, but my field,' says the querulous farmer, ' only holds the world together.' I quote another man's saying; unluckily that other withdraws himself in the same way, and quotes me. 'T is the trick of nature thus to degrade to-day; a good deal of buzz, and somewhere a result slipped magically in. Every roof is agreeable to the eye until it is lifted; then we find tragedy and moaning women and hard-eyed husbands and deluges of lethe, and the men ask, ' What 's the news?' as if the old were so bad. How many individuals can we count in society? how many actions? how many opinions? So much of our time is preparation, so much is routine, and so much retrospect, that the pith of each man's genius contracts itself to a very few hours. The history of literature — take the net result of Tiraboschi, Warton, or Schlegel ' — is a sum of very few ideas and of very few original tales; all the rest being variation of these. So in this great society wide lying around us, a critical analysis would find very few spontaneous actions. It is almost all custom and gross sense. There are even few opinions, and these seem organic in the speakers, and do not disturb the universal necessity.

What opium is instilled into all disaster! It shows formidable as we approach it, but there is at last no rough rasping friction, but the most slippery sliding surfaces; we fall soft on a thought; *Ate Dea* is gentle, —

> " Over men's heads walking aloft,
> With tender feet treading so soft." [1]

People grieve and bemoan themselves, but it is not half so bad with them as they say. There are moods in which we court suffering, in the hope that here at least we shall find reality, sharp peaks and edges of truth. But it turns out to be scene-painting and counterfeit. The only thing grief has taught me is to know how shallow it is. That, like all the rest, plays about the surface, and never introduces me into the reality, for contact with which we would even pay the costly price of sons and lovers. Was it Boscovich [2] who found out that bodies never come in contact? Well, souls never touch their objects. An innavigable sea washes with silent waves between us and the things we aim at and converse with. Grief too will make us idealists. In the death of my son, now more than two years ago, I seem to have lost a beautiful estate, — no more. [3] I cannot get it nearer to me. If to-morrow I should be informed of the bankruptcy of my principal debtors, the loss of my property would be a great inconvenience to me, perhaps, for many years; but it would leave me as it found me, — neither better nor worse. So is it with this calamity; it does not touch me; something which I fancied was a part of me, which could not be torn away without tearing me nor enlarged without enriching me, falls off from me and leaves no scar. It was caducous. I grieve that grief can teach me nothing, nor carry me one step into real nature. The Indian ' who was laid under a curse that the wind should not blow on him, nor water flow to him, nor fire burn him, is a type of us all. The dearest events are summer-rain, and we the Para coats that shed every drop. Nothing is left us now but death. We look to that with a grim satisfaction, saying, There at least is reality that will not dodge us.

I take this evanescence and lubricity of all objects, which lets them slip through our fingers then when we clutch hardest, to be the most unhandsome part of our condition. Nature does not like to be observed, and likes that we should be her fools and playmates. We may have the sphere for our cricket-ball, but not a berry for our philosophy. Direct strokes she never gave us power to make; all our blows glance, all our hits are accidents. Our relations to each other are oblique and casual.

Dream delivers us to dream, and there is no end to illusion.[1] Life is a train of moods like a string of beads, and as we pass through them they prove to be many-colored lenses which paint the world their own hue, and each shows only what lies in its focus. From the mountain you see the mountain. We animate what we can, and we see only what we animate. Nature and books belong to the eyes that see them. It depends on the mood of the man whether he shall see the sunset or the fine poem. There are always sunsets, and there is always genius; but only a few hours so serene that we can relish nature or criticism. The more or less depends on structure or temperament. Temperament is the iron wire on which the beads are strung. Of what use is fortune or talent to a cold and defective nature? Who cares what sensibility or discrimination a man has at some time shown, if he falls asleep in his chair? or if he laugh and giggle? or if he apologize?[2] or is infected with egotism? or thinks of his dollar? or cannot go by food? or has gotten a child in his boyhood? Of what use

is genius, if the organ is too convex or too con-
cave and cannot find a focal distance within the
actual horizon of human life?' Of what use,
if the brain is too cold or too hot, and the man
does not care enough for results to stimulate
him to experiment, and hold him up in it? or
if the web is too finely woven, too irritable by
pleasure and pain, so that life stagnates from
too much reception without due outlet? Of
what use to make heroic vows of amendment,
if the same old law-breaker is to keep them?
What cheer can the religious sentiment yield,
when that is suspected to be secretly dependent
on the seasons of the year and the state of the
blood? I knew a witty physician² who found
the creed in the biliary duct, and used to affirm
that if there was disease in the liver, the man
became a Calvinist, and if that organ was sound,
he became a Unitarian. Very mortifying is the
reluctant experience that some unfriendly excess
or imbecility neutralizes the promise of genius.
We see young men who owe us a new world,
so readily and lavishly they promise, but they
never acquit the debt; they die young and dodge
the account; or if they live they lose themselves
in the crowd.

Temperament also enters fully into the system of illusions and shuts us in a prison of glass which we cannot see. There is an optical illusion about every person we meet. In truth they are all creatures of given temperament, which will appear in a given character, whose boundaries they will never pass; but we look at them, they seem alive, and we presume there is impulse in them. In the moment it seems impulse; in the year, in the lifetime, it turns out to be a certain uniform tune which the revolving barrel of the music-box must play. Men resist the conclusion in the morning, but adopt it as the evening wears on, that temper prevails over everything of time, place and condition, and is inconsumable in the flames of religion.[1] Some modifications the moral sentiment avails to impose, but the individual texture holds its dominion, if not to bias the moral judgments, yet to fix the measure of activity and of enjoyment.

I thus express the law as it is read from the platform of ordinary life, but must not leave it without noticing the capital exception. For temperament is a power which no man willingly hears any one praise but himself. On the platform of physics we cannot resist the contracting influences of so-called science. Temperament puts all divinity to rout. I know the mental

proclivity of physicians. I hear the chuckle of
the phrenologists. Theoretic kidnappers and
slave-drivers, they esteem each man the victim
of another, who winds him round his finger by
knowing the law of his being; and, by such
cheap signboards as the color of his beard or
the slope of his occiput, reads the inventory
of his fortunes and character. The grossest ignorance does not disgust like this impudent
knowingness.[1] The physicians say they are not
materialists; but they are: — Spirit is matter
reduced to an extreme thinness: O *so* thin! —
But the definition of *spiritual* should be, *that
which is its own evidence.*[2] What notions do
they attach to love! what to religion! One
would not willingly pronounce these words
in their hearing, and give them the occasion
to profane them. I saw a gracious gentleman
who adapts his conversation to the form of the
head of the man he talks with! I had fancied
that the value of life lay in its inscrutable pos-
sibilities; in the fact that I never know, in
addressing myself to a new individual, what
may befall me. I carry the keys of my castle
in my hand, ready to throw them at the feet of
my lord, whenever and in what disguise soever
he shall appear. I know he is in the neigh-

borhood, hidden among vagabonds. Shall I
preclude my future by taking a high seat and
kindly adapting my conversation to the shape
of heads? When I come to that, the doctors
shall buy me for a cent. — 'But, sir, medical
history; the report to the Institute; the proven
facts!' — I distrust the facts and the inferences.
Temperament is the veto or limitation-power
in the constitution, very justly applied to restrain an opposite excess in the constitution,
but absurdly offered as a bar to original equity.
When virtue is in presence, all subordinate
powers sleep. On its own level, or in view of
nature, temperament is final. I see not, if one
be once caught in this trap of so-called sciences, any escape for the man from the links of
the chain of physical necessity. Given such an
embryo, such a history must follow. On this
platform one lives in a sty of sensualism, and
would soon come to suicide. But it is impossible that the creative power should exclude
itself. Into every intelligence there is a door
which is never closed, through which the creator
passes. The intellect, seeker of absolute truth,
or the heart, lover of absolute good, intervenes
for our succor, and at one whisper of these high
powers we awake from ineffectual struggles with

this nightmare.[1] We hurl it into its own hell, and cannot again contract ourselves to so base a state.

The secret of the illusoriness is in the necessity of a succession of moods or objects. Gladly we would anchor, but the anchorage is quicksand. This onward trick of nature is too strong for us : *Pero si muove.*[2] When at night I look at the moon and stars, I seem stationary, and they to hurry. Our love of the real draws us to permanence, but health of body consists in circulation, and sanity of mind in variety or facility of association. We need change of objects. Dedication to one thought is quickly odious. We house with the insane, and must humor them ; then conversation dies out. Once I took such delight in Montaigne that I thought I should not need any other book ; before that, in Shakspeare ; then in Plutarch ; then in Plotinus ; at one time in Bacon ; afterwards in Goethe ; even in Bettine ; but now I turn the pages of either of them languidly, whilst I still cherish their genius. So with pictures ; each will bear an emphasis of attention once, which it cannot retain, though we fain would continue to be pleased in that manner. How strongly I have

felt of pictures that when you have seen one
well, you must take your leave of it; you shall
never see it again. I have had good lessons
from pictures which I have since seen without
emotion or remark. A deduction must be made
from the opinion which even the wise express
on a new book or occurrence. Their opinion
gives me tidings of their mood, and some vague
guess at the new fact, but is nowise to be trusted
as the lasting relation between that intellect and
that thing. The child asks, ' Mamma, why don't
I like the story as well as when you told it me
yesterday?' Alas! child, it is even so with the
oldest cherubim of knowledge. But will it
answer thy question to say, Because thou wert
born to a whole and this story is a particular?'
The reason of the pain this discovery causes us
(and we make it late in respect to works of
art and intellect) is the plaint of tragedy which
murmurs from it in regard to persons, to friendship and love.

That immobility and absence of elasticity
which we find in the arts, we find with more
pain in the artist. (There is no power of expansion in men. Our friends early appear to us as
representatives of certain ideas which they never
pass or exceed.) They stand on the brink of the

ocean of thought and power, but they never take the single step that would bring them there. A man is like a bit of Labrador spar, which has no lustre as you turn it in your hand until you come to a particular angle ; then it shows deep and beautiful colors. There is no adaptation or universal applicability in men, but each has his special talent, and the mastery of successful men consists in adroitly keeping themselves where and when that turn shall be oftenest to be practised. We do what we must, and call it by the best names we can, and would fain have the praise of having intended the result which ensues. I cannot recall any form of man who is not superfluous sometimes. But is not this pitiful ? Life is not worth the taking, to do tricks in.

Of course it needs the whole society to give the symmetry we seek. The party-colored wheel must revolve very fast to appear white. Something is earned too by conversing with so much folly and defect. In fine, whoever loses, we are always of the gaining party. Divinity is behind our failures and follies also. The plays of children are nonsense, but very educative nonsense. So it is with the largest and solemnest things, with commerce, government, church, marriage, and so with the history of every man's bread, and the ways by which he is to come by it. Like a bird which alights nowhere, but hops perpetually from bough to bough, is the Power which abides in no man and in no woman, but for a moment speaks from this one, and for another moment from that one.

But what help from these fineries or pedantries? What help from thought? Life is not dialectics.[1] We, I think, in these times, have had lessons enough of the futility of criticism. Our young people have thought and written much on labor and reform, and for all that they have written, neither the world nor themselves have got on a step. Intellectual tasting of life will not supersede muscular activity. If a man should consider the nicety of the passage of a piece of bread down his throat, he would starve. At Education Farm the noblest theory of life sat on the noblest figures of young men and maidens, quite powerless and melancholy. It would not rake or pitch a ton of hay; it would not rub down a horse; and the men and maidens it left pale and hungry.[2] A political orator wittily compared our party promises to western roads, which opened stately enough, with planted

trees on either side to tempt the traveller, but
soon became narrow and narrower and ended in
a squirrel-track and ran up a tree. So does
culture with us; it ends in headache. Unspeak-
ably sad and barren does life look to those
who a few months ago were dazzled with the
splendor of the promise of the times. "There
is now no longer any right course of action nor
any self-devotion left among the Iranis." [1] Objections and criticism we have had our fill of.
There are objections to every course of life and
action, and the practical wisdom infers an indif-
ferency, from the omnipresence of objection.
The whole frame of things preaches indiffer-
ency. Do not craze yourself with thinking, but
go about your business anywhere. Life is not
intellectual or critical, but sturdy. Its chief good
is for well-mixed people who can enjoy what
they find, without question. Nature hates peep-
ing, and our mothers speak her very sense when
they say, " Children, eat your victuals, and say
no more of it." To fill the hour, — that is
happiness; to fill the hour and leave no crev-
ice for a repentance or an approval. [2] We live
amid surfaces, and the true art of life is to skate
well on them. Under the oldest mouldiest conventions a man of native force prospers just as

well as in the newest world, and that by skill
of handling and treatment. He can take hold
anywhere. Life itself is a mixture of power
and form, and will not bear the least excess of
either. To finish the moment, to find the journey's end in every step of the road, to live the
greatest number of good hours, is wisdom. It
is not the part of men, but of fanatics, or of
mathematicians if you will, to say that, the shortness of life considered, it is not worth caring
whether for so short a duration we were sprawl-
ing in want or sitting high. Since our office is
with moments, let us husband them. Five minutes of to-day are worth as much to me as five
minutes in the next millennium. Let us be
poised, and wise, and our own, to-day. Let us
treat the men and women well; treat them as if
they were real; perhaps they are. Men live in
their fancy, like drunkards whose hands are too
soft and tremulous for successful labor. It is a
tempest of fancies, and the only ballast I know
is a respect to the present hour. Without any
shadow of doubt, amidst this vertigo of shows
and politics, I settle myself ever the firmer in
the creed that we should not postpone and refer
and wish, but do broad justice where we are, by
whomsoever we deal with, accepting our actual

companions and circumstances, however humble or odious, as the mystic officials to whom the universe has delegated its whole pleasure for us. If these are mean and malignant, their contentment, which is the last victory of justice, is a more satisfying echo to the heart than the voice of poets and the casual sympathy of admirable persons. I think that however a thoughtful man may suffer from the defects and absurdities of his company, he cannot without affectation deny to any set of men and women a sensibility to extraordinary merit. The coarse and frivolous have an instinct of superiority, if they have not a sympathy, and honor it in their blind capricious way with sincere homage.[1]

The fine young people despise life, but in me, and in such as with me are free from dyspepsia, and to whom a day is a sound and solid good, it is a great excess of politeness to look scornful and to cry for company. I am grown by sympathy a little eager and sentimental, but leave me alone and I should relish every hour and what it brought me, the potluck of the day, as heartily as the oldest gossip in the bar-room. I am thankful for small mercies. I compared notes with one of my friends who expects everything of the universe and is disappointed when anything is less than the best, and I found that I begin at the other extreme, expecting nothing, and am always full of thanks for moderate goods.¹ I accept the clangor and jangle of contrary tendencies. I find my account in sots and bores also. They give a reality to the circumjacent picture which such a vanishing meteorous appearance can ill spare. In the morning I awake and find the old world, wife, babes and mother, Concord and Boston, the dear old spiritual world and even the dear old devil not far off. If we will take the good we find, asking no questions, we shall have heaping measures. The great gifts are not got by analysis. Everything good is on the highway. The middle region of our being is the temperate zone. We may climb into the thin and cold realm of pure geometry and lifeless science, or sink into that of sensation. Between these extremes is the equator of life, of thought, of spirit, of poetry, — a narrow belt. Moreover, in popular experience everything good is on the highway. A collector peeps into all the picture-shops of Europe for a landscape of Poussin, a crayon-sketch of Salvator; but the Transfiguration, the Last Judgment, the Communion of Saint Jerome, and what are as

transcendent as these, are on the walls of the
Vatican, the Uffizi, or the Louvre, where every
footman may see them; to say nothing of Nature's pictures in every street, of sunsets and
sunrises every day, and the sculpture of the
human body never absent. A collector recently
bought at public auction, in London, for one
hundred and fifty-seven guineas, an autograph
of Shakspeare; but for nothing a school-boy
can read Hamlet and can detect secrets of highest concernment yet unpublished therein. I
think I will never read any but the commonest
books, — the Bible, Homer, Dante, Shakspeare
and Milton. Then we are impatient of so public a life and planet, and run hither and thither
for nooks and secrets. The imagination delights
in the woodcraft of Indians, trappers and bee-
hunters. We fancy that we are strangers, and
not so intimately domesticated in the planet as
the wild man and the wild beast and bird. But
the exclusion reaches them also; reaches the
climbing, flying, gliding, feathered and four-
footed man. Fox and woodchuck, hawk and
snipe and bittern, when nearly seen, have no
more root in the deep world than man, and
are just such superficial tenants of the globe.
Then the new molecular philosophy shows as-

tronomical interspaces betwixt atom and atom, shows that the world is all outside; it has no inside.

The mid-world is best. Nature, as we know her, is no saint. The lights of the church, the ascetics, Gentoos and corn-eaters, she does not distinguish by any favor. She comes eating and drinking and sinning. Her darlings, the great, the strong, the beautiful, are not children of our law; do not come out of the Sunday School, nor weigh their food, nor punctually keep the commandments. If we will be strong with her strength we must not harbor such disconsolate consciences, borrowed too from the consciences of other nations. We must set up the strong present tense against all the rumors of wrath, past or to come.[1] So many things are unsettled which it is of the first importance to settle; — and, pending their settlement, we will do as we do. Whilst the debate goes forward on the equity of commerce, and will not be closed for a century or two, New and Old England may keep shop. Law of copyright and international copyright is to be discussed, and in the interim we will sell our books for the most we can. Expediency of literature, reason of literature, lawfulness of writing down a thought, is questioned; much is to say on both sides, and, while the fight waxes hot, thou, dearest scholar, stick to thy foolish task, add a line every hour, and between whiles add a line. Right to hold land, right of property, is disputed, and the conventions convene, and before the vote is taken, dig away in your garden, and spend your earnings as a waif or godsend to all serene and beautiful purposes. Life itself is a bubble and a scepticism, and a sleep within a sleep. Grant it, and as much more as they will, — but thou, God's darling! heed thy private dream; thou wilt not be missed in the scorning and scepticism; there are enough of them; stay there in thy closet and toil until the rest are agreed what to do about it. Thy sickness, they say, and thy puny habit require that thou do this or avoid that, but know that thy life is a flitting state, a tent for a night, and do thou, sick or well, finish that stint. Thou art sick, but shalt not be worse, and the universe, which holds thee dear, shall be the better.'

Human life is made up of the two elements, power and form, and the proportion must be invariably kept if we would have it sweet and sound. Each of these elements in excess makes a mischief as hurtful as its defect. Everything

III

runs to excess; every good quality is noxious if unmixed, and, to carry the danger to the edge of ruin, nature causes each man's peculiarity to superabound. Here, among the farms, we adduce the scholars as examples of this treachery. They are nature's victims of expression. You who see the artist, the orator, the poet, too near, and find their life no more excellent than that of mechanics or farmers, and themselves victims of partiality, very hollow and haggard, and pronounce them failures, not heroes, but quacks, — conclude very reasonably that these arts are not for man, but are disease. Yet nature will not bear you out. Irresistible nature made men such, and makes legions more of such, every day. You love the boy reading in a book, gazing at a drawing or a cast; yet what are these millions who read and behold, but incipient writers and sculptors? Add a little more of that quality which now reads and sees, and they will seize the pen and chisel. And if one remembers how innocently he began to be an artist, he perceives that nature joined with his enemy. A man is a golden impossibility. The line he must walk is a hair's breadth. The wise through excess of wisdom is made a fool.[1]

How easily, if fate would suffer it, we might
keep forever these beautiful limits, and adjust
ourselves, once for all, to the perfect calculation
of the kingdom of known cause and effect. In
the street and in the newspapers, life appears so
plain a business that manly resolution and ad-
herence to the multiplication-table through all
weathers will insure success. But ah ! presently
comes a day, or is it only a half-hour, with its
angel-whispering, — which discomfits the conclusions of nations and of years ! To-morrow
again every thing looks real and angular, the
habitual standards are reinstated, common-sense
is as rare as genius, — is the basis of genius, and
experience is hands and feet to every enterprise;
— and yet, he who should do his business on
this understanding would be quickly bankrupt.
Power keeps quite another road than the turn-
pikes of choice and will ; namely the subterra-
nean and invisible tunnels and channels of life.
It is ridiculous that we are diplomatists, and
doctors, and considerate people ; there are no
dupes like these. Life is a series of surprises,
and would not be worth taking or keeping if it
were not. God delights to isolate us every day,
and hide from us the past and the future. We
would look about us, but with grand politeness

he draws down before us an impenetrable screen of purest sky, and another behind us of purest sky. 'You will not remember,' he seems to say, 'and you will not expect.' All good conversation, manners and action come from a spontaneity which forgets usages and makes the moment great. Nature hates calculators; her methods are saltatory and impulsive. Man lives by pulses; our organic movements are such; and the chemical and ethereal agents are undulatory and alternate; and the mind goes antagonizing on, and never prospers but by fits. We thrive by casualties. Our chief experiences have been casual. The most attractive class of people are those who are powerful obliquely and not by the direct stroke;¹ men of genius, but not yet accredited; one gets the cheer of their light without paying too great a tax. Theirs is the beauty of the bird or the morning light, and not of art. In the thought of genius there is always a surprise; and the moral sentiment is well called "the newness," for it is never other; as new to the oldest intelligence as to the young child; — "the kingdom that cometh without observation."² In like manner, for practical success, there must not be too much design. A man will not be observed in doing that which he can do best. There is a

certain magic about his properest action which
stupefies your powers of observation, so that
though it is done before you, you wist not of it.
The art of life has a pudency, and will not be
exposed. Every man is an impossibility until
he is born; every thing impossible until we see
a success. The ardors of piety agree at last with
the coldest scepticism, — that nothing is of us
or our works, — that all is of God.[1] Nature
will not spare us the smallest leaf of laurel. All
writing comes by the grace of God, and all doing and having. I would gladly be moral and
keep due metes and bounds, which I dearly love,
and allow the most to the will of man; but I
have set my heart on honesty in this chapter,
and I can see nothing at last, in success or failure, than more or less of vital force supplied from
the Eternal. The results of life are uncalculated
and uncalculable. The years teach much which
the days never know. The persons who compose our company converse, and come and go,
and design and execute many things, and somewhat comes of it all, but an unlooked-for result.
The individual is always mistaken. He designed
many things, and drew in other persons as co-
adjutors, quarrelled with some or all, blundered
much, and something is done; all are a little

advanced, but the individual is always mistaken. It turns out somewhat new and very unlike what he promised himself.

The ancients, struck with this irreducibleness of the elements of human life to calculation, exalted Chance into a divinity; but that is to stay too long at the spark, which glitters truly at one point, but the universe is warm with the latency of the same fire. The miracle of life which will not be expounded but will remain a miracle, introduces a new element. In the growth of the embryo, Sir Everard Home ' I think noticed that the evolution was not from one central point, but coactive from three or more points. Life has no memory. That which proceeds in succession might be remembered, but that which is coexistent, or ejaculated from a deeper cause, as yet far from being conscious, knows not its own tendency. So is it with us, now sceptical or without unity, because immersed in forms and effects all seeming to be of equal yet hostile value, and now religious, whilst in the reception of spiritual law. Bear with these distractions, with this coetaneous growth of the parts; they will one day be *members*, and obey one will. On that one will, on that secret cause, they nail

our attention and hope. Life is hereby melted
into an expectation or a religion. Underneath
the inharmonious and trivial particulars, is a musical perfection; the Ideal journeying always with
us, the heaven without rent or seam. 'Do but
observe the mode of our illumination. When I
converse with a profound mind, or if at any time
being alone I have good thoughts, I do not at
once arrive at satisfactions, as when, being thirsty,
I drink water; or go to the fire, being cold; no!
but I am at first apprised of my vicinity to a
new and excellent region of life. By persisting
to read or to think, this region gives further sign
of itself, as it were in flashes of light, in sudden
discoveries of its profound beauty and repose,
as if the clouds that covered it parted at intervals and showed the approaching traveller
the inland mountains, with the tranquil eternal
meadows spread at their base, whereon flocks
graze and shepherds pipe and dance. But every
insight from this realm of thought is felt as initial, and promises a sequel. I do not make it; 1
arrive there, and behold what was there already.
I make! O no! I clap my hands in infantine
joy and amazement before the first opening to
me of this august magnificence, old with the love
. and homage of innumerable ages, young with

the life of life, the sunbright Mecca of the desert.
And what a future it opens! I feel a new heart
beating with the love of the new beauty. I am
ready to die out of nature and be born again into
this new yet unapproachable America I have
found in the West: —

> " Since neither now nor yesterday began
>   These thoughts, which have been ever, nor yet can
>   A man be found who their first entrance knew." [1]

If I have described life as a flux of moods, I
must now add that there is that in us which
changes not and which ranks all sensations and
states of mind. The consciousness in each man
is a sliding scale, which identifies him now with
the First Cause, and now with the flesh of his
body; life above life, in infinite degrees. The
sentiment from which it sprung determines the
dignity of any deed, and the question ever is, not
what you have done or forborne, but at whose
command you have done or forborne it.

Fortune, Minerva, Muse, Holy Ghost, —
these are quaint names, too narrow to cover
this unbounded substance. The baffled intellect must still kneel before this cause, which
refuses to be named, — ineffable cause, which
every fine genius has essayed to represent by
some emphatic symbol, as, Thales by water, An-.

aximenes by air, Anaxagoras by (Noῦς) thought, Zoroaster by fire, Jesus and the moderns by love; and the metaphor of each has become a national religion. The Chinese Mencius has not been the least successful in his generalization. "I fully understand language," he said, "and nourish well my vast-flowing vigor." — "I beg to ask what you call vast-flowing vigor?" said his companion. "The explanation," replied Mencius, "is difficult. This vigor is supremely great, and in the highest degree unbending. Nourish it correctly and do it no injury, and it will fill up the vacancy between heaven and earth. This vigor accords with and assists justice and reason, and leaves no hunger." — In our more correct writing we give to this generalization the name of Being, and thereby confess that we have arrived as far as we can go. Suffice it for the joy of the universe that we have not arrived at a wall, but at interminable oceans. Our life seems not present so much as prospective; not for the affairs on which it is wasted, but as a hint of this vast-flowing vigor. Most of life seems to be mere advertisement of faculty; information is given us not to sell ourselves cheap; that we are very great. So, in particulars, our greatness is always in a tendency

or direction, not in an action. It is for us to
believe in the rule, not in the exception. The
noble are thus known from the ignoble. So in
accepting the leading of the sentiments, it is not
what we believe concerning the immortality of
the soul or the like, but *the universal impulse to
believe*, that is the material circumstance and is
the principal fact in the history of the globe.[1]
Shall we describe this cause as that which works
directly? The spirit is not helpless or needful
of mediate organs. It has plentiful powers and
direct effects. I am explained without explain-
ing, I am felt without acting, and where I am
not. Therefore all just persons are satisfied with
their own praise. They refuse to explain themselves, and are content that new actions should
do them that office. They believe that we communicate without speech and above speech, and
that no right action of ours is quite unaffecting to our friends, at whatever distance; for
the influence of action is not to be measured
by miles. Why should I fret myself because
a circumstance has occurred which hinders my
presence where I was expected? If I am not at
the meeting, my presence where I am should be
as useful to the commonwealth of friendship
and wisdom, as would be my presence in that

place. I exert the same quality of power in all places. Thus journeys the mighty Ideal before us; it never was known to fall into the rear. No man ever came to an experience which was satiating, but his good is tidings of a better. Onward and onward! In liberated moments we know that a new picture of life and duty is already possible; the elements already exist in many minds around you of a doctrine of life which shall transcend any written record we have. The new statement will comprise the scepticisms as well as the faiths of society, and out of unbeliefs a creed shall be formed. For scepticisms are not gratuitous or lawless, but are limitations of the affirmative statement, and the new philosophy must take them in and make affirmations outside of them, just as much as it must include the oldest beliefs.[1]

It is very unhappy, but too late to be helped, the discovery we have made that we exist.[2] That discovery is called the Fall of Man. Ever afterwards we suspect our instruments. We have learned that we do not see directly, but mediately, and that we have no means of correcting these colored and distorting lenses which we are, or of computing the amount of their errors.

Perhaps these subject-lenses have a creative power; perhaps there are no objects. Once we lived in what we saw; now, the rapaciousness of this new power, which threatens to absorb all things, engages us. Nature, art, persons, letters, religions, objects, successively tumble in, and God is but one of its ideas. Nature and literature are subjective phenomena; every evil and every good thing is a shadow which we cast. The street is full of humiliations to the proud. As the fop contrived to dress his bailiffs in his livery and make them wait on his guests at table, so the chagrins which the bad heart gives off as bubbles, at once take form as ladies and gentlemen in the street, shopmen or bar-keepers in hotels, and threaten or insult whatever is threatenable and insultable in us. 'T is the same with our idolatries. People forget that it is the eye which makes the horizon, and the rounding mind's eye which makes this or that man a type or representative of humanity, with the name of hero or saint. Jesus, the " providential man," is a good man on whom many people are agreed that these optical laws shall take effect. By love on one part and by forbearance to press objection on the other part, it is for a time settled that we will look at him in the centre of the horizon,

and ascribe to him the properties that will attach
to any man so seen. But the longest love or
aversion has a speedy term. The great and cres-
cive self, rooted in absolute nature, supplants
all relative existence and ruins the kingdom
of mortal friendship and love. Marriage (in
what is called the spiritual world) is impossible,
because of the inequality between every subject
and every object. The subject is the receiver of
Godhead, and at every comparison must feel his
being enhanced by that cryptic might. Though
not in energy, yet by presence, this magazine
of substance cannot be otherwise than felt; nor
can any force of intellect attribute to the object
the proper deity which sleeps or wakes forever
in every subject. Never can love make consciousness and ascription equal in force. There
will be the same gulf between every me and
thee as between the original and the picture.
The universe is the bride of the soul. All private sympathy is partial. Two human beings
are like globes, which can touch only in a point,
and whilst they remain in contact all other points
of each of the spheres are inert; their turn must
also come, and the longer a particular union lasts
the more energy of appetency the parts not in
union acquire.

Life will be imaged, but cannot be divided nor doubled. Any invasion of its unity would be chaos. The soul is not twin-born but the only begotten, and though revealing itself as child in time, child in appearance, is of a fatal and universal power, admitting no co-life. Every day, every act betrays the ill-concealed deity. We believe in ourselves as we do not believe in others. We permit all things to ourselves, and that which we call sin in others is experiment for us. It is an instance of our faith in ourselves that men never speak of crime as lightly as they think; or every man thinks a latitude safe for himself which is nowise to be indulged to another. The act looks very differently on the inside and on the outside; in its quality and in its consequences. Murder in the murderer is no such ruinous thought as poets and romancers will have it; it does not unsettle him or fright him from his ordinary notice of trifles; it is an act quite easy to be contemplated; but in its sequel it turns out to be a horrible jangle and confounding of all relations. Especially the crimes that spring from love seem right and fair from the actor's point of view, but when acted are found destructive of society. No man at last believes that he can be lost, or that the

crime in him is as black as in the felon. Because
the intellect qualifies in our own case the moral
judgments. For there is no crime to the intellect. That is antinomian or hypernomian, and
judges law as well as fact. " It is worse than a
crime, it is a blunder," said Napoleon, speaking
the language of the intellect. To it, the world is
a problem in mathematics or the science of quantity, and it leaves out praise and blame and all
weak emotions. All stealing is comparative. If
you come to absolutes, pray who does not steal ?
Saints are sad, because they behold sin (even
when they speculate) from the point of view of
the conscience, and not of the intellect ; a confusion of thought. Sin, seen from the thought, is
a diminution, or *less* ; seen from the conscience
or will, it is pravity or *bad*. The intellect names
it shade, absence of light, and no essence. The
conscience must feel it as essence, essential evil.
This it is not ; it has an objective existence, but
no subjective.[1]

Thus inevitably does the universe wear our
color, and every object fall successively into the
subject itself. The subject exists, the subject en-
larges ; all things sooner or later fall into place.
As I am, so I see ; use what language we will,
we can never say anything but what we are ;

Hermes, Cadmus, Columbus, Newton, Bonaparte, are the mind's ministers. Instead of feeling a poverty when we encounter a great man, let us treat the new-comer like a travelling geologist who passes through our estate and shows us good slate, or limestone, or anthracite, in our brush pasture. The partial action of each strong mind in one direction is a telescope for the objects on which it is pointed. But every other part of knowledge is to be pushed to the same extravagance, ere the soul attains her due sphericity. Do you see that kitten chasing so prettily her own tail? If you could look with her eyes you might see her surrounded with hundreds of figures performing complex dramas, with tragic and comic issues, long conversations, many characters, many ups and downs of fate, — and meantime it is only puss and her tail. How long before our masquerade will end its noise of tambourines, laughter and shouting, and we shall find it was a solitary performance? A subject and an object, — it takes so much to make the galvanic circuit complete, but magnitude adds nothing. What imports it whether it is Kepler and the sphere, Columbus and America, a reader and his book, or puss with her tail?

It is true that all the muses and love and

religion hate these developments, and will find a
way to punish the chemist who publishes in the
parlor the secrets of the laboratory. And we
cannot say too little of our constitutional necessity of seeing things under private aspects, or
saturated with our humors. And yet is the God
the native of these bleak rocks. That need
makes in morals the capital virtue of self-trust.
We must hold hard to this poverty, however
scandalous, and by more vigorous self-recover-
ies, after the sallies of action, possess our axis
more firmly. The life of truth is cold and so
far mournful; but it is not the slave of tears,
contritions and perturbations. It does not attempt another's work, nor adopt another's facts.
It is a main lesson of wisdom to know your own
from another's. I have learned that I cannot
dispose of other people's facts; but I possess
such a key to my own as persuades me, against
all their denials, that they also have a key to
theirs.[1] (A sympathetic person is placed in the
dilemma of a swimmer among drowning men,
who all catch at him, and if he give so much as
a leg or a finger they will drown him.) They
wish to be saved from the mischiefs of their
vices, but not from their vices. Charity would
be wasted on this poor waiting on the symp-

toms. A wise and hardy physician will say, *Come out of that*, as the first condition of advice.

In this our talking America we are ruined by our good nature and listening on all sides. This compliance takes away the power of being greatly useful. A man should not be able to look other than directly and forthright. A preoccupied attention is the only answer to the importunate frivolity of other people; an attention, and to an aim which makes their wants frivolous. This is a divine answer, and leaves no appeal and no hard thoughts. In Flaxman's drawing of the Eumenides of Æschylus, Orestes supplicates Apollo, whilst the Furies sleep on the threshold. The face of the god expresses a shade of regret and compassion, but is calm with the conviction of the irreconcilableness of the two spheres. He is born into other politics, into the eternal and beautiful. The man at his feet asks for his interest in turmoils of the earth, into which his nature cannot enter. And the Eumenides there lying express pictorially this disparity. The god is surcharged with his divine destiny.

Illusion, Temperament, Succession, Surface, Surprise, Reality, Subjectiveness, — these are

threads on the loom of time, these are the lords
of life. I dare not assume to give their order,
but I name them as I find them in my way. I
know better than to claim any completeness for
my picture. I am a fragment, and this is a fragment of me. I can very confidently announce
one or another law, which throws itself into relief and form, but I am too young yet by some
ages to compile a code. I gossip for my hour
concerning the eternal politics. I have seen
many fair pictures not in vain. A wonderful
time I have lived in. I am not the novice I was
fourteen, nor yet seven years ago. Let who will
ask, Where is the fruit? I find a private fruit
sufficient. This is a fruit, — that I should not
ask for a rash effect from meditations, counsels
and the hiving of truths. I should feel it pitiful
to demand a result on this town and county, an
overt effect on the instant month and year. The
effect is deep and secular as the cause. It works
on periods in which mortal lifetime is lost. All
I know is reception; I am and I have: but I
do not get, and when I have fancied I had
gotten anything, I found I did not. I worship
with wonder the great Fortune. My reception
has been so large, that I am not annoyed by
receiving this or that superabundantly. I say to

the Genius, if he will pardon the proverb, *In for a mill, in for a million*. When I receive a new gift, I do not macerate my body to make the account square, for if I should die I could not make the account square. The benefit overran the merit the first day, and has overrun the merit ever since. The merit itself, so-called, I reckon part of the receiving.

Also that hankering after an overt or practical effect seems to me an apostasy. In good earnest I am willing to spare this most unnecessary deal of doing. Life wears to me a visionary face. Hardest roughest action is visionary also. It is but a choice between soft and turbulent dreams. People disparage knowing and the intellectual life, and urge doing. I am very content with knowing, if only I could know. That is an august entertainment, and would suffice me a great while. To know a little would be worth the expense of this world. I hear always the law of Adrastia, "that every soul which had acquired any truth, should be safe from harm until another period." [1]

I know that the world I converse with in the city and in the farms, is not the world I *think*. I observe that difference, and shall observe it. One day I shall know the value and law of this

discrepance. But I have not found that much
was gained by manipular attempts to realize the
world of thought. Many eager persons successively make an experiment in this way, and make
themselves ridiculous. They acquire democratic
manners, they foam at the mouth, they hate and
deny. Worse, I observe that in the history of
mankind there is never a solitary example of
success, — taking their own tests of success. I
say this polemically, or in reply to the inquiry,
Why not realize your world ? But far be from
me the despair which prejudges the law by a
paltry empiricism ; — since there never was a
right endeavor but it succeeded. Patience and
patience, we shall win at the last. We must be
very suspicious of the deceptions of the element
of time. It takes a good deal of time to eat or
to sleep, or to earn a hundred dollars, and a
very little time to entertain a hope and an insight
which becomes the light of our life. We dress
our garden, eat our dinners, discuss the household with our wives, and these things make no
impression, are forgotten next week ; but, in the
solitude to which every man is always returning, he has a sanity and revelations which in
his passage into new worlds he will carry with
him. Never mind the ridicule, never mind the

defeat; up again, old heart!—it seems to say,
—there is victory yet for all justice; and the
true romance which the world exists to realize
will be the transformation of genius into practical power.[1]

III

CHARACTER

THE sun set ; but set not his hope:
Stars rose ; his faith was earlier up: .
Fixed on the enormous galaxy,
Deeper and older seemed his eye:
And matched his sufferance sublime
The taciturnity of time.
He spoke, and words more soft than rain
Brought the Age of Gold again:
His action won such reverence sweet,
As hid all measure of the feat.

Work of his hand
He nor commends nor grieves:
Pleads for itself the fact;
As unrepenting Nature leaves
Her every act.

CHARACTER

I HAVE read that those who listened to Lord Chatham felt that there was something finer in the man than anything which he said. It has been complained of our brilliant English historian of the French Revolution that when he has told all his facts about Mirabeau, they do not justify his estimate of his genius. The Gracchi, Agis, Cleomenes, and others of Plutarch's heroes, do not in the record of facts equal their own fame. Sir Philip Sidney, the Earl of Essex, Sir Walter Raleigh, are men of great figure and of few deeds. We cannot find the smallest part of the personal weight of Washington in the narrative of his exploits. The authority of the name of Schiller is too great for his books. This inequality of the reputation to the works or the anecdotes is not accounted for by saying that the reverberation is longer than the thunder-clap, but somewhat resided in these men which begot an expectation that outran all their performance. The largest part of their power was latent. This is that which we call Character, — a reserved force, which acts directly by presence and without means. It is conceived of

as a certain undemonstrable force, a Familiar or
Genius, by whose impulses the man is guided,
but whose counsels he cannot impart; which is
company for him, so that such men are often
solitary, or if they chance to be social, do not
need society but can entertain themselves very
well alone. The purest literary talent appears
at one time great, at another time small, but
character is of a stellar and undiminishable
greatness. What others effect by talent or by
eloquence, this man accomplishes by some magnetism. "Half his strength he put not forth."
His victories are by demonstration of superiority, and not by crossing of bayonets. He con-
quers because his arrival alters the face of affairs.
"O Iole! how did you know that Hercules
was a god?" "Because," answered Iole, "I
was content the moment my eyes fell on him.
When I beheld Theseus, I desired that I might
see him offer battle, or at least guide his horses
in the chariot-race; but Hercules did not wait
for a contest; he conquered whether he stood,
or walked, or sat, or whatever thing he did."
Man, ordinarily a pendant to events, only half
attached, and that awkwardly, to the world he
lives in, in these examples appears to share the
life of things, and to be an expression of the

same laws which control the tides and the sun, numbers and quantities.

But to use a more modest illustration and nearer home, I observe that in our political elections, where this element, if it appears at all, can only occur in its coarsest form, we sufficiently understand its incomparable rate. The people know that they need in their representative much more than talent, namely the power to make his talent trusted. They cannot come at their ends by sending to Congress a learned, acute and fluent speaker, if he be not one who, before he was appointed by the people to represent them, was appointed by Almighty God to stand for a fact, — invincibly persuaded of that fact in himself, — so that the most confident and the most violent persons learn that here is resistance on which both impudence and terror are wasted, namely faith in a fact.[1] The men who carry their points do not need to inquire of their constituents what they should say, but are themselves the country which they represent; nowhere are its emotions or opinions so instant and true as in them ; nowhere so pure from a selfish infusion. The constituency at home hearkens to their words, watches the color of their cheek, and therein, as in a glass, dresses

its own. Our public assemblies are pretty good
tests of manly force. Our frank countrymen
of the west and south have a taste for character, and like to know whether the New Eng-
lander is a substantial man, or whether the hand
can pass through him.

The same motive force appears in trade.
There are geniuses in trade, as well as in war,
or the State, or letters; and the reason why
this or that man is fortunate is not to be told.
It lies in the man; that is all anybody can tell
you about it.' See him and you will know as
easily why he succeeds, as, if you see Napoleon,
you would comprehend his fortune. In the new
objects we recognize the old game, the habit of
fronting the fact, and not dealing with it at second hand, through the perceptions of somebody
else. Nature seems to authorize trade, as soon
as you see the natural merchant, who appears
not so much a private agent as her factor and
Minister of Commerce. His natural probity
combines with his insight into the fabric of
society to put him above tricks, and he communicates to all his own faith that contracts
are of no private interpretation. The habit of
his mind is a reference to standards of natural
equity and public advantage; and he inspires

respect and the wish to deal with him, both for
the quiet spirit of honor which attends him, and
for the intellectual pastime which the spectacle
of so much ability affords. This immensely
stretched trade, which makes the capes of the
Southern Ocean his wharves and the Atlantic
Sea his familiar port, centres in his brain only;
and nobody in the universe can make his place
good. In his parlor I see very well that he
has been at hard work this morning, with that
knitted brow and that settled humor, which
all his desire to be courteous cannot shake off.
I see plainly how many firm acts have been
done; how many valiant *noes* have this day
been spoken, when others would have uttered
ruinous *yeas*. I see, with the pride of art and
skill of masterly arithmetic and power of remote combination, the consciousness of being
an agent and playfellow of the original laws
of the world. He too believes that none can
supply him, and that a man must be born to
trade or he cannot learn it.[1]

This virtue draws the mind more when it
appears in action to ends not so mixed. It
works with most energy in the smallest companies and in private relations. In all cases it is
an extraordinary and incomputable agent. The

excess of physical strength is paralyzed by it.
Higher natures overpower lower ones by affect-
ing them with a certain sleep. The faculties are
locked up, and offer no resistance. Perhaps
that is the universal law. When the high cannot bring up the low to itself, it benumbs it, as
man charms down the resistance of the lower
animals. Men exert on each other a similar
occult power. How often has the influence of a
true master realized all the tales of magic! A
river of command seemed to run down from
his eyes into all those who beheld him, a torrent
of strong sad light, like an Ohio or Danube,
which pervaded them with his thoughts and
colored all events with the hue of his mind.
"What means did you employ?" was the question asked of the wife of Concini, in regard
to her treatment of Mary of Medici; and the
answer was, "Only that influence which every
strong mind has over a weak one." ' Cannot
Cæsar in irons shuffle off the irons and transfer
them to the person of Hippo or Thraso the
turnkey? Is an iron handcuff so immutable
a bond? Suppose a slaver on the coast of
Guinea should take on board a gang of negroes
which should contain persons of the stamp of
Toussaint L'Ouverture: or, let us fancy, under

these swarthy masks he has a gang of Washingtons in chains. When they arrive at Cuba, will the relative order of the ship's company be the same? Is there nothing but rope and iron? Is there no love, no reverence? Is there never a glimpse of right in a poor slave-captain's mind; and cannot these be supposed available to break or elude or in any manner overmatch the tension of an inch or two of iron ring?

This is a natural power, like light and heat, and all nature coöperates with it. The reason why we feel one man's presence and do not feel another's is as simple as gravity. Truth is the summit of being; justice is the application of it to affairs. All individual natures stand in a scale, according to the purity of this element in them. The will of the pure runs down from them into other natures, as water runs down from a higher into a lower vessel. This natural force is no more to be withstood than any other natural force. We can drive a stone upward for a moment into the air, but it is yet true that all stones will forever fall; and whatever instances can be quoted of unpunished theft, or of a lie which somebody credited, justice must prevail, and it is the privilege of truth to make itself believed. Character is this moral order seen through the medium of an individual nature. An individual is an encloser. Time and space, liberty and necessity, truth and thought, are left at large no longer. Now, the universe is a close or pound. All things exist in the man tinged with the manners of his soul. With what quality is in him he infuses all nature that he can reach ; nor does he tend to lose himself in vastness, but, at how long a curve soever, all his regards return into his own good at last.[1] He animates all he can, and he sees only what he animates. He encloses the world, as the patriot does his country, as a material basis for his character, and a theatre for action. A healthy soul stands united with the Just and the True, as the magnet arranges itself with the pole ; so that he stands to all beholders like a transparent object betwixt them and the sun, and whoso journeys towards the sun, journeys towards that person. He is thus the medium of the highest influence to all who are not on the same level. Thus men of character are the conscience of the society to which they belong.[2]

The natural measure of this power is the resistance of circumstances. Impure men consider life as it is reflected in opinions, events and persons. They cannot see the action until it is done. Yet its moral element preëxisted in the actor, and its quality as right or wrong it was easy to predict. Everything in nature is bipolar, or has a positive and a negative pole. There is a male and a female, a spirit and a fact, a north and a south. Spirit is the positive, the event is the negative. Will is the north, action the south pole. Character may be ranked as having its natural place in the north. It shares the magnetic currents of the system. The feeble souls are drawn to the south or negative pole. They look at the profit or hurt of the action. They never behold a principle until it is lodged in a person. They do not wish to be lovely, but to be loved. Men of character like to hear of their faults ; the other class do not like to hear of faults ; they worship events ; secure to them a fact, a connection, a certain chain of circumstances, and they will ask no more. The hero sees that the event is ancillary ; it must follow *him*.[1] A given order of events has no power to secure to him the satisfaction which the imagination attaches to it ; the soul of goodness escapes from any set of circumstances ; whilst prosperity belongs to a certain mind, and will introduce that power and victory which is its natural fruit, into any order of events. No change

III

of circumstances can repair a defect of character. We boast our emancipation from many superstitions; but if we have broken any idols it is through a transfer of the idolatry. What have I gained, that I no longer immolate a bull to Jove or to Neptune, or a mouse to Hecate; that I do not tremble before the Eumenides, or the Catholic Purgatory, or the Calvinistic Judgment-day, — if I quake at opinion, the public opinion as we call it; or at the threat of assault, or contumely, or bad neighbors, or poverty, or mutilation, or at the rumor of revolution, or of murder? If I quake, what matters it what I quake at? Our proper vice takes form in one or another shape, according to the sex, age, or temperament of the person, and, if we are capable of fear, will readily find terrors.[1] The covetousness or the malignity which saddens me when I ascribe it to society, is my own. I am always environed by myself. On the other part, rectitude is a perpetual victory, celebrated not by cries of joy but by serenity, which is joy fixed or habitual. It is disgraceful to fly to events for confirmation of our truth and worth. The capitalist does not run every hour to the broker to coin his advantages into current money of the realm; he is satisfied to read in the quotations of the market that his stocks have risen. The same transport which the occurrence of the best events in the best order would occasion me, I must learn to taste purer in the perception that my position is every hour meliorated, and does already command those events I desire. That exultation is only to be checked by the foresight of an order of things so excellent as to throw all our prosperities into the deepest shade.

The face which character wears to me is self-sufficingness. I revere the person who is riches; so that I cannot think of him as alone, or poor, or exiled, or unhappy, or a client, but as perpetual patron, benefactor and beatified man. Character is centrality, the impossibility of being displaced or overset. A man should give us a sense of mass. Society is frivolous, and shreds its day into scraps, its conversation into ceremonies and escapes. But if I go to see an ingenious man I shall think myself poorly entertained if he give me nimble pieces of benevolence and etiquette; rather he shall stand stoutly in his place and let me apprehend, if it were only his resistance; know that I have encountered a new and positive quality; — great refreshment for both of us. It is much that he

does not accept the conventional opinions and
practices. That non-conformity will remain a
goad and remembrancer, and every inquirer will
have to dispose of him, in the first place. There
is nothing real or useful that is not a seat of war.
Our houses ring with laughter and personal
and critical gossip, but it helps little. But the
uncivil, unavailable man, who is a problem and
a threat to society, whom it cannot let pass in
silence but must either worship or hate, — and
to whom all parties feel related, both the leaders of opinion and the obscure and eccentric, —
he helps ; he puts America and Europe in the
wrong, and destroys the scepticism which says,
'Man is a doll, let us eat and drink, 't is the
best we can do,' by illuminating the untried and
unknown. Acquiescence in the establishment
and appeal to the public, indicate infirm faith,
heads which are not clear, and which must see
a house built before they can comprehend the
plan of it. The wise man not only leaves out
of his thought the many, but leaves out the
few. Fountains,¹ the self-moved, the absorbed,
the commander because he is commanded, the
assured, the primary, — they are good ; for
these announce the instant presence of supreme
power.

Our action should rest mathematically on our substance. In nature there are no false valuations. A pound of water in the ocean-tempest has no more gravity than in a midsummer pond. All things work exactly according to their quality and according to their quantity; attempt nothing they cannot do, except man only. He has pretension; he wishes and attempts things beyond his force. I read in a book of English memoirs, " Mr. Fox (afterwards Lord Holland) said, he must have the Treasury; he had served up to it, and would have it." Xenophon and his Ten Thousand were quite equal to what they attempted, and did it; so equal, that it was not suspected to be a grand and inimitable exploit. Yet there stands that fact unrepeated, a high-water mark in military history. Many have attempted it since, and not been equal to it. It is only on reality that any power of action can be based. No institution will be better than the institutor. I knew an amiable and accomplished person who undertook a practical reform, yet I was never able to find in him the enterprise of love he took in hand. He adopted it by ear and by the understanding from the books he had been reading. All his action was tentative, a piece of the city carried out into the fields, and was the city still, and no new fact, and could not inspire enthusiasm. Had there been something latent in the man, a terrible undemonstrated genius agitating and embarrassing his demeanor, we had watched for its advent. It is not enough that the intellect should see the evils and their remedy. We shall still postpone our existence, nor take the ground to which we are entitled, whilst it is only a thought and not a spirit that incites us. We have not yet served up to it.

These are properties of life, and another trait is the notice of incessant growth. Men should be intelligent and earnest. They must also make us feel that they have a controlling happy future opening before them, whose early twilights already kindle in the passing hour.[1] The hero is misconceived and misreported; he cannot therefore wait to unravel any man's blunders; he is again on his road, adding new powers and honors to his domain and new claims on your heart, which will bankrupt you if you have loitered about the old things and have not kept your relation to him by adding to your wealth. New actions are the only apologies and explanations of old ones which the

noble can bear to offer or to receive. If your
friend has displeased you, you shall not sit down
to consider it, for he has already lost all memory
of the passage, and has doubled his power to
serve you, and ere you can rise up again will
burden you with blessings.

We have no pleasure in thinking of a benevolence that is only measured by its works.
Love is inexhaustible, and if its estate is wasted,
its granary emptied, still cheers and enriches,
and the man, though he sleep, seems to purify
the air and his house to adorn the landscape
and strengthen the laws. People always recognize this difference. We know who is benevolent, by quite other means than the amount
of subscription to soup-societies. It is only low
merits that can be enumerated. Fear, when
your friends say to you what you have done
well, and say it through; but when they stand
with uncertain timid looks of respect and half-
dislike, and must suspend their judgment for
years to come, you may begin to hope.[1] Those
who live to the future must always appear selfish to those who live to the present. Therefore it was droll in the good Riemer, who has
written memoirs of Goethe, to make out a list
of his donations and good deeds, as, so many

hundred thalers given to Stilling, to Hegel, to Tischbein; a lucrative place found for Professor Voss, a post under the Grand Duke for Herder, a pension for Meyer, two professors recommended to foreign universities; etc., etc. The longest list of specifications of benefit would look very short. A man is a poor creature if he is to be measured so. For all these of course are exceptions, and the rule and hodiurnal life of a good man is benefaction. The true charity of Goethe is to be inferred from the account he gave Dr. Eckermann of the way in which he had spent his fortune. "Each *bonmot* of mine has cost a purse of gold. Half a million of my own money, the fortune I inherited, my salary and the large income derived from my writings for fifty years back, have been expended to instruct me in what I now know. I have besides seen," etc.

I own it is but poor chat and gossip to go to enumerate traits of this simple and rapid power, and we are painting the lightning with charcoal; but in these long nights and vacations I like to console myself so. Nothing but itself can copy it. A word warm from the heart enriches me. I surrender at discretion. How death-cold is literary genius before this fire of life ! These are the touches that reanimate my heavy soul and give it eyes to pierce the dark of nature. I find, where I thought myself poor, there was I most rich. Thence comes a new intellectual exaltation, to be again rebuked by some new exhibition of character. Strange alternation of attraction and repulsion ! Character repudiates intellect, yet excites it ; and character passes into thought, is published so, and then is ashamed before new flashes of moral worth.

Character is nature in the highest form. It is of no use to ape it or to contend with it. Somewhat is possible of resistance, and of persistence, and of creation, to this power, which will foil all emulation.

This masterpiece is best where no hands but nature's have been laid on it. Care is taken that the greatly-destined shall slip up into life in the shade, with no thousand-eyed Athens to watch and blazon every new thought, every blushing emotion of young genius. Two persons lately, very young children of the most high God, have given me occasion for thought. When I explored the source of their sanctity and charm for the imagination, it seemed as if each answered, ' From my non-conformity ; I

never listened to your people's law, or to what
they call their gospel, and wasted my time. I
was content with the simple rural poverty of
my own; hence this sweetness; my work never
reminds you of that, — is pure of that.' And
nature advertises me in such persons that in democratic America she will not be democratized.[1]
How cloistered and constitutionally sequestered
from the market and from scandal! It was
only this morning that I sent away some wild
flowers of these wood-gods. They are a relief
from literature, — these fresh draughts from the
sources of thought and sentiment; as we read,
in an age of polish and criticism, the first lines
of written prose and verse of a nation. How
captivating is their devotion to their favorite
books, whether Æschylus, Dante, Shakspeare,
or Scott, as feeling that they have a stake in
that book; who touches that, touches them, —
and especially the total solitude of the critic,
the Patmos of thought from which he writes,
in unconsciousness of any eyes that shall ever
read this writing. Could they dream on still,
as angels, and not wake to comparisons and to
be flattered! Yet some natures are too good to
be spoiled by praise, and wherever the vein of
thought reaches down into the profound, there

is no danger from vanity. Solemn friends will
warn them of the danger of the head's being
turned by the flourish of trumpets, but they
can afford to smile. I remember the indignation of an eloquent Methodist at the kind
admonitions of a Doctor of Divinity, — 'My
friend, a man can neither be praised nor in-
sulted.' ¹ But forgive the counsels ; they are
very natural. I remember the thought which
occurred to me when some ingenious and spiritual foreigners came to America, was, Have
you been victimized in being brought hither?
— or, prior to that, answer me this, ' Are you
victimizable?' ²

As I have said, Nature keeps these sovereign-
ties in her own hands, and however pertly our
sermons and disciplines would divide some share
of credit, and teach that the laws fashion the citizen, she goes her own gait and puts the wisest
in the wrong. She makes very light of gospels
and prophets, as one who has a great many
more to produce and no excess of time to spare
on any one. There is a class of men, individuals
of which appear at long intervals, so eminently
endowed with insight and virtue that they have
been unanimously saluted as *divine*, and who
seem to be an accumulation of that power we

consider. Divine persons are character born, or,
to borrow a phrase from Napoleon, they are
victory organized. They are usually received
with ill-will, because they are new and because
they set a bound to the exaggeration that has
been made of the personality of the last divine
person. Nature never rhymes her children, nor
makes two men alike. When we see a great man
we fancy a resemblance to some historical person, and predict the sequel of his character and
fortune ; a result which he is sure to disappoint.
None will ever solve the problem of his character according to our prejudice, but only in his
own high unprecedented way. Character wants
room ; must not be crowded on by persons nor
be judged from glimpses got in the press of affairs or on few occasions. It needs perspective,
as a great building. It may not, probably does
not, form relations rapidly ; and we should not
require rash explanation, either on the popular
ethics, or on our own, of its action.

I look on Sculpture as history. I do not
think the Apollo and the Jove impossible in
flesh and blood. Every trait which the artist
recorded in stone he had seen in life, and better
than his copy. We have seen many counterfeits,
but we are born believers in great men. How

easily we read in old books, when men were few,
of the smallest action of the patriarchs. We
require that a man should be so large and co-
lumnar in the landscape, that it should deserve
to be recorded that he arose, and girded up his
loins, and departed to such a place. The most
credible pictures are those of majestic men who
prevailed at their entrance, and convinced the
senses ; as happened to the eastern magian who
was sent to test the merits of Zertusht or Zoroaster. " When the Yunâni sage arrived at
Balkh, the Persians tell us, Gushtasp appointed
a day on which the Mobeds of every country
should assemble, and a golden chair was placed
for the Yunâni sage. Then the beloved of Yez-
dam, the prophet Zertusht, advanced into the
midst of the assembly. The Yunâni sage, on
seeing that chief, said, ' This form and this gait
cannot lie, and nothing but truth can proceed
from them.' " [1] Plato said it was impossible not
to believe in the children of the gods, " though
they should speak without probable or necessary
arguments." [2] I should think myself very unhappy in my associates if I could not credit the
best things in history. " John Bradshaw," says
Milton, " appears like a consul, from whom the
fasces are not to depart with the year ; so that

not on the tribunal only, but throughout his life,
you would regard him as sitting in judgment
upon kings." [1] I find it more credible, since it
is anterior information, that one man should
know heaven, as the Chinese say, than that so
many men should know the world. " The virtuous prince confronts the gods, without any
misgiving. He waits a hundred ages till a sage
comes, and does not doubt. He who confronts
the gods, without any misgiving, knows heaven;
he who waits a hundred ages until a sage comes,
without doubting, knows men. Hence the virtuous prince moves, and for ages shows empire
the way." But there is no need to seek remote
examples. He is a dull observer whose experience has not taught him the reality and force
of magic, as well as of chemistry. The coldest
precisian cannot go abroad without encounter-
ing inexplicable influences. One man fastens an
eye on him and the graves of the memory render up their dead; the secrets that make him
wretched either to keep or to betray must be
yielded; — another, and he cannot speak, and
the bones of his body seem to lose their carti-
lages; the entrance of a friend adds grace, bold-
ness and eloquence to him; and there are persons he cannot choose but remember, who gave

a transcendent expansion to his thought, and
kindled another life in his bosom.

What is so excellent as strict relations of
amity, when they spring from this deep root?
The sufficient reply to the skeptic who doubts
the power and the furniture of man, is in that
possibility of joyful intercourse with persons,
which makes the faith and practice of all reasonable men. I know nothing which life has to
offer so satisfying as the profound good understanding which can subsist, after much exchange
of good offices, between two virtuous men, each
of whom is sure of himself and sure of his friend.
It is a happiness which postpones all other grati-
fications, and makes politics, and commerce, and
churches, cheap. For when men shall meet as
they ought, each a benefactor, a shower of stars,
clothed with thoughts, with deeds, with accom-
plishments, it should be the festival of nature
which all things announce. Of such friendship,
love in the sexes is the first symbol, as all other
things are symbols of love. Those relations to
the best men, which, at one time, we reckoned
the romances of youth, become, in the progress
of the character, the most solid enjoyment.

If it were possible to live in right relations
with men! — if we could abstain from asking

anything of them, from asking their praise, or help, or pity, and content us with compelling them through the virtue of the eldest laws! Could we not deal with a few persons, — with one person, — after the unwritten statutes, and make an experiment of their efficacy? Could we not pay our friend the compliment of truth, of silence, of forbearing? Need we be so eager to seek him? If we are related, we shall meet. It was a tradition of the ancient world that no metamorphosis could hide a god from a god; and there is a Greek verse which runs, —

"The Gods are to each other not unknown." [1]

Friends also follow the laws of divine necessity; they gravitate to each other, and cannot otherwise : —

When each the other shall avoid,
Shall each by each be most enjoyed. [2]

Their relation is not made, but allowed. The gods must seat themselves without seneschal in our Olympus, and as they can instal themselves by seniority divine. Society is spoiled if pains are taken, if the associates are brought a mile to meet. And if it be not society, it is a mischievous, low, degrading jangle, though made up of the best. All the greatness of each is kept back and every foible in painful activity, as if the Olympians should meet to exchange snuff-boxes.

Life goes headlong. We chase some flying scheme, or we are hunted by some fear or command behind us. But if suddenly we encounter a friend, we pause; our heat and hurry look foolish enough; now pause, now possession is required, and the power to swell the moment from the resources of the heart. The moment is all, in all noble relations.

A divine person is the prophecy of the mind; a friend is the hope of the heart. Our beatitude waits for the fulfilment of these two in one. The ages are opening this moral force. All force is the shadow or symbol of that. Poetry is joyful and strong as it draws its inspiration thence. Men write their names on the world as they are filled with this. History has been mean; our nations have been mobs; we have never seen a man: that divine form we do not yet know, but only the dream and prophecy of such: we do not know the majestic manners which belong to him, which appease and exalt the beholder. We shall one day see that the most private is the most public energy, that quality atones for quantity, and grandeur of character acts in the

III

dark, and succors them who never saw it. What greatness has yet appeared is beginnings and encouragements to us in this direction. The history of those gods and saints which the world has written and then worshipped, are documents of character. The ages have exulted in the manners of a youth who owed nothing to fortune, and who was hanged at the Tyburn of his nation, who, by the pure quality of his nature, shed an epic splendor around the facts of his death which has transfigured every particular into an universal symbol for the eyes of mankind. This great defeat is hitherto our highest fact. But the mind requires a victory to the senses ; a force of character which will convert judge, jury, soldier and king ; which will rule animal and mineral virtues, and blend with the courses of sap, of rivers, of winds, of stars, and of moral agents.

If we cannot attain at a bound to these grandeurs, at least let us do them homage. In society, high advantages are set down to the possessor as disadvantages. It requires the more wariness in our private estimates. I do not forgive in my friends the failure to know a fine character and to entertain it with thankful hospitality.[1] When at last that which we have always longed for is arrived and shines on us with glad rays out of that far celestial land, then to be coarse, then to be critical and treat such a visitant with the jabber and suspicion of the streets, argues a vulgarity that seems to shut the doors of heaven. This is confusion, this the right insanity, when the soul no longer knows its own, nor where its allegiance, its religion, are due. Is there any religion but this, to know that wherever in the wide desert of being the holy sentiment we cherish has opened into a flower, it blooms for me ? if none sees it, I see it ; I am aware, if I alone, of the greatness of the fact. Whilst it blooms, I will keep sabbath or holy time, and suspend my gloom and my folly and jokes. Nature is indulged by the presence of this guest. There are many eyes that can detect and honor the prudent and household virtues ; there are many that can discern Genius on his starry track, though the mob is incapable ; but when that love which is all-suffering, all-abstaining, all-aspiring, which has vowed to itself that it will be a wretch and also a fool in this world sooner than soil its white hands by any compliances, comes into our streets and houses,—only the pure and aspiring can know its face, and the only compliment they can pay it is to own it.

IV

MANNERS

" How near to good is what is fair!
  Which we no sooner see,
  But with the lines and outward air
  Our senses taken be.

  Again yourselves compose,
  And now put all the aptness on
  Of Figure, that Proportion
      Or Color can disclose ;
  That if those silent arts were lost,
  Design and Picture, they might boast
      From you a newer ground,
  Instructed by the heightening sense
  Of dignity and reverence
      In their true motions found.''

                              Ben Jonson.

MANNERS

HALF the world, it is said, knows not how the other half live. Our Exploring Expedition saw the Feejee islanders getting their dinner off human bones; and they are said to eat their own wives and children. The husbandry of the modern inhabitants of Gournou (west of old Thebes) is philosophical to a fault. To set up their housekeeping nothing is requisite but two or three earthen pots, a stone to grind meal, and a mat which is the bed. The house, namely a tomb, is ready without rent or taxes. No rain can pass through the roof, and there is no door, for there is no want of one, as there is nothing to lose. If the house do not please them, they walk out and enter another, as there are several hundreds at their command. " It is somewhat singular," adds Belzoni, to whom we owe this account, "to talk of happiness among people who live in sepulchres, among the corpses and rags of an ancient nation which they know nothing of." In the deserts of Borgoo the rock-Tibboos still dwell in caves, like cliff-swallows, and the language of these negroes is compared by their neighbors to the shrieking of bats and

to the whistling of birds. Again, the Bornoos
have no proper names; individuals are called
after their height, thickness, or other accidental
quality, and have nicknames merely. But the
salt, the dates, the ivory, and the gold, for which
these horrible regions are visited, find their way
into countries where the purchaser and consumer
can hardly be ranked in one race with these can-
nibals and man-stealers; countries where man
serves himself with metals, wood, stone, glass,
gum, cotton, silk and wool; honors himself
with architecture;[1] writes laws, and contrives to
execute his will through the hands of many nations; and, especially, establishes a select society,
running through all the countries of intelligent
men, a self-constituted aristocracy, or fraternity
of the best, which, without written law or exact
usage of any kind, perpetuates itself, colonizes
every new-planted island and adopts and makes
its own whatever personal beauty or extraordinary native endowment anywhere appears.

- [What fact more conspicuous in modern history than the creation of the gentleman? Chivalry is that, and loyalty is that, and in English
literature half the drama, and all the novels,
from Sir Philip Sidney to Sir Walter Scott, paint
this figure. The word *gentleman*, which, like the

word *Christian*, must hereafter characterize the
present and the few preceding centuries by the
importance attached to it, is a homage to personal and incommunicable properties.' Frivolous and fantastic additions have got associated
with the name, but the steady interest of mankind in it must be attributed to the valuable properties which it designates. An element which
unites all the most forcible persons of every
country, makes them intelligible and agreeable
to each other, and is somewhat so precise that it
is at once felt if an individual lack the masonic
sign, — cannot be any casual product, but must
be an average result of the character and faculties universally found in men. It seems a certain
permanent average ; as the atmosphere is a permanent composition, whilst so many gases are
combined only to be decompounded. *Comme il
faut*, is the Frenchman's description of good
society : *as we must be.* It is a spontaneous fruit
of talents and feelings of precisely that class who
have most vigor, who take the lead in the world
of this hour, and though far from pure, far from
constituting the gladdest and highest tone of
human feeling, it is as good as the whole society
permits it to be. It is made of the spirit, more
than of the talent of men, and is a compound

result into which every great force enters as an ingredient, namely virtue, wit, beauty, wealth and power.

There is something equivocal in all the words in use to express the excellence of manners and social cultivation, because the quantities are fluxional, and the last effect is assumed by the senses as the cause. The word *gentleman* has not any correlative abstract to express the quality. *Gentility* is mean, and *gentilesse*[1] is obsolete. But we must keep alive in the vernacular the distinction between *fashion*, a word of narrow and often sinister meaning, and the heroic character which *the gentleman* imports. The usual words, however, must be respected; they will be found to contain the root of the matter. The point of distinction in all this class of names, as courtesy, chivalry, fashion, and the like, is that the flower and fruit, not the grain of the tree, are contemplated. It is beauty which is the aim this time, and not worth.[2] The result is now in question, although our words intimate well enough the popular feeling that the appearance supposes a substance. The gentleman is a man of truth, lord of his own actions, and expressing that lordship in his behavior; not in any manner dependent and servile, either on persons, or opin-

ions, or possessions. Beyond this fact of truth
and real force, the word denotes good-nature or
benevolence: manhood first, and then gentle-
ness. The popular notion certainly adds a condition of ease and fortune; but that is a natural
result of personal force and love, that they should
possess and dispense the goods of the world. In
times of violence, every eminent person must
fall in with many opportunities to approve his
stoutness and worth; therefore every man's name
that emerged at all from the mass in the feudal
ages rattles in our ear like a flourish of trumpets. But personal force never goes out of fashion.' That is still paramount to-day, and in the
moving crowd of good society the men of valor
and reality are known and rise to their natural
place. The competition is transferred from war
to politics and trade, but the personal force
appears readily enough in these new arenas.

Power first, or no leading class. In politics
and in trade, bruisers and pirates are of better
promise than talkers and clerks. God knows
that all sorts of gentlemen knock at the door;²
but whenever used in strictness and with any
emphasis, the name will be found to point at
original energy. It describes a man standing
in his own right and working after untaught

methods. In a good lord there must first be a good animal, at least to the extent of yielding the incomparable advantage of animal spirits. The ruling class must have more, but they must have these, giving in every company the sense of power, which makes things easy to be done which daunt the wise.[1] The society of the energetic class, in their friendly and festive meetings, is full of courage and of attempts which intimidate the pale scholar. The courage which girls exhibit is like a battle of Lundy's Lane, or a sea-fight. The intellect relies on memory to make some supplies to face these extemporaneous squadrons. But memory is a base mendicant with basket and badge, in the presence of these sudden masters. The rulers of society must be up to the work of the world, and equal to their versatile office: men of the right Cæsarian pattern, who have great range of affinity. I am far from believing the timid maxim of Lord Falkland (" that for ceremony there must go two to it; since a bold fellow will go through the cunningest forms "), and am of opinion that the gentleman is the bold fellow whose forms are not to be broken through; and only that plenteous nature is rightful master which is the complement of whatever person it converses with.

My gentleman gives the law where he is; he
will outpray saints in chapel, outgeneral veterans
in the field, and outshine all courtesy in the hall.
He is good company for pirates and good with
academicians; so that it is useless to fortify yourself against him; he has the private entrance to
all minds, and I could as easily exclude myself,
as him. The famous gentlemen of Asia and
Europe have been of this strong type; Saladin,
Sapor, the Cid,¹ Julius Cæsar, Scipio, Alexander,
Pericles, and the lordliest personages. They
sat very carelessly in their chairs, and were too
excellent themselves, to value any condition at
a high rate.

A plentiful fortune is reckoned necessary, in
the popular judgment, to the completion of this
man of the world; and it is a material deputy
which walks through the dance which the first
has led. Money is not essential, but this wide
affinity is, which transcends the habits of clique
and caste and makes itself felt by men of all
classes. If the aristocrat is only valid in fashion-
able circles and not with truckmen, he will never
be a leader in fashion; and if the man of the
people cannot speak on equal terms with the
gentleman, so that the gentleman shall perceive
that he is already really of his own order, he is

not to be feared. Diogenes, Socrates, and Epaminondas, are gentlemen of the best blood who
have chosen the condition of poverty when that
of wealth was equally open to them. I use these
old names, but the men I speak of are my contemporaries.[1] Fortune will not supply to every
generation one of these well-appointed knights,
but every collection of men furnishes some example of the class; and the politics of this country, and the trade of every town, are controlled
by these hardy and irresponsible doers, who have
invention to take the lead, and a broad sympathy
which puts them in fellowship with crowds, and
makes their action popular.

The manners of this class are observed and
caught with devotion by men of taste. The association of these masters with each other and
with men intelligent of their merits, is mutually
agreeable and stimulating. The good forms, the
happiest expressions of each, are repeated and
adopted. By swift consent everything superfluous is dropped, everything graceful is renewed.
Fine manners show themselves formidable to
the uncultivated man. They are a subtler science of defence to parry and intimidate; but
once matched by the skill of the other party,
they drop the point of the sword, — points and

fences disappear, and the youth finds himself in
a more transparent atmosphere, wherein life is
a less troublesome game, and not a misunderstanding rises between the players. Manners
aim to facilitate life, to get rid of impediments
and bring the man pure to energize. They aid
our dealing and conversation as a railway aids
travelling, by getting rid of all avoidable ob-
structions of the road and leaving nothing to be
conquered but pure space.¹ These forms very
soon become fixed, and a fine sense of propriety
is cultivated with the more heed that it becomes
a badge of social and civil distinctions. Thus
grows up Fashion, an equivocal semblance, the ·
most puissant, the most fantastic and frivolous,
the most feared and followed, and which morals
and violence assault in vain.

There exists a strict relation between the class
of power and the exclusive and polished circles.
The last are always filled or filling from the first.
The strong men usually give some allowance
even to the petulances of fashion, for that affinity they find in it. Napoleon, child of the revolution, destroyer of the old noblesse, never
ceased to court the Faubourg St. Germain;
doubtless with the feeling that fashion is a homage to men of his stamp. Fashion, though ·

strange way, represents all manly virtue. It is virtue gone to seed : it is a kind of posthumous honor. It does not often caress the great, but the children of the great : it is a hall of the Past.]￢ It usually sets its face against the great of this hour. Great men are not commonly in its halls ; they are absent in the field : they are working, not triumphing. Fashion is made up of their children ; of those who through the value and virtue of somebody, have acquired lustre to their name, marks of distinction, means of cultivation and generosity, and in their physical organization a certain health and excellence which secure to them, if not the highest power to work, yet high power to enjoy. The class of power, the working heroes, the Cortez, the Nelson, the Napoleon, see that this is the festivity and permanent celebration of such as they ; that fashion is funded talent ; is Mexico, Marengo and Trafalgar beaten out thin ; that the brilliant names of fashion run back to just such busy names as their own, fifty or sixty years ago. They are the sowers, their sons shall be the reapers, and *their* sons, in the ordinary course of things, must yield the possession of the harvest to new competitors with keener eyes and stronger frames. The city is recruited from the country. In the year 1805, it is said, every legitimate monarch in Europe was imbecile. The city would have died out, rotted and exploded, long ago, but that it was reinforced from the fields. It is only country which came to town day before yesterday that is city and court to-day.[1]

Aristocracy and fashion are certain inevitable results. These mutual selections are indestructible. If they provoke anger in the least favored class, and the excluded majority revenge themselves on the excluding minority by the strong hand and kill them, at once a new class finds itself at the top, as certainly as cream rises in a bowl of milk: and if the people should destroy class after class, until two men only were left, one of these would be the leader and would be involuntarily served and copied by the other. You may keep this minority out of sight and out of mind, but it is tenacious of life, and is one of the estates of the realm. I am the more struck with this tenacity, when I see its work. It respects the administration of such unimportant matters, that we should not look for any durability in its rule. We sometimes meet men under some strong moral influence, as a patriotic, a literary, a religious movement, and feel that the moral sentiment rules man and nature.

III

We think all other distinctions and ties will be slight and fugitive, this of caste or fashion for example; yet come from year to year and see how permanent that is, in this Boston or New York life of man, where too it has not the least countenance from the law of the land. Not in Egypt or in India a firmer or more impassable line. Here are associations whose ties go over and under and through it, a meeting of merchants, a military corps, a college class, a fire-club, a professional association, a political, a religious convention; — the persons seem to draw inseparably near; yet, that assembly once dispersed, its members will not in the year meet again. Each returns to his degree in the scale of good society, porcelain remains porcelain, and earthen earthen. The objects of fashion may be frivolous, or fashion may be objectless, but the nature of this union and selection can be neither frivolous nor accidental. Each man's rank in that perfect graduation depends on some symmetry in his structure or some agreement in his structure to the symmetry of society. Its doors unbar instantaneously to a natural claim of their own kind. A natural gentleman finds his way in, and will keep the oldest patrician out who has lost his intrinsic rank.[1] Fashion understands itself; good-breeding and personal superiority of whatever country readily fraternize with those of every other. The chiefs of savage tribes have distinguished themselves in London and Paris by the purity of their tournure.

To say what good of fashion we can, it rests on reality, and hates nothing so much as pretenders; to exclude and mystify pretenders and send them into everlasting 'Coventry,' is its delight. We contemn in turn every other gift of men of the world; but the habit even in little and the least matters of not appealing to any but our own sense of propriety, constitutes the foundation of all chivalry. There is almost no kind of self-reliance, so it be sane and proportioned, which fashion does not occasionally adopt and give it the freedom of its saloons. A sainted soul is always elegant, and, if it will, passes unchallenged into the most guarded ring. But so will Jock the teamster pass, in some crisis that brings him thither, and find favor, as long as his head is not giddy with the new circumstance, and the iron shoes do not wish to dance in waltzes and cotillons. For there is nothing settled in manners, but the laws of behavior yield to the energy of the individual. The maiden at her first ball, the countryman at a city dinner,

believes that there is a ritual according to which
every act and compliment must be performed,
or the failing party must be cast out of this presence.   Later they learn that good sense and
character make their own forms every moment,
and speak or abstain, take wine or refuse it, stay
or go, sit in a chair or sprawl with children on
the floor, or stand on their head, or what else
soever, in a new and aboriginal way; and that
strong will is always in fashion, let who will
be unfashionable. All that fashion demands is
composure and self-content.[1] A circle of men
perfectly well-bred would be a company of sensible persons in which every man's native manners
and character appeared. If the fashionist have
not this quality, he is nothing. We are such
lovers of self-reliance that we excuse in a man
many sins if he will show us a complete satisfaction in his position, which asks no leave to
be, of mine, or any man's good opinion.[2] But
any deference to some eminent man or woman
of the world, forfeits all privilege of nobility.
He is an underling: I have nothing to do with
him; I will speak with his master. A man
should not go where he cannot carry his whole
sphere or society with him, — not bodily, the
whole circle of his friends, but atmospherically.

He should preserve in a new company the same attitude of mind and reality of relation which his daily associates draw him to, else he is shorn of his best beams, and will be an orphan in the merriest club. " If you could see Vich Ian Vohr with his tail on ! — " But Vich Ian Vohr must always carry his belongings in some fashion, if not added as honor, then severed as disgrace.[1]

There will always be in society certain persons who are mercuries of its approbation, and whose glance will at any time determine for the curious their standing in the world. These are the chamberlains of the lesser gods. Accept their coldness as an omen of grace with the loftier deities, and allow them all their privilege. They are clear in their office, nor could they be thus formidable without their own merits. But do not measure the importance of this class by their pretension, or imagine that a fop can be the dispenser of honor and shame. They pass also at their just rate; for how can they otherwise, in circles which exist as a sort of herald's office for the sifting of character ?

As the first thing man requires of man is reality, so that appears in all the forms of society. We pointedly, and by name, introduce the parties to each other. Know you before all heaven

and earth, that this is Andrew, and this is Greg-
ory, — they look each other in the eye; they
grasp each other's hand, to identify and signal-
ize each other. It is a great satisfaction. A
gentleman never dodges; his eyes look straight
forward, and he assures the other party, first
of all, that he has been met. For what is it
that we seek, in so many visits and hospitalities?
Is it your draperies, pictures, and decorations?
Or do we not insatiably ask, Was a man in the
house? I may easily go into a great household
where there is much substance, excellent pro-
vision for comfort, luxury and taste, and yet
not encounter there any Amphitryon who shall
subordinate these appendages. I may go into
a cottage, and find a farmer who feels that he
is the man I have come to see, and fronts me
accordingly. It was therefore a very natural
point of old feudal etiquette that a gentleman
who received a visit, though it were of his sovereign, should not leave his roof, but should
wait his arrival at the door of his house.[1] No
house, though it were the Tuileries or the Es-
curial, is good for anything without a master.
And yet we are not often gratified by this hospitality. Everybody we know surrounds himself with a fine house, fine books, conservatory,

gardens, equipage and all manner of toys, as screens to interpose between himself and his guest. Does it not seem as if man was of a very sly, elusive nature, and dreaded nothing so much as a full rencontre front to front with his fellow? It were unmerciful, I know, quite to abolish the use of these screens, which are of eminent convenience, whether the guest is too great or too little. We call together many friends who keep each other in play, or by luxuries and ornaments we amuse the young people, and guard our retirement. Or if perchance a searching realist comes to our gate, before whose eye we have no care to stand, then again we run to our curtain, and hide ourselves as Adam at the voice of the Lord God in the garden. Cardinal Caprara, the Pope's legate at Paris, defended himself from the glances of Napoleon by an immense pair of green spectacles. Napoleon remarked them, and speedily managed to rally them off: and yet Napoleon, in his turn, was not great enough, with eight hundred thousand troops at his back, to face a pair of freeborn eyes, but fenced himself with etiquette and within triple barriers of reserve; and, as all the world knows from Madame de Staël, was wont, when he found himself observed, to discharge his face of all expression. But emperors and rich men are by no means the most skilful masters of good manners. No rent-roll nor army-list can dignify skulking and dissimulation; and the first point of courtesy must always be truth, as really all the forms of good-breeding point that way.

I have just been reading, in Mr. Hazlitt's translation, Montaigne's account of his journey into Italy, and am struck with nothing more agreeably than the self-respecting fashions of the time. His arrival in each place, the arrival of a gentleman of France, is an event of some consequence. Wherever he goes he pays a visit to whatever prince or gentleman of note resides upon his road, as a duty to himself and to civilization. When he leaves any house in which he has lodged for a few weeks, he causes his arms to be painted and hung up as a perpetual sign to the house, as was the custom of gentlemen.

The complement of this graceful self-respect, and that of all the points of good-breeding I most require and insist upon, is deference. I like that every chair should be a throne, and hold a king. I prefer a tendency to stateliness to an excess of fellowship. Let the incommunicable objects of nature and the metaphysical isolation of man teach us independence. Let us not be too much acquainted. I would have a man enter his house through a hall filled with heroic and sacred sculptures, that he might not want the hint of tranquillity and self-poise.[1] We should meet each morning as from foreign countries, and, spending the day together, should depart at night, as into foreign countries. In all things I would have the island of a man inviolate. Let us sit apart as the gods, talking from peak to peak all round Olympus. No degree of affection need invade this religion. This is myrrh and rosemary to keep the other sweet. Lovers should guard their strangeness.[2] If they forgive too much, all slides into confusion and meanness. It is easy to push this deference to a Chinese etiquette; but coolness and absence of heat and haste indicate fine qualities. A gentleman makes no noise; a lady is serene. Proportionate is our disgust at those invaders who fill a studious house with blast and running, to secure some paltry convenience. Not less I dislike a low sympathy of each with his neighbor's needs. Must we have a good understanding with one another's palates? as foolish people who have lived long together know when each wants salt or sugar. I pray my

companion, if he wishes for bread, to ask me for
bread, and if he wishes for sassafras or arsenic,
to ask me for them, and not to hold out his
plate as if I knew already. Every natural func-
tion can be dignified by deliberation and privacy.
Let us leave hurry to slaves. The compliments
and ceremonies of our breeding should recall,[1]
however remotely, the grandeur of our destiny.

The flower of courtesy does not very well
bide handling, but if we dare to open another
leaf and explore what parts go to its conforma-
tion, we shall find also an intellectual quality.
To the leaders of men, the brain as well as the
flesh and the heart must furnish a proportion.
Defect in manners is usually the defect of fine
perceptions. Men are too coarsely made for the
delicacy of beautiful carriage and customs. It is
not quite sufficient to good-breeding, a union of
kindness and independence. We imperatively
require a perception of, and a homage to beauty
in our companions. Other virtues are in request
in the field and workyard, but a certain degree
of taste is not to be spared in those we sit with.
I could better eat with one who did not respect
the truth or the laws than with a sloven and
unpresentable person. Moral qualities rule the
world, but at short distances the senses are

despotic. The same discrimination of fit and
fair runs out, if with less rigor, into all parts of
life. The average spirit of the energetic class is
good sense, acting under certain limitations and
to certain ends. It entertains every natural gift.
Social in its nature, it respects everything which
tends to unite men. It delights in measure.
The love of beauty is mainly the love of measure or proportion. The person who screams,
or uses the superlative degree, or converses with
heat, puts whole drawing-rooms to flight. If
you wish to be loved, love measure.[1] You must
have genius or a prodigious usefulness if you
will hide the want of measure. This perception
comes in to polish and perfect the parts of the
social instrument. Society will pardon much to
genius and special gifts, but, being in its nature
a convention, it loves what is conventional, or
what belongs to coming together.[2] That makes
the good and bad of manners, namely what
helps or hinders fellowship. For fashion is not
good sense absolute, but relative ; not good
sense private, but good sense entertaining company. It hates corners and sharp points of
character, hates quarrelsome, egotistical, solitary
and gloomy people ; hates whatever can interfere with total blending of parties ; whilst it

values all peculiarities as in the highest degree refreshing, which can consist with good fellowship. And besides the general infusion of wit to heighten civility, the direct splendor of intellectual power is ever welcome in fine society as the costliest addition to its rule and its credit.

The dry light must shine in to adorn our festival, but it must be tempered and shaded, or that will also offend.[1] Accuracy is essential to beauty, and quick perceptions to politeness, but not too quick perceptions. One may be too punctual and too precise. He must leave the omniscience of business at the door, when he comes into the palace of beauty. Society loves creole natures, and sleepy languishing manners, so that they cover sense, grace and good-will: the air of drowsy strength, which disarms criticism; perhaps because such a person seems to reserve himself for the best of the game, and not spend himself on surfaces; an ignoring eye,[2] which does not see the annoyances, shifts and inconveniences that cloud the brow and smother the voice of the sensitive.

— [Therefore besides personal force and so much perception as constitutes unerring taste, society demands in its patrician class another element already intimated, which it significantly terms

good-nature, — expressing all degrees of generosity, from the lowest willingness and faculty
to oblige, up to the heights of magnanimity
and love. Insight we must have, or we shall
run against one another and miss the way to our
food ; but intellect is selfish and barren. The
secret of success in society is a certain heartiness
and sympathy. A man who is not happy in the
company cannot find any word in his memory
that will fit the occasion. All his information is
a little impertinent. A man who is happy there,
finds in every turn of the conversation equally
lucky occasions for the introduction of that
which he has to say. The favorites of society,
and what it calls *whole souls*, are able men and
of more spirit than wit, who have no uncom-
fortable egotism, but who exactly fill the hour
and the company ; contented and contenting, at
a marriage or a funeral, a ball or a jury, a water-
party or a shooting-match. England, which is
rich in gentlemen, furnished, in the beginning
of the present century, a good model of that
genius which the world loves, in Mr. Fox, who
added to his great abilities the most social disposition and real love of men. Parliamentary
history has few better passages than the debate
in which Burke and Fox separated in the House

of Commons; when Fox urged on his old friend the claims of old friendship with such tenderness that the house was moved to tears. Another anecdote is so close to my matter, that I must hazard the story. A tradesman who had long dunned him for a note of three hundred guineas, found him one day counting gold, and demanded payment. "No," said Fox, "I owe this money to Sheridan; it is a debt of honor; if an accident should happen to me, he has nothing to show." "Then," said the creditor, "I change my debt into a debt of honor," and tore the note in pieces. Fox thanked the man for his confidence and paid him, saying, "his debt was of older standing, and Sheridan must wait." Lover of liberty, friend of the Hindoo, friend of the African slave, he possessed a great personal popularity; and Napoleon said of him on the occasion of his visit to Paris, in 1805, "Mr. Fox will always hold the first place in an assembly at the Tuileries."

We may easily seem ridiculous in our eulogy of courtesy, whenever we insist on benevolence as its foundation. The painted phantasm Fashion rises to cast a species of derision on what we say. But I will neither be driven from some allowance to Fashion as a symbolic institution, nor from the belief that love is the basis of courtesy.[1] We must obtain *that*, if we can ; but by all means we must affirm *this*. Life owes much of its spirit to these sharp contrasts. Fashion, which affects to be honor, is often, in all men's experience, only a ballroom code. Yet so long as it is the highest circle in the imagination of the best heads on the planet, there is something necessary and excellent in it ; for it is not to be supposed that men have agreed to be the dupes of anything preposterous ; and the respect which these mysteries inspire in the most rude and sylvan characters, and the curiosity with which details of high life are read, betray the universality of the love of cultivated manners. I know that a comic disparity would be felt, if we should enter the acknowledged ' first circles ' and apply these terrific standards of justice, beauty and benefit to the individuals actually found there. Monarchs and heroes, sages and lovers, these gallants are not. Fashion has many classes and many rules of probation and admission, and not the best alone. There is not only the right of conquest, which genius pretends, — the individual demonstrating his natural aristocracy best of the best ; — but less claims will pass for the time ; for Fash-

ion loves lions, and points like Circe to her
horned company.¹ This gentleman is this after-
noon arrived from Denmark ; and that is my
Lord Ride, who came yesterday from Bagdat ;
here is Captain Friese, from Cape Turnagain ;
and Captain Symmes, from the interior of the
earth ; and Monsieur Jovaire, who came down
this morning in a balloon ; Mr. Hobnail, the
reformer ; and Reverend Jul Bat, who has con-
verted the whole torrid zone in his Sunday
school ; and Signor Torre del Greco, who ex-
tinguished Vesuvius by pouring into it the Bay
of Naples ; Spahi, the Persian ambassador ; and
Tul Wil Shan, the exiled nabob of Nepaul,
whose saddle is the new moon. — But these are
monsters of one day, and to-morrow will be dis-
missed to their holes and dens ; for in these
rooms every chair is waited for. The artist, the
scholar, and, in general, the clerisy, win their
way up into these places and get represented
here, somewhat on this footing of conquest.
Another mode is to pass through all the degrees,
spending a year and a day in St. Michael's
Square, being steeped in Cologne water, and
perfumed, and dined, and introduced, and properly grounded in all the biography and politics
and anecdotes of the boudoirs.

Yet these fineries may have grace and wit. Let there be grotesque sculpture about the gates and offices of temples. Let the creed and commandments even have the saucy homage of parody. The forms of politeness universally express benevolence in superlative degrees. What if they are in the mouths of selfish men, and used as means of selfishness? What if the false gentleman almost bows the true out of the world? What if the false gentleman contrives so to address his companion as civilly to exclude all others from his discourse, and also to make them feel excluded? Real service will not lose its nobleness. All generosity is not merely French and sentimental; nor is it to be concealed that living blood and a passion of kindness does at last distinguish God's gentleman from Fashion's. The epitaph of Sir Jenkin Grout is not wholly unintelligible to the present age : " Here lies Sir Jenkin Grout, who loved his friend and persuaded his enemy : what his mouth ate, his hand paid for : what his servants robbed, he restored : if a woman gave him pleasure, he supported her in pain : he never forgot his children ; and whoso touched his finger, drew after it his whole body." ' Even the line of heroes is not utterly extinct. There is still ever some admirable person in plain clothes, standing on the wharf, who jumps in to rescue a drowning man ; there is still some absurd inventor of charities ; some guide and comforter of runaway slaves; some friend of Poland; some Philhellene ; some fanatic who plants shade-trees for the second and third generation, and orchards when he is grown old ; some well-concealed piety ; some just man happy in an ill fame ; some youth ashamed of the favors of fortune and impatiently casting them on other shoulders. And these are the centres of society, on which it returns for fresh impulses. These are the creators of Fashion, which is an attempt to organize beauty of behavior. The beautiful and the generous are, in the theory, the doctors and apostles of this church: Scipio, and the Cid,[1] and Sir Philip Sidney, and Washington, and every pure and valiant heart who worshipped Beauty by word and by deed. The persons who constitute the natural aristocracy are not found in the actual aristocracy, or only on its edge ; as the chemical energy of the spectrum is found to be greatest just outside of the spectrum. Yet that is the infirmity of the seneschals, who do not know their sovereign when he appears. The theory of society supposes the existence and sovereignty of these. It divines afar off their coming. It says with the elder gods, —

> " As Heaven and Earth are fairer far
> Than Chaos and blank Darkness, though once chiefs;
> And as we show beyond that Heaven and Earth
> In form and shape compact and beautiful; . . .
> So on our heels a fresh perfection treads,
> A power more strong in beauty, born of us
> And fated to excel us, as we pass
> In glory that old Darkness. . . .
> . . . For 't is the eternal law
> That first in beauty shall be first in might." [1]

Therefore, within the ethnical circle of good society there is a narrower and higher circle, concentration of its light, and flower of courtesy, to which there is always a tacit appeal of pride and reference, as to its inner and imperial court; the parliament of love and chivalry. And this is constituted of those persons in whom heroic dispositions are native; with the love of beauty, the delight in society, and the power to embellish the passing day. If the individuals who compose the purest circles of aristocracy in Europe, the guarded blood of centuries, should pass in review, in such manner as that we could at leisure and critically inspect their behavior, we might find no gentleman and

no lady; for although excellent specimens of
courtesy and high-breeding would gratify us
in the assemblage, in the particulars we should
detect offence. Because elegance comes of no
breeding, but of birth. There must be romance
of character, or the most fastidious exclusion of
impertinencies will not avail. It must be genius which takes that direction: it must be not
courteous, but courtesy. High behavior is as
rare in fiction as it is in fact. Scott is praised
for the fidelity with which he painted the demeanor and conversation of the superior classes.
Certainly, kings and queens, nobles and great
ladies, had some right to complain of the absurdity that had been put in their mouths before
the days of Waverley; but neither does Scott's
dialogue bear criticism. His lords brave each
other in smart epigrammatic speeches, but the
dialogue is in costume, and does not please on
the second reading: it is not warm with life.
In Shakspeare alone the speakers do not strut
and bridle, the dialogue is easily great, and he
adds to so many titles that of being the best-
bred man in England and in Christendom.
Once or twice in a lifetime we are permitted
to enjoy the charm of noble manners, in the
presence of a man or woman who have no bar

in their nature, but whose character emanates freely in their word and gesture. A beautiful form is better than a beautiful face; a beautiful behavior is better than a beautiful form: it gives a higher pleasure than statues or pictures; it is the finest of the fine arts. A man is but a little thing in the midst of the objects of nature, yet, by the moral quality radiating from his countenance he may abolish all considerations of magnitude, and in his manners equal the majesty of the world. I have seen an individual whose manners, though wholly within the conventions of elegant society, were never learned there, but were original and commanding and held out protection and prosperity; one who did not need the aid of a court-suit, but carried the holiday in his eye; who exhilarated the fancy by flinging wide the doors of new modes of existence; who shook off the captivity of etiquette, with happy, spirited bearing, good-natured and free as Robin Hood; yet with the port of an emperor, if need be, — calm, serious and fit to stand the gaze of millions.

The open air and the fields, the street and public chambers are the places where Man executes his will; let him yield or divide the sceptre at the door of the house. Woman, with

her instinct of behavior, instantly detects in
man a love of trifles, any coldness or imbecility, or, in short, any want of that large, flowing
and magnanimous deportment which is indispensable as an exterior in the hall. Our American institutions have been friendly to her, and
at this moment I esteem it a chief felicity of
this country, that it excels in women. A certain awkward consciousness of inferiority in the
men may give rise to the new chivalry in be-
half of Woman's Rights. Certainly let her be
as much better placed in the laws and in social
forms as the most zealous reformer can ask,
but I confide so entirely in her inspiring and
musical nature, that I believe only herself can
show us how she shall be served.[1] The wonderful generosity of her sentiments raises her
at times into heroical and godlike regions,
and verifies the pictures of Minerva, Juno, or
Polymnia; and by the firmness with which
she treads her upward path, she convinces the
coarsest calculators that another road exists
than that which their feet know. But besides
those who make good in our imagination the
place of muses and of Delphic Sibyls, are there
not women who fill our vase with wine and
roses to the brim, so that the wine runs over

and fills the house with perfume; who inspire
us with courtesy; who unloose our tongues and
we speak; who anoint our eyes and we see?
We say things we never thought to have said;
for once, our walls of habitual reserve vanished
and left us at large; we were children playing
with children in a wide field of flowers. Steep
us, we cried, in these influences, for days, for
weeks, and we shall be sunny poets and will
write out in many-colored words the romance
that you are. Was it Hafiz or Firdousi that
said of his Persian Lilla, She was an elemental
force, and astonished me by her amount of life,
when I saw her day after day radiating, every
instant, redundant joy and grace on all around
her? She was a solvent powerful to reconcile
all heterogeneous persons into one society: like
air or water, an element of such a great range
of affinities that it combines readily with a thousand substances. Where she is present all others
will be more than they are wont. She was a unit
and whole, so that whatsoever she did, became
her. She had too much sympathy and desire
to please, than that you could say her manners
were marked with dignity, yet no princess could
surpass her clear and erect demeanor on each
occasion. She did not study the Persian gram-

mar, nor the books of the seven poets, but all the poems of the seven seemed to be written upon her. For though the bias of her nature was not to thought, but to sympathy, yet was she so perfect in her own nature as to meet intellectual persons by the fulness of her heart, warming them by her sentiments; believing, as she did, that by dealing nobly with all, all would show themselves noble.[1]

I know that this Byzantine pile of chivalry or Fashion, which seems so fair and picturesque to those who look at the contemporary facts for science or for entertainment, is not equally pleasant to all spectators. The constitution of our society makes it a giant's castle to the ambitious youth who have not found their names enrolled in its Golden Book, and whom it has excluded from its coveted honors and privileges. They have yet to learn that its seeming grandeur is shadowy and relative: it is great by their allowance; its proudest gates will fly open at the approach of their courage and virtue. For the present distress, however, of those who are predisposed to suffer from the tyrannies of this caprice, there are easy remedies. To remove your residence a couple of miles, or at most four, will commonly relieve the most extreme susceptibility.[1] For the advantages which fashion values are plants which thrive in very confined localities, in a few streets namely. Out of this precinct they go for nothing; are of no use in the farm, in the forest, in the market, in war, in the nuptial society, in the literary or scientific circle, at sea, in friendship, in the heaven of thought or virtue.

But we have lingered long enough in these painted courts. The worth of the thing signified must vindicate our taste for the emblem. Everything that is called fashion and courtesy humbles itself before the cause and fountain of honor, creator of titles and dignities, namely the heart of love.[2] This is the royal blood, this the fire, which, in all countries and contingencies, will work after its kind and conquer and expand all that approaches it. This gives new meanings to every fact. This impoverishes the rich, suffering no grandeur but its own. What *is* rich? Are you rich enough to help anybody? to succor the unfashionable and the eccentric? rich enough to make the Canadian in his wagon, the itinerant with his consul's paper which commends him " To the charitable," the swarthy Italian with his few broken words of English,

the lame pauper hunted by overseers from town
to town, even the poor insane or besotted wreck
of man or woman, feel the noble exception of
your presence and your house from the general
bleakness and stoniness; to make such feel that
they were greeted with a voice which made them
both remember and hope? What is vulgar but
to refuse the claim on acute and conclusive
reasons? What is gentle, but to allow it, and
give their heart and yours one holiday from
the national caution? Without the rich heart,
wealth is an ugly beggar. The king of Schiraz
could not afford to be so bountiful as the poor
Osman who dwelt at his gate. Osman had a
humanity so broad and deep that although his
speech was so bold and free with the Koran as
to disgust all the dervishes, yet was there never
a poor outcast, eccentric, or insane man, some
fool who had cut off his beard, or who had
been mutilated under a vow, or had a pet madness in his brain, but fled at once to him; that
great heart lay there so sunny and hospitable in
the centre of the country, that it seemed as if
the instinct of all sufferers drew them to his
side. And the madness which he harbored he
did not share.' Is not this to be rich? this only
to be rightly rich?

But I shall hear without pain that I play the courtier very ill, and talk of that which I do not well understand. It is easy to see that what is called by distinction society and fashion has good laws as well as bad, has much that is necessary, and much that is absurd. Too good for banning, and too bad for blessing, it reminds us of a tradition of the pagan mythology, in any attempt to settle its character. ' I overheard Jove, one day,' said Silenus, ' talking of destroying the earth ; he said it had failed ; they were all rogues and vixens, who went from bad to worse, as fast as the days succeeded each other. Minerva said she hoped not ; they were only ridiculous little creatures, with this odd circumstance, that they had a blur, or indeterminate aspect, seen far or seen near; if you called them bad, they would appear so ; if you called them good, they would appear so ; and there was no one person or action among them which would not puzzle her owl, much more all Olympus, to know whether it was fundamentally bad or good.' '

V

GIFTS

Gifts of one who loved me, —
'T was high time they came ;
When he ceased to love me,
Time they stopped for shame.

GIFTS

IT is said that the world is in a state of bankruptcy; that the world owes the world more than the world can pay, and ought to go into chancery and be sold. I do not think this general insolvency, which involves in some sort all the population, to be the reason of the difficulty experienced at Christmas and New Year and other times, in bestowing gifts; since it is always so pleasant to be generous, though very vexatious to pay debts. But the impediment lies in the choosing. If at any time it comes into my head that a present is due from me to somebody, I am puzzled what to give, until the opportunity is gone. Flowers and fruits are always fit presents; flowers, because they are a proud assertion that a ray of beauty outvalues all the utilities of the world. These gay natures contrast with the somewhat stern countenance of ordinary nature: they are like music heard out of a work-house. Nature does not cocker us; we are children, not pets; she is not fond; everything is dealt to us without fear or favor, after severe universal laws. Yet these delicate flowers look like the frolic and interference of love and

beauty. Men use to tell us that we love flattery
even though we are not deceived by it, because
it shows that we are of importance enough to
be courted. Something like that pleasure, the
flowers give us : what am I to whom these sweet
hints are addressed ? Fruits are acceptable gifts,
because they are the flower of commodities, and
admit of fantastic values being attached to them.
If a man should send to me to come a hundred
miles to visit him and should set before me a
basket of fine summer-fruit, I should think there
was some proportion between the labor and the
reward.[1]

For common gifts, necessity makes perti-
nences and beauty every day, and one is glad
when an imperative leaves him no option ; since
if the man at the door have no shoes, you have
not to consider whether you could procure him
a paint-box. And as it is always pleasing to see
a man eat bread, or drink water, in the house
or out of doors, so it is always a great satisfaction to supply these first wants. Necessity does
everything well. In our condition of universal
dependence it seems heroic to let the petitioner
be the judge of his necessity, and to give all
that is asked, though at great inconvenience.
If it be a fantastic desire, it is better to leave to

others the office of punishing him. I can think of many parts I should prefer playing to that of the Furies.[1] Next to things of necessity, the rule for a gift, which one of my friends prescribed, is that we might convey to some person that which properly belonged to his character, and was easily associated with him in thought. But our tokens of compliment and love are for the most part barbarous. Rings and other jewels are not gifts, but apologies for gifts. The only gift is a portion of thyself. Thou must bleed for me. Therefore the poet brings his poem; the shepherd, his lamb; the farmer, corn; the miner, a gem; the sailor, coral and shells; the painter, his picture; the girl, a handkerchief of her own sewing. This is right and pleasing, for it restores society in so far to the primary basis, when a man's biography is conveyed in his gift, and every man's wealth is an index of his merit.[2] But it is a cold lifeless business when you go to the shops to buy me something which does not represent your life and talent, but a goldsmith's. This is fit for kings, and rich men who represent kings, and a false state of property, to make presents of gold and silver stuffs, as a kind of symbolical sin-offering, or payment of blackmail.

III

The law of benefits is a difficult channel, which requires careful sailing, or rude boats. It is not the office of a man to receive gifts. How dare you give them? We wish to be self-sustained. We do not quite forgive a giver. The hand that feeds us is in some danger of being bitten. We can receive anything from love, for that is a way of receiving it from ourselves ; but not from any one who assumes to bestow. We sometimes hate the meat which we eat, because there seems something of degrading dependence in living by it : —

> "Brother, if Jove to thee a present make,
> Take heed that from his hands thou nothing take." [1]

We ask the whole. Nothing less will content us. We arraign society if it do not give us, besides earth and fire and water, opportunity, love, reverence and objects of veneration.

He is a good man who can receive a gift well. We are either glad or sorry at a gift, and both emotions are unbecoming. Some violence I think is done, some degradation borne, when I rejoice or grieve at a gift. I am sorry when my independence is invaded, or when a gift comes from such as do not know my spirit, and so the act is not supported ; [2] and if the gift pleases me overmuch, then I should be ashamed

that the donor should read my heart, and see
that I love his commodity, and not him. The
gift, to be true, must be the flowing of the giver
unto me, correspondent to my flowing unto him.
When the waters are at level, then my goods
pass to him, and his to me.¹ All his are mine,
all mine his. I say to him, How can you give
me this pot of oil or this flagon of wine when
all your oil and wine is mine, which belief of
mine this gift seems to deny? Hence the fitness of beautiful, not useful things, for gifts.
This giving is flat usurpation, and therefore
when the beneficiary is ungrateful, as all bene-
ficiaries hate all Timons, not at all considering
the value of the gift but looking back to the
greater store it was taken from, — I rather sympathize with the beneficiary than with the anger
of my lord Timon. For the expectation of
gratitude is mean, and is continually punished
by the total insensibility of the obliged person.
It is a great happiness to get off without injury and heart-burning from one who has had
the ill-luck to be served by you. It is a very
onerous business, this of being served, and the
debtor naturally wishes to give you a slap. A
golden text for these gentlemen is that which
I so admire in the Buddhist, who never thanks,

and who says, "Do not flatter your benefactors."

The reason of these discords I conceive to be that there is no commensurability between a man and any gift. You cannot give anything to a magnanimous person. After you have served him he at once puts you in debt by his magnanimity. The service a man renders his friend is trivial and selfish compared with the service he knows his friend stood in readiness to yield him, alike before he had begun to serve his friend, and now also. Compared with that good-will I bear my friend, the benefit it is in my power to render him seems small. Besides, our action on each other, good as well as evil, is so incidental and at random that we can seldom hear the acknowledgments of any person who would thank us for a benefit, without some shame and humiliation. We can rarely strike a direct stroke, but must be content with an oblique one; we seldom have the satisfaction of yielding a direct benefit which is directly received. But rectitude scatters favors on every side without knowing it, and receives with wonder the thanks of all people.

I fear to breathe any treason against the majesty of love, which is the genius and god

of gifts, and to whom we must not affect to pre-
scribe. Let him give kingdoms of flower-leaves
indifferently.¹ There are persons from whom we
always expect fairy-tokens; let us not cease to
expect them. This is prerogative, and not to be
limited by our municipal rules. For the rest, I
like to see that we cannot be bought and sold.
The best of hospitality and of generosity is also
not in the will, but in fate. I find that I am not
much to you; you do not need me; you do not
feel me; then am I thrust out of doors, though
you proffer me house and lands. No services
are of any value, but only likeness. When I
have attempted to join myself to others by services, it proved an intellectual trick, — no more.
They eat your service like apples, and leave you
out. But love them, and they feel you and delight in you all the time.

VI

NATURE

THE rounded world is fair to see,
Nine times folded in mystery:
Though baffled seers cannot impart
The secret of its laboring heart,
Throb thine with Nature's throbbing breast,
And all is clear from east to west.
Spirit that lurks each form within
Beckons to spirit of its kin;
Self-kindled every atom glows,
And hints the future which it owes.

NATURE

THERE are days which occur in this climate, at almost any season of the year, wherein the world reaches its perfection; when the air, the heavenly bodies and the earth, make a harmony, as if nature would indulge her offspring; when, in these bleak upper sides of the planet, nothing is to desire that we have heard of the happiest latitudes, and we bask in the shining hours of Florida and Cuba; when everything that has life gives sign of satisfaction, and the cattle that lie on the ground seem to have great and tranquil thoughts.[1] These halcyons may be looked for with a little more assurance in that pure October weather which we distinguish by the name of the Indian summer. The day, immeasurably long, sleeps over the broad hills and warm wide fields. To have lived through all its sunny hours, seems longevity enough. The solitary places do not seem quite lonely. At the gates of the forest, the surprised man of the world is forced to leave his city estimates of great and small, wise and foolish. The knapsack of custom falls off his back with the first step he takes into these precincts. Here is sanctity which shames our religions, and reality which discredits our heroes. Here we find Nature to be the circumstance which dwarfs every other circumstance, and judges like a god all men that come to her. We have crept out of our close and crowded houses into the night and morning, and we see what majestic beauties daily wrap us in their bosom. How willingly we would escape the barriers which render them comparatively impotent, escape the sophistication and second thought, and suffer nature to intrance us. The tempered light of the woods is like a perpetual morning, and is stimulating and heroic. The anciently-reported spells of these places creep on us. The stems of pines, hemlocks and oaks almost gleam like iron on the excited eye. The incommunicable trees begin to persuade us to live with them, and quit our life of solemn trifles. Here no history, or church, or state, is interpolated on the divine sky and the immortal year. How easily we might walk onward into the opening landscape, absorbed by new pictures and by thoughts fast succeeding each other, until by degrees the recollection of home was crowded out of the mind, all memory obliterated by the tyranny of the present, and we were led in triumph by nature.

These enchantments are medicinal, they sober
and heal us. These are plain pleasures, kindly
and native to us. We come to our own, and
make friends with matter, which the ambitious
chatter of the schools would persuade us to
despise. We never can part with it; the mind
loves its old home: as water to our thirst, so
is the rock, the ground, to our eyes and hands
and feet. It is firm water; it is cold flame;
what health, what affinity! Ever an old friend,
ever like a dear friend and brother when we
chat affectedly with strangers, comes in this
honest face, and takes a grave liberty with us,
and shames us out of our nonsense. Cities give
not the human senses room enough. We go
out daily and nightly to feed the eyes on the
horizon, and require so much scope, just as
we need water for our bath. There are all degrees of natural influence, from these quarantine
powers of nature, up to her dearest and gravest
ministrations to the imagination and the soul.
There is the bucket of cold water from the
spring, the wood-fire to which the chilled traveller rushes for safety, — and there is the sublime moral of autumn and of noon. We nestle
in nature, and draw our living as parasites from
her roots and grains, and we receive glances

from the heavenly bodies, which call us to solitude and foretell the remotest future. The blue
zenith is the point in which romance and reality
meet. I think if we should be rapt away into
all that and dream of heaven, and should converse with Gabriel and Uriel, the upper sky
would be all that would remain of our furniture.

It seems as if the day was not wholly profane
in which we have given heed to some natural
object. The fall of snowflakes in a still air,
preserving to each crystal its perfect form; the
blowing of sleet over a wide sheet of water, and
over plains; the waving rye-field; the mimic
waving of acres of houstonia, whose innumerable florets whiten and ripple before the eye;
the reflections of trees and flowers in glassy
lakes; the musical, steaming, odorous south
wind, which converts all trees to wind-harps;
the crackling and spurting of hemlock in the
flames, or of pine logs, which yield glory to
the walls and faces in the sitting-room, — these
are the music and pictures of the most ancient
religion. My house stands in low land, with
limited outlook, and on the skirt of the village.
But I go with my friend to the shore of our
little river, and with one stroke of the paddle
I leave the village politics and personalities,

yes, and the world of villages and personalities, behind, and pass into a delicate realm of sunset and moonlight, too bright almost for spotted man to enter without novitiate and probation. We penetrate bodily this incredible beauty; we dip our hands in this painted element; our eyes are bathed in these lights and forms.[1] A holiday, a *villeggiatura*, a royal revel, the proudest, most heart-rejoicing festival that valor and beauty, power and taste, ever decked and enjoyed, establishes itself on the instant. These sunset clouds, these delicately emerging stars, with their private and ineffable glances, signify it and proffer it.[2] I am taught the poorness of our invention, the ugliness of towns and palaces. Art and luxury have early learned that they must work as enhancement and sequel to this original beauty. I am over-instructed for my return. Henceforth I shall be hard to please. I cannot go back to toys. I am grown expensive and sophisticated. I can no longer live without elegance, but a countryman shall be my master of revels. He who knows the most; he who knows what sweets and virtues are in the ground, the waters, the plants, the heavens, and how to come at these enchantments, — is the rich and royal man. Only as far as the masters

of the world have called in nature to their aid,
can they reach the height of magnificence. This
is the meaning of their hanging-gardens, villas,
garden-houses, islands, parks and preserves, to
back their faulty personality with these strong
accessories. I do not wonder that the landed
interest should be invincible in the State with
these dangerous auxiliaries. These bribe and
invite; not kings, not palaces, not men, not
women, but these tender and poetic stars, eloquent of secret promises. We heard what the
rich man said, we knew of his villa, his grove,
his wine and his company, but the provocation
and point of the invitation came out of these
beguiling stars. In their soft glances I see what
men strove to realize in some Versailles, or
Paphos, or Ctesiphon. Indeed, it is the magi-
cal lights of the horizon and the blue sky for
the background which save all our works of art,
which were otherwise bawbles. When the rich
tax the poor with servility and obsequiousness,
they should consider the effect of men reputed
to be the possessors of nature, on imaginative
minds. Ah! if the rich were rich as the poor
fancy riches! A boy hears a military band play
on the field at night, and he has kings and
queens and famous chivalry palpably before

him. He hears the echoes of a horn in a hill
country, in the Notch Mountains, for example,
which converts the mountains into an Æolian
harp, — and this supernatural *tiralira* restores
to him the Dorian mythology, Apollo, Diana,
and all divine hunters and huntresses.[1] Can a
musical note be so lofty, so haughtily beautiful!
To the poor young poet, thus fabulous is his
picture of society; he is loyal; he respects the
rich; they are rich for the sake of his imagination; how poor his fancy would be, if they were
not rich! That they have some high-fenced
grove which they call a park; that they live in
larger and better-garnished saloons than he has
visited, and go in coaches, keeping only the
society of the elegant, to watering-places and
to distant cities, — these make the groundwork
from which he has delineated estates of romance,
compared with which their actual possessions
are shanties and paddocks. The muse herself
betrays her son, and enhances the gifts of wealth
and well-born beauty by a radiation out of the
air, and clouds, and forests that skirt the road,
— a certain haughty favor, as if from patrician
genii to patricians, a kind of aristocracy in nature, a prince of the power of the air.[2]

The moral sensibility which makes Edens and

Tempes so easily, may not be always found,
but the material landscape is never far off. We
can find these enchantments without visiting the
Como Lake, or the Madeira Islands. We exaggerate the praises of local scenery. In every
landscape the point of astonishment is the meeting of the sky and the earth, and that is seen
from the first hillock as well as from the top of
the Alleghanies. The stars at night stoop down
over the brownest, homeliest common with all
the spiritual magnificence which they shed on
the Campagna, or on the marble deserts of
Egypt. The uprolled clouds and the colors of
morning and evening will transfigure maples and
alders. The difference between landscape and
landscape is small, but there is great difference
in the beholders. There is nothing so wonderful in any particular landscape as the necessity
of being beautiful under which every landscape
lies. Nature cannot be surprised in undress.
Beauty breaks in everywhere.

But it is very easy to outrun the sympathy
of readers on this topic, which schoolmen called
natura naturata, or nature passive.[1] One can
hardly speak directly of it without excess. It is
as easy to broach in mixed companies what is
called " the subject of religion." A susceptible

person does not like to indulge his tastes in this kind without the apology of some trivial necessity : he goes to see a wood-lot, or to look at the crops, or to fetch a plant or a mineral from a remote locality, or he carries a fowling-piece or a fishing-rod. I suppose this shame must have a good reason. A dilettanteism in nature is barren and unworthy. The fop of fields is no better than his brother of Broadway. Men are naturally hunters and inquisitive of wood-craft, and I suppose that such a gazetteer as wood-cutters and Indians should furnish facts for, would take place in the most sumptuous drawing-rooms of all the " Wreaths " and " Flora's chaplets" of the bookshops ; yet ordinarily, whether we are too clumsy for so subtle a topic, or from whatever cause, as soon as men begin to write on nature, they fall into euphuism. Frivolity is a most unfit tribute to Pan, who ought to be represented in the mythology as the most continent of gods. I would not be frivolous before the admirable reserve and prudence of time, yet I cannot renounce the right of returning often to this old topic. The multitude of false churches accredits the true religion. Literature, poetry, science are the homage of man to this unfathomed secret, concerning which no

III

sane man can affect an indifference or incurios-
ity. Nature is loved by what is best in us. It
is loved as the city of God, although, or rather
because there is no citizen. The sunset is unlike
anything that is underneath it: it wants men.
And the beauty of nature must always seem unreal and mocking, until the landscape has human
figures that are as good as itself. If there were
good men, there would never be this rapture
in nature. If the king is in the palace, nobody
looks at the walls. It is when he is gone, and
the house is filled with grooms and gazers, that
we turn from the people to find relief in the
majestic men that are suggested by the pictures
and the architecture. The critics who complain
of the sickly separation of the beauty of nature
from the thing to be done, must consider that
our hunting of the picturesque is inseparable
from our protest against false society. Man is
fallen; nature is erect, and serves as a differen-
tial thermometer, detecting the presence or absence of the divine sentiment in man. By fault
of our dulness and selfishness we are looking up
to nature, but when we are convalescent, nature
will look up to us. We see the foaming brook
with compunction: if our own life flowed with
the right energy, we should shame the brook.[1]

The stream of zeal sparkles with real fire, and not with reflex rays of sun and moon. Nature may be as selfishly studied as trade. Astronomy to the selfish becomes astrology; psychology, mesmerism (with intent to show where our spoons are gone); and anatomy and physiology become phrenology and palmistry.[1]

But taking timely warning, and leaving many things unsaid on this topic, let us not longer omit our homage to the Efficient Nature, *natura naturans*, the quick cause before which all forms flee as the driven snows; itself secret, its works driven before it in flocks and multitudes, (as the ancients represented nature by Proteus, a shepherd,) and in undescribable variety. It publishes itself in creatures, reaching from particles and spiculæ through transformation on transformation to the highest symmetries, arriving at consummate results without a shock or a leap. A little heat, that is a little motion, is all that differences the bald, dazzling white and deadly cold poles of the earth from the prolific tropical climates. All changes pass without violence, by reason of the two cardinal conditions of boundless space and boundless time. Geology has initiated us into the secularity of nature, and taught us to disuse our dame-school measures, and ex-

change our Mosaic and Ptolemaic schemes for.
her large style. We knew nothing rightly, for
want of perspective. Now we learn what patient
periods must round themselves before the rock
is formed; then before the rock is broken, and
the first lichen race has disintegrated the thinnest
external plate into soil, and opened the door for
the remote Flora, Fauna, Ceres, and Pomona to
come in. How far off yet is the trilobite! how far
the quadruped! how inconceivably remote is
man! All duly arrive, and then race after race of
men. It is a long way from granite to the oyster;
farther yet to Plato and the preaching of the
immortality of the soul. Yet all must come, as
surely as the first atom has two sides.[1]

Motion or change and identity or rest are
the first and second secrets of nature: Motion
and Rest. The whole code of her laws may
be written on the thumbnail, or the signet of
a ring. The whirling bubble on the surface of a
brook admits us to the secret of the mechanics
of the sky. Every shell on the beach is a key
to it. A little water made to rotate in a cup ex-
plains the formation of the simpler shells; the
addition of matter from year to year arrives at
last at the most complex forms; and yet so poor
is nature with all her craft, that from the begin-

ning to the end of the universe she has but one
stuff, — but one stuff with its two ends, to serve
up all her dream-like variety. Compound it how
she will, star, sand, fire, water, tree, man, it is
still one stuff, and betrays the same properties.[1]

Nature is always consistent, though she feigns
to contravene her own laws. She keeps her
laws, and seems to transcend them. She arms
and equips an animal to find its place and living in the earth, and at the same time she arms
and equips another animal to destroy it. Space
exists to divide creatures; but by clothing the
sides of a bird with a few feathers she gives him
a petty omnipresence. The direction is forever
onward, but the artist still goes back for materials and begins again with the first elements
on the most advanced stage: otherwise all goes
to ruin. If we look at her work, we seem to
catch a glance of a system in transition. Plants
are the young of the world, vessels of health
and vigor; but they grope ever upward towards
consciousness; the trees are imperfect men, and
seem to bemoan their imprisonment, rooted in
the ground.[2] The animal is the novice and
probationer of a more advanced order. The
men, though young, having tasted the first drop
from the cup of thought, are already dissipated:

the maples and ferns are still uncorrupt; yet
no doubt when they come to consciousness they
too will curse and swear. Flowers so strictly
belong to youth that we adult men soon come
to feel that their beautiful generations concern
not us: we have had our day; now let the
children have theirs. The flowers jilt us, and
we are old bachelors with our ridiculous tenderness.

Things are so strictly related, that according
to the skill of the eye, from any one object the
parts and properties of any other may be pre-
dicted. If we had eyes to see it, a bit of stone
from the city wall would certify us of the necessity that man must exist, as readily as the city.
That identity makes us all one, and reduces to
nothing great intervals on our customary scale.
We talk of deviations from natural life, as if
artificial life were not also natural. The smooth-
est curled courtier in the boudoirs of a palace
has an animal nature, rude and aboriginal as a
white bear, omnipotent to its own ends, and is
directly related, there amid essences and billets-
doux, to Himmaleh mountain-chains and the
axis of the globe. If we consider how much
we are nature's, we need not be superstitious
about towns, as if that terrific or benefic force

did not find us there also, and fashion cities. Nature, who made the mason, made the house. We may easily hear too much of rural influences. The cool disengaged air of natural objects makes them enviable to us, chafed and irritable creatures with red faces, and we think we shall be as grand as they if we camp out and eat roots ; but let us be men instead of woodchucks and the oak and the elm shall gladly serve us, though we sit in chairs of ivory on carpets of silk.

This guiding identity.runs through all the surprises and contrasts of the piece, and characterizes every law. Man carries the world in his head, the whole astronomy and chemistry suspended in a thought. Because the history of nature is charactered in his brain, therefore is he the prophet and discoverer of her secrets. Every known fact in natural science was divined by the presentiment of somebody, before it was actually verified. A man does not tie his shoe without recognizing laws which bind the farthest regions of nature: moon, plant, gas, crystal, are concrete geometry and numbers. Common sense knows its own, and recognizes the fact at first sight in chemical experiment. The common sense ' of Franklin, Dalton, Davy and Black is the same common sense' which made the arrangements which now it discovers.

If the identity expresses organized rest, the counter action runs also into organization. The astronomers said, ' Give us matter and a little motion and we will construct the universe. It is not enough that we should have matter, we must also have a single impulse, one shove to launch the mass and generate the harmony of the centrifugal and centripetal forces. Once heave the ball from the hand, and we can show how all this mighty order grew.' — ' A very unreasonable postulate,' said the metaphysicians, ' and a plain begging of the question. Could you not prevail to know the genesis of projection, as well as the continuation of it ? ' Nature, meanwhile, had not waited for the discussion, but, right or wrong, bestowed the impulse, and the balls rolled.' It was no great affair, a mere push, but the astronomers were right in making much of it, for there is no end to the consequences of the act. That famous aboriginal push propagates itself through all the balls of the system, and through every atom of every ball; through all the races of creatures, and through the history and performances of every individual. Exaggeration is in the course

of things. Nature sends no creature, no man
into the world without adding a small excess of
his proper quality. Given the planet, it is still
necessary to add the impulse; so to every creature nature added a little violence of direction
in its proper path, a shove to put it on its way;
in every instance a slight generosity, a drop too
much. Without electricity the air would rot,
and without this violence of direction which
men and women have, without a spice of bigot
and fanatic, no excitement, no efficiency. We
aim above the mark to hit the mark. Every
act hath some falsehood of exaggeration in it.
And when now and then comes along some sad,
sharp-eyed man, who sees how paltry a game
is played, and refuses to play but blabs the
secret; — how then? Is the bird flown? O no,
the wary Nature sends a new troop of fairer
forms, of lordlier youths, with a little more
excess of direction to hold them fast to their
several aim; makes them a little wrong-headed
in that direction in which they are rightest, and
on goes the game again with new whirl, for a
generation or two more. The child with his
sweet pranks, the fool of his senses, commanded
by every sight and sound, without any power
to compare and rank his sensations, abandoned

to a whistle or a painted chip, to a lead dragoon
or a gingerbread-dog, individualizing everything,
generalizing nothing, delighted with every new
thing, lies down at night overpowered by the
fatigue which this day of continual pretty madness has incurred. But Nature has answered
her purpose with the curly, dimpled lunatic.
She has tasked every faculty, and has secured
the symmetrical growth of the bodily frame by
all these attitudes and exertions, — an end of
the first importance, which could not be trusted
to any care less perfect than her own. This
glitter, this opaline lustre plays round the top
of every toy to his eye to insure his fidelity,
and he is deceived to his good.[1] We are made
alive and kept alive by the same arts. Let the
stoics say what they please, we do not eat for
the good of living, but because the meat is
savory and the appetite is keen. The vege-
table life does not content itself with casting
from the flower or the tree a single seed, but it
fills the air and earth with a prodigality of seeds,
that, if thousands perish, thousands may plant
themselves ; that hundreds may come up, that
tens may live to maturity ; that at least one
may replace the parent. All things betray the
same calculated profusion. The excess of fear

with which the animal frame is hedged round, shrinking from cold, starting at sight of a snake or at a sudden noise, protects us, through a multitude of groundless alarms, from some one real danger at last. The lover seeks in marriage his private felicity and perfection, with no prospective end; and nature hides in his happiness her own end, namely progeny, or the perpetuity of the race.

But the craft with which the world is made, runs also into the mind and character of men. No man is quite sane; each has a vein of folly in his composition, a slight determination of blood to the head, to make sure of holding him hard to some one point which nature had taken to heart. Great causes are never tried on their merits; but the cause is reduced to particulars to suit the size of the partisans, and the contention is ever hottest on minor matters. Not less remarkable is the overfaith of each man in the importance of what he has to do or say. The poet, the prophet, has a higher value for what he utters than any hearer, and therefore it gets spoken. The strong, self-complacent Luther declares with an emphasis not to be mistaken, that " God himself cannot do without wise men." Jacob Behmen and George Fox betray their egotism in the pertinacity of their controversial tracts, and James Naylor once suffered himself to be worshipped as the Christ.[1] Each prophet comes presently to identify himself with his thought, and to esteem his hat and shoes sacred. However this may discredit such persons with the judicious, it helps them with the people, as it gives heat, pungency and publicity to their words. A similar experience is not infrequent in private life. Each young and ardent person writes a diary, in which, when the hours of prayer and penitence arrive, he inscribes his soul. The pages thus written are to him burning and fragrant; he reads them on his knees by midnight and by the morning star; he wets them with his tears; they are sacred; too good for the world, and hardly yet to be shown to the dearest friend. This is the man-child that is born to the soul, and her life still circulates in the babe. The umbilical cord has not yet been cut. After some time has elapsed, he begins to wish to admit his friend to this hallowed experience, and with hesitation, yet with firmness, exposes the pages to his eye. Will they not burn his eyes? The friend coldly turns them over, and passes from the writing to conversation, with easy transition, which strikes the other

party with astonishment and vexation. He cannot suspect the writing itself. Days and nights
of fervid life, of communion with angels of darkness and of light have engraved their shadowy
characters on that tear-stained book. He sus-
pects the intelligence or the heart of his friend.
Is there then no friend? He cannot yet credit
that one may have impressive experience and
yet may not know how to put his private fact
into literature : and perhaps the discovery that
wisdom has other tongues and ministers than
we, that though we should hold our peace the
truth would not the less be spoken, might check
injuriously the flames of our zeal. A man can
only speak so long as he does not feel his speech
to be partial and inadequate. It is partial, but
he does not see it to be so whilst he utters it.
As soon as he is released from the instinctive
and particular and sees its partiality, he shuts
his mouth in disgust. For no man can write
anything who does not think that what he writes
is for the time the history of the world ; or do
anything well who does not esteem his work to
be of importance. My work may be of none,
but I must not think it of none, or I shall not
do it with impunity.

In like manner, there is throughout nature

something mocking, something that leads us on
and on, but arrives nowhere ; keeps no faith
with us. All promise outruns the performance.
We live in a system of approximations. Every
end is prospective of some other end, which is
also temporary ; a round and final success nowhere. We are encamped in nature, not domesticated. Hunger and thirst lead us on to eat and
to drink ; but bread and wine, mix and cook
them how you will, leave us hungry and thirsty,
after the stomach is full. It is the same with
all our arts and performances. Our music, our
poetry, our language itself are not satisfactions,
but suggestions. The hunger for wealth, which
reduces the planet to a garden, fools the eager
pursuer. What is the end sought? Plainly to
secure the ends of good sense and beauty from
the intrusion of deformity or vulgarity of any
kind. But what an operose method! What a
train of means to secure a little conversation!
This palace of brick and stone, these servants,
this kitchen, these stables, horses and equipage,
this bank-stock and file of mortgages ; trade to
all the world, country-house and cottage by the
waterside, all for a little conversation, high, clear
and spiritual! Could it not be had as well by
beggars on the highway? No, all these things

came from successive efforts of these beggars to remove friction from the wheels of life, and give opportunity. Conversation, character, were the avowed ends; wealth was good as it appeased the animal cravings, cured the smoky chimney, silenced the creaking door, brought friends together in a warm and quiet room, and kept the children and the dinner-table in a different apartment. Thought, virtue, beauty, were the ends; but it was known that men of thought and virtue sometimes had the headache, or wet feet, or could lose good time whilst the room was getting warm in winter days. Unluckily, in the exertions necessary to remove these inconveniences, the main attention has been diverted to this object; the old aims have been lost sight of, and to remove friction has come to be the end. That is the ridicule of rich men; and Boston, London, Vienna, and now the governments generally of the world, are cities and governments of the rich; and the masses are not men, but *poor men*, that is, men who would be rich; this is the ridicule of the class, that they arrive with pains and sweat and fury nowhere; when all is done, it is for nothing. They are like one who has interrupted the conversation of a company to make his speech, and now has forgotten what he went to

say. The appearance strikes the eye everywhere
of an aimless society, of aimless nations. Were
the ends of nature so great and cogent as to exact
this immense sacrifice of men?

Quite analogous to the deceits in life, there
is, as might be expected, a similar effect on the
eye from the face of external nature. There is
in woods and waters a certain enticement and
flattery, together with a failure to yield a present satisfaction. This disappointment is felt in
every landscape. I have seen the softness and
beauty of the summer clouds floating feathery
overhead, enjoying, as it seemed, their height
and privilege of motion, whilst yet they appeared
not so much the drapery of this place and hour,
as forelooking to some pavilions and gardens of
festivity beyond. It is an odd jealousy, but the
poet finds himself not near enough to his object.
The pine-tree, the river, the bank of flowers
before him does not seem to be nature. Nature
is still elsewhere. This or this is but outskirt
and a far-off reflection and echo of the triumph
that has passed by and is now at its glancing
splendor and heyday, perchance in the neighbor-
ing fields, or, if you stand in the field, then in
the adjacent woods.[1] The present object shall
give you this sense of stillness that follows a

pageant which has just gone by. What splendid distance, what recesses of ineffable pomp and loveliness in the sunset ! But who can go where they are, or lay his hand or plant his foot thereon ? Off they fall from the round world forever and ever. It is the same among the men and women as among the silent trees ; always a referred existence, an absence, never a presence and satisfaction. Is it that beauty can never be grasped ? in persons and in landscape is equally inaccessible ? The accepted and betrothed lover has lost the wildest charm of his maiden in her acceptance of him. She was heaven whilst he pursued her as a star : she cannot be heaven if she stoops to such a one as he.[1]

What shall we say of this omnipresent appearance of that first projectile impulse, of this flattery and balking of so many well-meaning creatures ? Must we not suppose somewhere in the universe a slight treachery and derision ? Are we not engaged to a serious resentment of this use that is made of us ? Are we tickled trout, and fools of nature ? One look at the face of heaven and earth lays all petulance at rest, and soothes us to wiser convictions. To the intelligent, nature converts itself into a vast promise, and will not be rashly explained.[2] Her secret is

III

untold. Many and many an Œdipus arrives;
he has the whole mystery teeming in his brain.
Alas! the same sorcery has spoiled his skill;
no syllable can he shape on his lips. Her mighty
orbit vaults like the fresh rainbow into the deep,
but no archangel's wing was yet strong enough
to follow it and report of the return of the curve.
But it also appears that our actions are seconded
and disposed to greater conclusions than we designed. We are escorted on every hand through
life by spiritual agents, and a beneficent purpose
lies in wait for us. We cannot bandy words
with Nature, or deal with her as we deal with
persons.. If we measure our individual forces
against hers we may easily feel as if we were the
sport of an insuperable destiny. But if, instead
of identifying ourselves with the work, we feel
that the soul of the Workman streams through
us, we shall find the peace of the morning dwell-
ing first in our hearts, and the fathomless powers
of gravity and chemistry, and, over them, of
life, preëxisting within us in their highest form.[1]

The uneasiness which the thought of our
helplessness in the chain of causes occasions us,
results from looking too much at one condition of nature, namely, Motion. But the drag
is never taken from the wheel. Wherever the

impulse exceeds, the Rest or Identity insinuates
its compensation. All over the wide fields of
earth grows the prunella or self-heal.[1] After
every foolish day we sleep off the fumes and
furies of its hours; and though we are always
engaged with particulars, and often enslaved to
them, we bring with us to every experiment the
innate universal laws. These, while they exist
in the mind as ideas, stand around us in nature
forever embodied, a present sanity to expose
and cure the insanity of men. Our servitude
to particulars betrays us into a hundred foolish
expectations. We anticipate a new era from
the invention of a locomotive, or a balloon; the
new engine brings with it the old checks. They
say that by electro-magnetism your salad shall be
grown from the seed whilst your fowl is roast-
ing for dinner; it is a symbol of our modern
aims and endeavors, of our condensation and
acceleration of objects; — but nothing is gained;
nature cannot be cheated; man's life is but
seventy salads long, grow they swift or grow
they slow.[2] In these checks and impossibilities,
however, we find our advantage, not less than
in the impulses. Let the victory fall where it
will, we are on that side. And the knowledge
that we traverse the whole scale of being, from

the centre to the poles of nature, and have some stake in every possibility, lends that sublime lustre to death, which philosophy and religion have too outwardly and literally striven to express in the popular doctrine of the immortality of the soul. The reality is more excellent than the report. Here is no ruin, no discontinuity, no spent ball. The divine circulations never rest nor linger. Nature is the incarnation of a thought, and turns to a thought again, as ice becomes water and gas. The world is mind precipitated, and the volatile essence is forever escaping again into the state of free thought. Hence the virtue and pungency of the influence on the mind of natural objects, whether inorganic or organized. Man imprisoned, man crystallized, man vegetative, speaks to man impersonated.[1] That power which does not respect quantity, which makes the whole and the particle its equal channel, delegates its smile to the morning, and distils its essence into every drop of rain. Every moment instructs, and every object; for wisdom is infused into every form. It has been poured into us as blood; it convulsed us as pain; it slid into us as pleasure; it enveloped us in dull, melancholy days, or in days of cheerful labor; we did not guess its essence until after a long time.

VII

POLITICS

GOLD and iron are good
To buy iron and gold;
All earth's fleece and food
For their like are sold.
Boded Merlin wise,
Proved Napoleon great, —
Nor kind nor coinage buys
Aught above its rate.
Fear, Craft and Avarice
Cannot rear a State.
Out of dust to build
What is more than dust, —
Walls Amphion piled
Phœbus stablish must.
When the Muses nine
With the Virtues meet,
Find to their design
An Atlantic seat,
By green orchard boughs
Fended from the heat,
Where the statesman ploughs
Furrow for the wheat;
When the Church is social worth,
When the state-house is the hearth,
Then the perfect State is come,
The republican at home.

POLITICS

IN dealing with the State we ought to remember that its institutions are not aboriginal, though they existed before we were
born; that they are not superior to the citizen;
that every one of them was once the act of a
single man; every law and usage was a man's
expedient to meet a particular case; that they
all are imitable, all alterable; we may make as
good, we may make better. Society is an illusion to the young citizen. It lies before him in
rigid repose, with certain names, men and institutions rooted like oak-trees to the centre,
round which all arrange themselves the best
they can. But the old statesman knows that
society is fluid; there are no such roots and
centres, but any particle may suddenly become
the centre of the movement and compel the
system to gyrate round it; as every man of
strong will, like Pisistratus or Cromwell, does
for a time, and every man of truth, like Plato
or Paul, does forever.¹ But politics rest on necessary foundations, and cannot be treated with
levity. Republics abound in young civilians who
believe that the laws make the city, that grave

modifications of the policy and modes of living
and employments of the population, that commerce, education and religion may be voted in
or out; and that any measure, though it were
absurd, may be imposed on a people if only
you can get sufficient voices to make it a law.
But the wise know that foolish legislation is a
rope of sand which perishes in the twisting; [1]
that the State must follow and not lead the
character and progress of the citizen; the
strongest usurper is quickly got rid of; and they
only who build on Ideas, build for eternity; and
that the form of government which prevails is
the expression of what cultivation exists in the
population which permits it. The law is only
a memorandum. We are superstitious, and esteem the statute somewhat: so much life as it
has in the character of living men is its force.
The statute stands there to say, Yesterday we
agreed so and so, but how feel ye this article
to-day? Our statute is a currency which we
stamp with our own portrait: it soon becomes
unrecognizable, and in process of time will return to the mint. [2] Nature is not democratic,
nor limited-monarchical, but despotic, and will
not be fooled or abated of any jot of her authority by the pertest of her sons; and as fast as

Central Part of Concord, 1839

modi·
and c
merc
or o·
absu
you
But
rop
tha
ch
st
o
t·
t

the public mind is opened to more intelligence, ·
the code is seen to be brute and stammering.
It speaks not articulately, and must be made to.
Meantime the education of the general mind
never stops. The reveries of the true and simple are prophetic. What the tender poetic youth
dreams, and prays, and paints to-day, but shuns
the ridicule of saying aloud, shall presently be
the resolutions of public bodies ; then shall be
carried as grievance and bill of rights through
conflict and war, and then shall be triumphant
law and establishment for a hundred years, until
it gives place in turn to new prayers and pic-
tures.¹ The history of the State sketches in
coarse outline the progress of thought, and follows at a distance the delicacy of culture and of
aspiration.

The theory of politics which has possessed the
mind of men, and which they have expressed the
best they could in their laws and in their revolutions, considers persons and property as the two
objects for whose protection government exists.
Of persons, all have equal rights, in virtue of
being identical in nature. This interest of course
with its whole power demands a democracy.
Whilst the rights of all as persons are equal,
in virtue of their access to reason, their rights

in property are very unequal. One man owns his clothes, and another owns a county. This accident, depending primarily on the skill and virtue of the parties, of which there is every degree, and secondarily on patrimony, falls unequally, and its rights of course are unequal. Personal rights, universally the same, demand a government framed on the ratio of the census; property demands a government framed on the ratio of owners and of owning. Laban, who has flocks and herds, wishes them looked after by an officer on the frontiers, lest the Midianites shall drive them off; and pays a tax to that end. Jacob has no flocks or herds and no fear of the Midianites, and pays no tax to the officer. It seemed fit that Laban and Jacob should have equal rights to elect the officer who is to defend their persons, but that Laban and not Jacob should elect the officer who is to guard the sheep and cattle. And if question arise whether additional officers or watch-towers should be provided, must not Laban and Isaac, and those who must sell part of their herds to buy protection for the rest, judge better of this, and with more right, than Jacob, who, because he is a youth and a traveller, eats their bread and not his own?

In the earliest society the proprietors made their own wealth, and so long as it comes to the owners in the direct way, no other opinion would arise in any equitable community than that property should make the law for property, and persons the law for persons.

But property passes through donation or inheritance to those who do not create it. Gift, in one case, makes it as really the new owner's, as labor made it the first owner's : in the other case, of patrimony, the law makes an ownership which will be valid in each man's view according to the estimate which he sets on the public tranquillity.

It was not, however, found easy to embody the readily admitted principle that property should make law for property, and persons for persons ; since persons and property mixed themselves in every transaction. At last it seemed settled that the rightful distinction was that the proprietors should have more elective franchise than non-proprietors, on the Spartan principle of "calling that which is just, equal; not that which is equal, just."

That principle no longer looks so self-evident as it appeared in former times, partly because doubts have arisen whether too much weight had not been allowed in the laws to property, and such a structure given to our usages as allowed the rich to encroach on the poor, and to keep them poor; but mainly because there is an instinctive sense, however obscure and yet inarticulate, that the whole constitution of property, on its present tenures, is injurious, and its influence on persons deteriorating and degrading; that truly the only interest for the consideration of the State is persons; that property will always follow persons; that the highest end of government is the culture of men; and that if men can be educated, the institutions will share their improvement and the moral sentiment will write the law of the land.

If it be not easy to settle the equity of this question, the peril is less when we take note of our natural defences. We are kept by better guards than the vigilance of such magistrates as we commonly elect. Society always consists in greatest part of young and foolish persons. The old, who have seen through the hypocrisy of courts and statesmen, die and leave no wisdom to their sons. They believe their own newspaper, as their fathers did at their age. With such an ignorant and deceivable majority, States would soon run to ruin, but that there are limitations beyond which the folly and ambition of governors cannot go. Things have their laws, as well as men ; and things refuse to be trifled with.[1] Property will be protected. Corn will not grow unless it is planted and manured ; but the farmer will not plant or hoe it unless the chances are a hundred to one that he will cut and harvest it.[2] Under any forms, persons and property must and will have their just sway. They exert their power, as steadily as matter its attraction. Cover up a pound of earth never so cunningly, divide and subdivide it ; melt it to liquid, convert it to gas ; it will always weigh a pound ; it will always attract and resist other matter by the full virtue of one pound weight : — and the attributes of a person, his wit and his moral energy, will exercise, under any law or extinguishing tyranny, their proper force, — if not overtly, then covertly ; if not for the law, then against it ; if not wholesomely, then poisonously ; with right, or by might.

The boundaries of personal influence it is impossible to fix, as persons are organs of moral or supernatural force. Under the dominion of an idea which possesses the minds of multitudes, as civil freedom, or the religious sentiment, the powers of persons are no longer subjects of calculation. A nation of men unanimously bent on freedom or conquest can easily confound the arithmetic of statists, and achieve extravagant actions, out of all proportion to their means; as the Greeks, the Saracens, the Swiss, the Americans, and the French have done.[1]

In like manner to every particle of property belongs its own attraction. A cent is the representative of a certain quantity of corn or other commodity. Its value is in the necessities of the animal man. It is so much warmth, so much bread, so much water, so much land. The law may do what it will with the owner of property; its just power will still attach to the cent. The law may in a mad freak say that all shall have power except the owners of property; they shall have no vote. Nevertheless, by a higher law, the property will, year after year, write every statute that respects property. The non-proprietor will be the scribe of the proprietor. What the owners wish to do, the whole power of property will do, either through the law or else in defiance of it. Of course I speak of all the property, not merely of the great estates. When the rich are outvoted, as frequently happens, it is the joint treasury of the poor which exceeds their accumulations. Every man owns something, if it is only a cow, or a wheelbarrow, or his arms, and so has that property to dispose of.[1]

The same necessity which secures the rights of person and property against the malignity or folly of the magistrate, determines the form and methods of governing, which are proper to each nation and to its habit of thought, and nowise transferable to other states of society. In this country we are very vain of our political institutions, which are singular in this, that they sprung, within the memory of living men, from the character and condition of the people, which they still express with sufficient fidelity, — and we ostentatiously prefer them to any other in history. They are not better, but only fitter for us. We may be wise in asserting the advantage in modern times of the democratic form, but to other states of society, in which religion consecrated the monarchical, that and not this was expedient. Democracy is better for us, because the religious sentiment of the present time accords better with it. Born democrats, we are nowise qualified to judge of monarchy, which, to our fathers living in the monarchical idea, was also relatively right. But our institutions, though in coincidence with the spirit of the age, have not any exemption from the practical defects which have discredited other forms. Every actual State is corrupt. Good men must not obey the laws too well.[1] What satire on government can equal the severity of censure conveyed in the word *politic*, which now for ages has signified *cunning*, intimating that the State is a trick?

The same benign necessity and the same practical abuse appear in the parties, into which each State divides itself, of opponents and defenders of the administration of the government. Parties are also founded on instincts, and have better guides to their own humble aims than the sagacity of their leaders. They have nothing perverse in their origin, but rudely mark some real and lasting relation. We might as wisely reprove the east wind or the frost, as a political party, whose members, for the most part, could give no account of their position, but stand for the defence of those interests in which they find themselves. Our quarrel with them begins when they quit this deep natural ground at the bidding of some leader, and obeying personal considerations, throw themselves into the maintenance and defence of points nowise belonging to their system. A party is perpetually corrupted by personality. Whilst we absolve the association from dishonesty, we cannot extend the same charity to their leaders. They reap the rewards of the docility and zeal of the masses which they direct. Ordinarily our parties are parties of circumstance, and not of principle; as the planting interest in conflict with the commercial; the party of capitalists and that of operatives : parties which are identical in their moral character, and which can easily change ground with each other in the support of many of their measures. Parties of principle, as, religious sects, or the party of free-trade, of universal suffrage, of abolition of slavery, of abolition of capital punishment,— degenerate into personalities, or would inspire enthusiasm. The vice of our leading parties in this country (which may be cited as a fair specimen of these societies of opinion) is that they do not plant themselves on the deep and necessary grounds to which they are respectively entitled, but lash themselves to fury in the carrying of some local and momentary measure, nowise useful to the commonwealth. Of the two great parties which at this hour almost share the nation between them, I should say that one has the best cause, and the other contains the best men. The philosopher, the poet, or the religious man,

III

will of course wish to cast his vote with the democrat, for free-trade, for wide suffrage, for the abolition of legal cruelties in the penal code, and for facilitating in every manner the access of the young and the poor to the sources of wealth and power. But he can rarely accept the persons whom the so-called popular party propose to him as representatives of these liberalities. They have not at heart the ends which give to the name of democracy what hope and virtue are in it. The spirit of our American radicalism is destructive and aimless : it is not loving ; it has no ulterior and divine ends, but is destructive only out of hatred and selfishness. On the other side, the conservative party, composed of the most moderate, able and cultivated part of the population, is timid, and merely defensive of property. It vindicates no right, it aspires to no real good, it brands no crime, it proposes no generous policy ; it does not build, nor write, nor cherish the arts, nor foster religion, nor establish schools, nor encourage science, nor emancipate the slave, nor befriend the poor, or the Indian, or the immigrant. From neither party, when in power, has the world any benefit to expect in science, art, or humanity, at all commensurate with the resources of the nation.

I do not for these defects despair of our republic. We are not at the mercy of any waves
of chance. In the strife of ferocious parties, human nature always finds itself cherished; as the
children of the convicts at Botany Bay are found
to have as healthy a moral sentiment as other
children. Citizens of feudal states are alarmed
at our democratic institutions lapsing into anarchy, and the older and more cautious among
ourselves are learning from Europeans to look
with some terror at our turbulent freedom. It
is said that in our license of construing the Constitution, and in the despotism of public opinion,
we have no anchor; and one foreign observer
thinks he has found the safeguard in the sanctity of Marriage among us; and another thinks
he has found it in our Calvinism. Fisher Ames
expressed the popular security more wisely, when
he compared a monarchy and a republic, saying
that a monarchy is a merchantman, which sails
well, but will sometimes strike on a rock and go
to the bottom; whilst a republic is a raft, which
would never sink, but then your feet are always
in water. No forms can have any dangerous
importance whilst we are befriended by the laws
of things. It makes no difference how many
tons' weight of atmosphere presses on our heads,

so long as the same pressure resists it within the lungs. Augment the mass a thousand-fold, it cannot begin to crush us, as long as reaction is equal to action. The fact of two poles, of two forces, centripetal and centrifugal, is universal, and each force by its own activity develops the other. Wild liberty develops iron conscience. Want of liberty, by strengthening law and decorum, stupefies conscience. ' Lynch-law ' prevails only where there is greater hardihood and self-subsistency in the leaders. A mob cannot be a permanency ; everybody's interest requires that it should not exist, and only justice satisfies all.

We must trust infinitely to the beneficent necessity which shines through all laws. Human nature expresses itself in them as characteristically as in statues, or songs, or railroads ; and an abstract of the codes of nations would be a transcript of the common conscience. Governments have their origin in the moral identity of men. Reason for one is seen to be reason for another, and for every other. There is a middle measure which satisfies all parties, be they never so many or so resolute for their own. Every man finds a sanction for his simplest claims and deeds, in decisions of his own mind, which he calls Truth and Holiness. In these decisions

all the citizens find a perfect agreement, and
only in these; not in what is good to eat, good
to wear, good use of time, or what amount of
land or of public aid each is entitled to claim.
This truth and justice men presently endeavor
to make application of to the measuring of land,
the apportionment of service, the protection of
life and property. Their first endeavors, no
doubt, are very awkward. Yet absolute right
is the first governor; or, every government is
an impure theocracy. The idea after which each
community is aiming to make and mend its law,
is the will of the wise man. The wise man it
cannot find in nature, and it makes awkward
but earnest efforts to secure his government by
contrivance; as by causing the entire people to
give their voices on every measure; or by a
double choice to get the representation of the
whole; or by a selection of the best citizens;
or to secure the advantages of efficiency and
internal peace by confiding the government to
one, who may himself select his agents. All
forms of government symbolize an immortal
government, common to all dynasties and independent of numbers, perfect where two men
exist, perfect where there is only one man.

Every man's nature is a sufficient advertisement to him of the character of his fellows. My right and my wrong is their right and their wrong. Whilst I do what is fit for me, and abstain from what is unfit, my neighbor and I shall often agree in our means, and work together for a time to one end. But whenever I find my dominion over myself not sufficient for me, and undertake the direction of him also, I overstep the truth, and come into false relations to him. I may have so much more skill or strength than he that he cannot express adequately his sense of wrong, but it is a lie, and hurts like a lie both him and me. Love and nature cannot maintain the assumption; it must be executed by a practical lie, namely by force. This undertaking for another is the blunder which stands in colossal ugliness in the governments of the world. It is the same thing in numbers, as in a pair, only not quite so intelligible. I can see well enough a great difference between my setting myself down to a self-control, and my going to make somebody else act after my views; but when a quarter of the human race assume to tell me what I must do, I may be too much disturbed by the circumstances to see so clearly the absurdity of their command. Therefore all public ends look vague and quixotic beside private ones.

For any laws but those which men make for themselves are laughable.[1] If I put myself in the place of my child, and we stand in one thought and see that things are thus or thus, that perception is law for him and me. We are both there, both act. But if, without carrying him into the thought, I look over into his plot, and, guessing how it is with him, ordain this or that, he will never obey me.[2] This is the history of governments, — one man does something which is to bind another. A man who cannot be acquainted with me, taxes me; looking from afar at me ordains that a part of my labor shall go to this or that whimsical end, — not as I, but as he happens to fancy. Behold the consequence. Of all debts men are least willing to pay the taxes. What a satire is this on government! Everywhere they think they get their money's worth, except for these.[3]

Hence the less government we have the better, — the fewer laws, and the less confided power. The antidote to this abuse of formal government is the influence of private character, the growth of the Individual; the appearance of the principal to supersede the proxy; the appearance of the wise man; of whom the existing government is, it must be owned, but a shabby imitation. That which all things tend to educe; which freedom, cultivation, intercourse, revolutions, go to form and deliver, is character; that is the end of Nature, to reach unto this coronation of her king. To educate the wise man the State exists, and with the appearance of the wise man the State expires. The appearance of character makes the State unnecessary. The wise man is the State. He needs no army, fort, or navy, — he loves men too well; no bribe, or feast, or palace, to draw friends to him; no vantage ground, no favorable circumstance. He needs no library, for he has not done thinking; no church, for he is a prophet; no statute-book, for he has the lawgiver; no money, for he is value; no road, for he is at home where he is; no experience, for the life of the creator shoots through him, and looks from his eyes. He has no personal friends, for he who has the spell to draw the prayer and piety of all men unto him needs not husband and educate a few to share with him a select and poetic life. His relation to men is angelic; his memory is myrrh to them; his presence, frankincense and flowers.[1]

We think our civilization near its meridian, but we are yet only at the cock-crowing and the morning star. In our barbarous society the influence of character is in its infancy. As a political power, as the rightful lord who is to tumble all rulers from their chairs, its presence is hardly yet suspected. Malthus and Ricardo quite omit it; the Annual Register is silent; in the Conversations' Lexicon it is not set down ; the President's Message, the Queen's Speech, have not mentioned it; and yet it is never nothing. Every thought which genius and piety throw into the world, alters the world.' The gladiators in the lists of power feel, through all their frocks of force and simulation, the presence of worth. I think the very strife of trade and ambition is confession of this divinity ; and successes in those fields are the poor amends, the fig-leaf with which the shamed soul attempts to hide its nakedness. I find the like unwilling homage in all quarters. It is because we know how much is due from us that we are impatient to show some petty talent as a substitute for worth. We are haunted by a conscience of this right to grandeur of character, and are false to it. But each of us has some talent, can do somewhat useful, or graceful, or formidable, or amusing, or lucrative. That we do, as an apology to others and to ourselves for not reaching the mark of a good and equal life. But it does not satisfy *us*, whilst we thrust it on the notice of our companions. It may throw dust in their eyes, but does not smooth our own brow, or give us the tranquillity of the strong when we walk abroad. We do penance as we go. Our talent is a sort of expiation, and we are constrained to reflect on our splendid moment with a certain humiliation, as somewhat too fine, and not as one act of many acts, a fair expression of our permanent energy. Most persons of ability meet in society with a kind of tacit appeal. Each seems to say, ' I am not all here.' Senators and presidents have climbed so high with pain enough, not because they think the place specially agreeable, but as an apology for real worth, and to vindicate their manhood in our eyes. This conspicuous chair is their compensation to themselves for being of a poor, cold, hard nature. They must do what they can. Like one class of forest animals, they have nothing but a prehensile tail ; climb they must, or crawl. If a man found himself so rich-natured that he could enter into strict relations with the best persons and make life serene around him by the dignity and sweetness of his behavior, could he afford to circumvent the favor of the caucus and the press, and covet relations so hollow and pompous as those of a politician? Surely nobody would be a charlatan who could afford to be sincere.

The tendencies of the times favor the idea of self-government, and leave the individual, for all code, to the rewards and penalties of his own constitution; which work with more energy than we believe whilst we depend on artificial restraints. The movement in this direction has been very marked in modern history. Much has been blind and discreditable, but the nature of the revolution is not affected by the vices of the revolters; for this is a purely moral force. It was never adopted by any party in history, neither can be. It separates the individual from all party, and unites him at the same time to the race. It promises a recognition of higher rights than those of personal freedom, or the security of property. A man has a right to be employed, to be trusted, to be loved, to be revered. The power of love, as the basis of a State, has never been tried. We must not imagine that all things are lapsing into confusion if every tender protestant be not compelled to bear his part in certain social conventions; nor doubt that roads can be built, letters carried, and the fruit of labor secured, when the government of force is at an end. Are our methods now so excellent that all competition is hopeless ? could not a nation of friends even devise better ways? On the other hand, let not the most conservative and timid fear anything from a premature surrender of the bayonet and the system of force. For, according to the order of nature, which is quite superior to our will, it stands thus ; there will always be a government of force where men are selfish ; and when they are pure enough to abjure the code of force they will be wise enough to see how these public ends of the post-office, of the highway, of commerce and the exchange of property, of museums and libraries, of institutions of art and science can be answered.

We live in a very low state of the world, and pay unwilling tribute to governments founded on force. There is not, among the most religious and instructed men of the most religious and civil nations, a reliance on the moral sentiment and a sufficient belief in the unity of things, to persuade them that society can be maintained without artificial restraints, as well as the solar system ; ' or that the private citizen might be reasonable and a good neighbor, without the hint of a jail or a confiscation. What is strange too, there never was in any man sufficient faith in the power of rectitude to inspire him with the broad design of renovating the State on the principle of right and love. All those who have pretended this design have been partial reformers, and have admitted in some manner the supremacy of the bad State. I do not call to mind a single human being who has steadily denied the authority of the laws, on the simple ground of his own moral nature. Such designs, full of genius and full of faith as they are, are not entertained except avowedly as air-pictures.[1] If the individual who exhibits them dare to think them practicable, he disgusts scholars and churchmen ; and men of talent and women of superior sentiments cannot hide their contempt. Not the less does nature continue to fill the heart of youth with suggestions of this enthusiasm, and there are now men, — if indeed I can speak in the plural number, — more exactly, I will say, I have just been conversing with one man, to whom no weight of adverse experience will make it for a moment appear impossible that thousands of human beings might exercise towards each other the grandest and simplest sentiments, as well as a knot of friends, or a pair of lovers.

VIII

NOMINALIST AND REALIST

In countless upward-striving waves
The moon-drawn tide-wave strives:
In thousand far-transplanted grafts
The parent fruit survives;
So, in the new-born millions,
The perfect Adam lives.
Not less are summer mornings dear
To every child they wake,
And each with novel life his sphere
Fills for his proper sake.

NOMINALIST AND REALIST

I CANNOT often enough say that a man is only a relative and representative nature. Each is a hint of the truth, but far enough from being that truth which yet he quite newly and inevitably suggests to us. If I seek it in him I shall not find it. Could any man conduct into me the pure stream of that which he pretends to be! Long afterwards I find that quality else-where which he promised me. The genius of the Platonists is intoxicating to the student, yet how few particulars of it can I detach from all their books. The man momentarily stands for the thought, but will not bear examination ; and a society of men will cursorily represent well enough a certain quality and culture, for example, chivalry or beauty of manners ; but separate them and there is no gentleman and no lady in the group.' The least hint sets us on the pur-suit of a character which no man realizes. We have such exorbitant eyes that on seeing the smallest arc we complete the curve, and when the curtain is lifted from the diagram which it seemed to veil, we are vexed to find that no more was drawn than just that fragment of an

III

arc which we first beheld. We are greatly too liberal in our construction of each other's faculty and promise. Exactly what the parties have already done they shall do again; but that which we inferred from their nature and inception, they will not do. That is in nature, but not in them. That happens in the world, which we often witness in a public debate. Each of the speakers expresses himself imperfectly; no one of them hears much that another says, such is the preoccupation of mind of each; and the audience, who have only to hear and not to speak, judge very wisely and superiorly how wrongheaded and unskilful is each of the debaters to his own affair. Great men or men of great gifts you shall easily find, but symmetrical men never.[1] When I meet a pure intellectual force or a generosity of affection, I believe here then is man; and am presently mortified by the discovery that this individual is no more available to his own or to the general ends than his companions; because the power which drew my respect is not supported by the total symphony of his talents. All persons exist to society by some shining trait of beauty or utility which they have. We borrow the proportions of the man from that one fine feature, and finish the portrait symmetrically; which is false, for the rest of his body is small or deformed. I observe a person who makes a good public appearance, and conclude thence the perfection of his private character, on which this is based; but he has no private character. He is a graceful cloak or lay-figure for holidays. All our poets, heroes and saints, fail utterly in some one or in many parts to satisfy our idea, fail to draw our spontaneous interest, and so leave us without any hope of realization but in our own future. Our exaggeration of all fine characters arises from the fact that we identify each in turn with the soul. But there are no such men as we fable; no Jesus, nor Pericles, nor Cæsar, nor Angelo, nor Washington, such as we have made. We consecrate a great deal of nonsense because it was allowed by great men. There is none without his foible. I believe that if an angel should come to chant the chorus of the moral law, he would eat too much gingerbread, or take liberties with private letters, or do some precious atrocity. It is bad enough that our geniuses cannot do anything useful, but it is worse that no man is fit for society who has fine traits. He is admired at a distance, but he cannot come near without appearing a cripple. The men of fine parts protect themselves by solitude, or by courtesy, or by satire, or by an acid worldly manner; each concealing as he best can his incapacity for useful association, but they want either love or self-reliance.

Our native love of reality joins with this experience to teach us a little reserve, and to dissuade a too sudden surrender to the brilliant qualities of persons. Young people admire talents or particular excellences; as we grow older we value total powers and effects, as the impression, the quality, the spirit of men and things. The genius is all. The man,—it is his system : we do not try a solitary word or act, but his habit. The acts which you praise, I praise not, since they are departures from his faith, and are mere compliances. The magnetism which arranges tribes and races in one polarity is alone to be respected ; the men are steel-filings. Yet we unjustly select a particle, and say, ' O steel-filing number one ! what heart-drawings I feel to thee ! what prodigious virtues are these of thine ! how constitutional to thee, and incommunicable ! ' Whilst we speak the loadstone is withdrawn ; down falls our filing in a heap with the rest, and we continue our mummery to the wretched shaving. Let us go for

universals; for the magnetism, not for the nee-
dles. Human life and its persons are poor em-
pirical pretensions. A personal influence is an
ignis fatuus. If they say it is great, it is great;
if they say it is small, it is small; you see it, and
you see it not, by turns; it borrows all its size
from the momentary estimation of the speakers :
the Will-of-the-wisp vanishes if you go too near,
vanishes if you go too far, and only blazes at
one angle. Who can tell if Washington be
a great man or no? Who can tell if Franklin
be? Yes, or any but the twelve, or six, or three
great gods of fame? And they too loom and
fade before the eternal.

We are amphibious creatures, weaponed for
two elements, having two sets of faculties, the
particular and the catholic. We adjust our instrument for general observation, and sweep the
heavens as easily as we pick out a single figure
in the terrestrial landscape. We are practically
skilful in detecting elements for which we have
no place in our theory, and no name. Thus we
are very sensible of an atmospheric influence in
men and in bodies of men, not accounted for in
an arithmetical addition of all their measurable
properties. There is a genius of a nation, which
is not to be found in the numerical citizens,

but which characterizes the society. England, strong, punctual, practical, well-spoken England I should not find if I should go to the island to seek it. In the parliament, in the play-house, at dinner-tables, I might see a great number of rich, ignorant, book-read, conventional, proud men, — many old women, — and not anywhere the Englishman who made the good speeches, combined the accurate engines, and did the bold and nervous deeds. It is even worse in America, where, from the intellectual quickness of the race, the genius of the country is more splendid in its promise and more slight in its performance.[1] Webster cannot do the work of Webster. We conceive distinctly enough the French, the Spanish, the German genius, and it is not the less real that perhaps we should not meet in either of those nations a single individual who corresponded with the type. We infer the spirit of the nation in great measure from the language, which is a sort of monument to which each forcible individual in a course of many hundred years has contributed a stone. And, universally, a good example of this social force is the veracity of language, which cannot be debauched. In any controversy concerning morals, an appeal may be made with safety to the sentiments which the language of the people expresses. Proverbs, words and grammar-inflections convey the public sense with more purity and precision than the wisest individual.

In the famous dispute with the Nominalists, the Realists had a good deal of reason.[1] General ideas are essences. They are our gods: they round and ennoble the most partial and sordid way of living. Our proclivity to details cannot quite degrade our life and divest it of poetry. The day-laborer is reckoned as standing at the foot of the social scale, yet he is saturated with the laws of the world. His measures are the hours; morning and night, solstice and equinox, geometry, astronomy and all the lovely accidents of nature play through his mind. Money, which represents the prose of life, and which is hardly spoken of in parlors without an apology, is, in its effects and laws, as beautiful as roses. Property keeps the accounts of the world, and is always moral. The property will be found where the labor, the wisdom and the virtue have been in nations, in classes [2] and (the whole life-time considered, with the compensations) in the individual also. How wise the world appears, when the laws and usages of nations are largely detailed, and the completeness of the municipal system is considered! Nothing is left out. If you go into the markets and the custom-houses, the insurers' and notaries' offices, the offices of sealers of weights and measures, of inspection of provisions, — it will appear as if one man had made it all. Wherever you go, a wit like your own has been before you, and has realized its thought. The Eleusinian mysteries, the Egyptian architecture, the Indian astronomy, the Greek sculpture, show that there always were seeing and knowing men in the planet. The world is full of masonic ties, of guilds, of secret and public legions of honor; that of scholars, for example; and that of gentlemen, fraternizing with the upper class of every country and every culture.[1]

I am very much struck in literature by the appearance that one person wrote all the books; as if the editor of a journal planted his body of reporters in different parts of the field of action, and relieved some by others from time to time; but there is such equality and identity both of judgment and point of view in the narrative that it is plainly the work of one all-seeing, all-hearing gentleman. I looked into Pope's Odyssey yesterday: it is as correct and elegant after our canon of to-day as if it were newly written. The

modernness of all good books seems to give me
an existence as wide as man.[1] What is well done
I feel as if I did; what is ill done I reck not
of. Shakspeare's passages of passion (for example, in Lear and Hamlet) are in the very dialect
of the present year. I am faithful again to the
whole over the members in my use of books.
I find the most pleasure in reading a book in
a manner least flattering to the author. I read
Proclus, and sometimes Plato, as I might read
a dictionary, for a mechanical help to the fancy
and the imagination. I read for the lustres, as
if one should use a fine picture in a chromatic
experiment, for its rich colors. 'T is not Proclus,
but a piece of nature and fate that I explore. It
is a greater joy to see the author's author, than
himself. A higher pleasure of the same kind
I found lately at a concert, where I went to hear
Handel's Messiah. As the master overpowered
the littleness and incapableness of the perform-
ers and made them conductors of his electricity,
so it was easy to observe what efforts nature was
making, through so many hoarse, wooden and
imperfect persons, to produce beautiful voices,
fluid and soul-guided men and women. The
genius of nature was paramount at the oratorio.[2]

This preference of the genius to the parts is

the secret of that deification of art, which is found in all superior minds. Art, in the artist, is proportion, or a habitual respect to the whole by an eye loving beauty in details. And the wonder and charm of it is the sanity in insanity which it denotes. Proportion is almost impossible to human beings. There is no one who does not exaggerate. In conversation, men are encumbered with personality, and talk too much. In modern sculpture, picture and poetry, the beauty is miscellaneous ; the artist works here and there and at all points, adding and adding, instead of unfolding the unit of his thought. Beautiful details we must have, or no artist ; but they must be means and never other. The eye must not lose sight for a moment of the purpose. Lively boys write to their ear and eye, and the cool reader finds nothing but sweet jingles in it. When they grow older, they respect the argument.

We obey the same intellectual integrity when we study in exceptions the law of the world. Anomalous facts, as the never quite obsolete rumors of magic and demonology, and the new allegations of phrenologists and neurologists, are of ideal use. They are good indications. Homœopathy is insignificant as an art of healing, but of great value as criticism on the hygeia or medical practice of the time. So with Mesmerism, Swedenborgism, Fourierism, and the Millennial Church; they are poor pretensions enough, but good criticism on the science, philosophy and preaching of the day. For these abnormal insights of the adepts ought to be normal, and things of course.[1]

All things show us that on every side we are very near to the best. It seems not worth while to execute with too much pains some one intellectual, or æsthetical, or civil feat, when presently the dream will scatter, and we shall burst into universal power. The reason of idleness and of crime is the deferring of our hopes. Whilst we are waiting we beguile the time with jokes, with sleep, with eating and with crimes.

Thus we settle it in our cool libraries, that all the agents with which we deal are subalterns, which we can well afford to let pass, and life will be simpler when we live at the centre and flout the surfaces. I wish to speak with all respect of persons, but sometimes I must pinch myself to keep awake and preserve the due decorum. They melt so fast into each other that they are like grass and trees, and it needs an

effort to treat them as individuals. Though the
uninspired man certainly finds persons a con-
veniency in household matters, the divine man
does not respect them; he sees them as a rack
of clouds, or a fleet of ripples which the wind
drives over the surface of the water.[1] But this
is flat rebellion. Nature will not be Buddhist:
she resents generalizing, and insults the philosopher in every moment with a million of fresh
particulars. It is all idle talking: as much as a
man is a whole, so is he also a part; and it were
partial not to see it. What you say in your
pompous distribution only distributes you into
your class and section. You have not got rid of
parts by denying them, but are the more partial. You are one thing, but Nature is *one thing
and the other thing*, in the same moment.[2] She
will not remain orbed in a thought, but rushes
into persons; and when each person, inflamed to
a fury of personality, would conquer all things
to his poor crotchet, she raises up against him
another person, and by many persons incarnates
again a sort of whole. She will have all. Nick
Bottom cannot play all the parts, work it how
he may; there will be somebody else, and the
world will be round. Everything must have its
flower or effort at the beautiful, coarser or finer

according to its stuff. They relieve and recommend each other, and the sanity of society is a balance of a thousand insanities. She punishes abstractionists, and will only forgive an induction which is rare and casual. We like to come to a height of land and see the landscape, just as we value a general remark in conversation. But it is not the intention of Nature that we should live by general views. We fetch fire and water, run about all day among the shops and markets, and get our clothes and shoes made and mended, and are the victims of these details; and once in a fortnight we arrive perhaps at a rational moment. If we were not thus infatuated, if we saw the real from hour to hour, we should not be here to write and to read, but should have been burned or frozen long ago. She would never get anything done, if she suffered Admirable Crichtons and universal geniuses. She loves better a wheelwright who dreams all night of wheels, and a groom who is part of his horse; for she is full of work, and these are her hands. As the frugal farmer takes care that his cattle shall eat down the rowen, and swine shall eat the waste of his house, and poultry shall pick the crumbs, — so our economical mother dispatches a new genius and

habit of mind into every district and condition
of existence, plants an eye wherever a new ray
of light can fall, and gathering up into some
man every property in the universe, establishes
thousand-fold occult mutual attractions among
her offspring, that all this wash and waste of
power may be imparted and exchanged.

Great dangers undoubtedly accrue from this
incarnation and distribution of the godhead, and
hence Nature has her maligners, as if she were
Circe; and Alphonso of Castile fancied he could
have given useful advice. But she does not go
unprovided; she has hellebore at the bottom
of the cup.[1] Solitude would ripen a plentiful
crop of despots. The recluse thinks of men as
having his manner, or as not having his manner; and as having degrees of it, more and less.
But when he comes into a public assembly he
sees that men have very different manners from
his own, and in their way admirable. In his
childhood and youth he has had many checks
and censures, and thinks modestly enough of
his own endowment. When afterwards he comes
to unfold it in propitious circumstance, it seems
the only talent; he is delighted with his success, and accounts himself already the fellow of
the great. But he goes into a mob, into a bank-

ing house, into a mechanic's shop, into a mill, into a laboratory, into a ship, into a camp, and in each new place he is no better than an idiot; other talents take place, and rule the hour. The rotation which whirls every leaf and pebble to the meridian, reaches to every gift of man, and we all take turns at the top.

For Nature, who abhors mannerism, has set her heart on breaking up all styles and tricks, and it is so much easier to do what one has done before than to do a new thing, that there is a perpetual tendency to a set mode. In every conversation, even the highest, there is a certain trick, which may be soon learned by an acute person, and then that particular style continued indefinitely. Each man too is a tyrant in tendency, because he would impose his idea on others; and their trick is their natural defence. Jesus would absorb the race; but Tom Paine or the coarsest blasphemer helps humanity by resisting this exuberance of power. Hence the immense benefit of party in politics, as it reveals faults of character in a chief, which the intellectual force of the persons, with ordinary opportunity and not hurled into aphelion by hatred, could not have seen. Since we are all so stupid, what benefit that there should be two stupidities! It is like that brute advantage so essential to astronomy, of having the diameter of the earth's orbit for a base of its triangles. Democracy is morose, and runs to anarchy, but in the State and in the schools it is indispensable to resist the consolidation of all men into a few men. If John was perfect, why are you and I alive?' As long as any man exists, there is some need of him; let him fight for his own. A new poet has appeared; a new character approached us; why should we refuse to eat bread until we have found his regiment and section in our old army-files? Why not a new man? Here is a new enterprise of Brook Farm, of Skeneateles, of Northampton:' why so impatient to baptize them Essenes, or Port-Royalists, or Shakers, or by any known and effete name? Let it be a new way of living. Why have only two or three ways of life, and not thousands? Every man is wanted, and no man is wanted much. We came this time for condiments, not for corn. We want the great genius only for joy; for one star more in our constellation, for one tree more in our grove. But he thinks we wish to belong to him, as he wishes to occupy us. He greatly mistakes us. I think I have done well if I have acquired a new word from a good author; and my business with him is to find my own, though it were only to melt him down into an epithet or an image for daily use:

"Into paint will I grind thee, my bride!" [1]

To embroil the confusion and make it impossible to arrive at any general statement, — when we have insisted on the imperfection of individuals, our affections and our experience urge that every individual is entitled to honor, and a very generous treatment is sure to be repaid. A recluse sees only two or three persons, and allows them all their room; they spread themselves at large. The statesman looks at many, and compares the few habitually with others, and these look less. Yet are they not entitled to this generosity of reception? and is not munificence the means of insight? For though gamesters say that the cards beat all the players, though they were never so skilful, yet in the contest we are now considering, the players are also the game, and share the power of the cards. If you criticise a fine genius, the odds are that you are out of your reckoning, and instead of the poet, are censuring your own caricature of him. For there is somewhat spheral and infinite in every man, especially in every genius,

III

which, if you can come very near him, sports with all your limitations. For rightly every man is a channel through which heaven floweth,[1] and whilst I fancied I was criticising him, I was censuring or rather terminating my own soul. After taxing Goethe as a courtier, artificial, unbelieving, worldly, — I took up this book of Helena, and found him an Indian of the wilderness, a piece of pure nature like an apple or an oak, large as morning or night, and virtuous as a brier-rose.

But care is taken that the whole tune shall be played. If we were not kept among surfaces, everything would be large and universal; now the excluded attributes burst in on us with the more brightness that they have been excluded. " Your turn now, my turn next," is the rule of the game.[2] The universality being hindered in its primary form, comes in the secondary form of *all sides;* the points come in succession to the meridian, and by the speed of rotation a new whole is formed. Nature keeps herself whole and her representation complete in the experience of each mind. She suffers no seat to be vacant in her college. It is the secret of the world that all things subsist and do not die, but only retire a little from sight and afterwards

return again. Whatever does not concern us is
concealed from us. As soon as a person is no
longer related to our present well-being, he is
concealed, or *dies*, as we say. Really, all things
and persons are related to us, but according to
our nature they act on us not at once but in
succession, and we are made aware of their presence one at a time. All persons, all things
which we have known, are here present, and
many more than we see; the world is full. As
the ancient said, the world is a *plenum* or solid;
and if we saw all things that really surround us
we should be imprisoned and unable to move.
For though nothing is impassable to the soul,
but all things are pervious to it and like high-
ways, yet this is only whilst the soul does not see
them. As soon as the soul sees any object, it
stops before that object. Therefore the divine
Providence which keeps the universe open in
every direction to the soul, conceals all the furniture and all the persons that do not concern
a particular soul, from the senses of that individual. Through solidest eternal things the man
finds his road as if they did not subsist, and does
not once suspect their being. As soon as he
needs a new object, suddenly he beholds it, and
no longer attempts to pass through it, but takes

another way. When he has exhausted for the time the nourishment to be drawn from any one person or thing, that object is withdrawn from his observation, and though still in his immediate neighborhood, he does not suspect its presence. Nothing is dead: men feign themselves dead, and endure mock funerals and mournful obituaries, and there they stand looking out of the window, sound and well, in some new and strange disguise. Jesus is not dead; he is very well alive: nor John, nor Paul, nor Mahomet, nor Aristotle; at times we believe we have seen them all, and could easily tell the names under which they go.

If we cannot make voluntary and conscious steps in the admirable science of universals, let us see the parts wisely, and infer the genius of nature from the best particulars with a becoming charity. What is best in each kind is an index of what should be the average of that thing. Love shows me the opulence of nature, by disclosing to me in my friend a hidden wealth, and I infer an equal depth of good in every other direction. It is commonly said by farmers that a good pear or apple costs no more time or pains to rear than a poor one; so I would have no work of art, no speech, or action, or thought, or friend, but the best.

The end and the means, the gamester and the game, — life is made up of the intermixture and reaction of these two amicable powers, whose marriage appears beforehand monstrous, as each denies and tends to abolish the other. We must reconcile the contradictions as we can, but their discord and their concord introduce wild absurdities into our thinking and speech. No sentence will hold the whole truth, and the only way in which we can be just, is by giving ourselves the lie ; Speech is better than silence ; silence is better than speech ; — All things are in contact ; every atom has a sphere of repulsion ; — Things are, and are not, at the same time ; — and the like. All the universe over, there is but one thing, this old Two-Face, creator-creature, mind-matter, right-wrong, of which any proposition may be affirmed or denied. Very fitly therefore I assert that every man is a partialist ; that nature secures him as an instrument by self-conceit, preventing the tendencies to religion and science ; and now further assert, that, each man's genius being nearly and affectionately explored, he is justified in his individuality, as his nature is found to be immense ; and now I add that every man is a universalist also, and, as our earth, whilst it spins on its own axis, spins

all the time around the sun through the celestial
spaces, so the least of its rational children, the
most dedicated to his private affair, works out,
though as it were under a disguise, the universal
problem. We fancy men are individuals; so are
pumpkins; but every pumpkin in the field goes
through every point of pumpkin history. The
rabid democrat, as soon as he is senator and rich
man, has ripened beyond possibility of sincere
radicalism, and unless he can resist the sun, he
must be conservative the remainder of his days.
Lord Eldon said in his old age that " if he were
to begin life again, he would be damned but he
would begin as agitator."

We hide this universality if we can, but it
appears at all points. We are as ungrateful as
children. There is nothing we cherish and strive
to draw to us but in some hour we turn and rend
it. We keep a running fire of sarcasm at ignorance and the life of the senses; then goes by,
perchance, a fair girl, a piece of life, gay and
happy, and making the commonest offices beautiful by the energy and heart with which she
does them; and seeing this we admire and love
her and them, and say, ' Lo! a genuine creature of the fair earth, not dissipated or too early
ripened by books, philosophy, religion, society,

or care ! ' insinuating a treachery and contempt for all we had so long loved and wrought in ourselves and others.

If we could have any security against moods ! If the profoundest prophet could be holden to his words, and the hearer who is ready to sell all and join the crusade could have any certificate that to-morrow his prophet shall not unsay his testimony ! But the Truth sits veiled there on the Bench, and never interposes an adamantine syllable ; and the most sincere and revolutionary doctrine, put as if the ark of God were carried forward some furlongs, and planted there for the succor of the world, shall in a few weeks be coldly set aside by the same speaker, as morbid; " I thought I was right, but I was not," — and the same immeasurable credulity demanded for new audacities.   If we were not of all opinions ! if we did not in any moment shift the platform on which we stand, and look and speak from another ! if there could be any regulation, any ' one-hour-rule,' that a man should never leave his point of view without sound of trumpet.   I am always insincere, as always knowing there are other moods.'

How sincere and confidential we can be, saying all that lies in the mind, and yet go away feeling that all is yet unsaid, from the incapacity of the parties to know each other, although they use the same words! My companion assumes to know my mood and habit of thought, and we go on from explanation to explanation until all is said which words can, and we leave matters just as they were at first, because of that vicious assumption. Is it that every man believes every other to be an incurable partialist, and himself a universalist? I talked yesterday with a pair of philosophers; I endeavored to show my good men that I liked everything by turns and nothing long; that I loved the centre, but doated on the superficies; that I loved man, if men seemed to me mice and rats; that I revered saints, but woke up glad that the old pagan world stood its ground and died hard; that I was glad of men of every gift and nobility, but would not live in their arms. Could they but once understand that I loved to know that they existed, and heartily wished them God-speed, yet, out of my poverty of life and thought, had no word or welcome for them when they came to see me, and could well consent to their living in Oregon for any claim I felt on them, — it would be a great satisfaction.[1]

IX

NEW ENGLAND REFORMERS

A LECTURE READ BEFORE THE SOCIETY IN AMORY
HALL, ON SUNDAY, MARCH 3, 1844

In the suburb, in the town,
On the railway, in the square,
Came a beam of goodness down
Doubling daylight everywhere :
Peace now each for malice takes,
Beauty for his sinful weeds,
For the angel Hope aye makes
Him an angel whom she leads.

NEW ENGLAND REFORMERS

WHOEVER has had opportunity of acquaintance with society in New England during the last twenty-five years, with those middle and with those leading sections that may constitute any just representation of the character and aim of the community, will have been struck with the great activity of thought and experimenting. His attention must be commanded by the signs that the Church, or religious party, is falling from the Church nominal, and is appearing in temperance and non-resistance societies; in movements of abolitionists and of socialists; and in very significant assemblies called Sabbath and Bible Conventions; [1] composed of ultraists, of seekers, of all the soul of the soldiery of dissent, and meeting to call in question the authority of the Sabbath, of the priesthood, and of the Church. In these movements nothing was more remarkable than the discontent they begot in the movers. The spirit of protest and of detachment drove the members of these Conventions to bear testimony against the Church, and immediately afterwards to declare their discontent with these Conventions, their independence of their colleagues, and their impatience of the methods whereby they were working. They defied each other, like a congress of kings, each of whom had a realm to rule, and a way of his own that made concert unprofitable. What a fertility of projects for the salvation of the world! One apostle thought all men should go to farming, and another that no man should buy or sell, that the use of money was the cardinal evil; another that the mischief was in our diet, that we eat and drink damnation. These made unleavened bread, and were foes to the death to fermentation. It was in vain urged by the housewife that God made yeast, as well as dough, and loves fermentation just as dearly as he loves vegetation; that fermentation develops the saccharine element in the grain, and makes it more palatable and more digestible. No: they wish the pure wheat, and will die but it shall not ferment. Stop, dear Nature, these incessant advances of thine; let us scotch these ever-rolling wheels! Others attacked the system of agriculture, the use of animal manures in farming, and the tyranny of man over brute nature; these abuses polluted his food. The ox must be taken from the plough and the horse from the cart, the hundred acres of the farm must be spaded, and the man must walk, wherever boats and locomotives will not carry him. Even the insect world was to be defended, — that had been too long neglected, and a society for the protection of ground-worms, slugs and mosquitos was to be incorporated without delay. With these appeared the adepts of homœopathy, of hydropathy, of mesmerism, of phrenology, and their wonderful theories of the Christian miracles! Others assailed particular vocations, as that of the lawyer, that of the merchant, of the manufacturer, of the clergyman, of the scholar. Others attacked the institution of marriage as the fountain of social evils. Others devoted themselves to the worrying of churches and meetings for public worship ; and the fertile forms of antinomianism ' among the elder. puritans seemed to have their match in the plenty of the new harvest of reform.

With this din of opinion and debate there was a keener scrutiny of institutions and domestic life than any we had known ; there was sincere protesting against existing evils, and there were changes of employment dictated by conscience. No doubt there was plentiful vaporing, and cases of backsliding might occur. But in each of these movements emerged a good result, a tendency to the adoption of simpler methods, and an assertion of the sufficiency of the private man. Thus it was directly in the spirit and genius of the age, what happened in one instance when a church censured and threatened to ex-communicate one of its members on account of the somewhat hostile part to the church which his conscience led him to take in the anti-slavery business; the threatened individual immediately excommunicated the church, in a public and formal process. This has been several times repeated: it was excellent when it was done the first time, but of course loses all value when it is copied. Every project in the history of re-form, no matter how violent and surprising, is good when it is the dictate of a man's genius and constitution, but very dull and suspicious when adopted from another. It is right and beautiful in any man to say, 'I will take this coat, or this book, or this measure of corn of yours,' — in whom we see the act to be original, and to flow from the whole spirit and faith of him; for then that taking will have a giving as free and divine; but we are very easily dis-posed to resist the same generosity of speech when we miss originality and truth to character in it.

There was in all the practical activities of New England for the last quarter of a century, a gradual withdrawal of tender consciences from the social organizations. There is observable throughout, the contest between mechanical and spiritual methods, but with a steady tendency of the thoughtful and virtuous to a deeper belief and reliance on spiritual facts.

In politics, for example, it is easy to see the progress of dissent. The country is full of rebellion; the country is full of kings. Hands off! let there be no control and no interference in the administration of the affairs of this kingdom of me. Hence the growth of the doctrine and of the party of Free Trade, and the willingness to try that experiment, in the face of what appear incontestable facts. I confess, the motto of the Globe newspaper is so attractive to me that I can seldom find much appetite to read what is below it in its columns: " The world is governed too much." So the country is frequently affording solitary examples of resistance to the government, solitary nullifiers, who throw themselves on their reserved rights; nay, who have reserved all their rights; who reply to the assessor and to the clerk of court that they do not know the State,' and embarrass the courts of law by non-juring and the commander-in-chief of the militia by non-resistance.'

The same disposition to scrutiny and dissent appeared in civil, festive, neighborly, and domestic society. A restless, prying, conscientious criticism broke out in unexpected quarters. Who gave me the money with which I bought my coat? Why should professional labor and that of the counting-house be paid so disproportionately to the labor of the porter and wood-sawyer? The whole business of Trade gives me to pause and think, as it constitutes false relations between men; inasmuch as I am prone to do unto others as does of any responsibility to behave well, and nobly to that person whom I owe it money; whereas if I had not that commodity, I should do unto me my good behavior of a commerce, and that would be a honorable to men, as long as himself the only certificate that he had a right to those acts and services what each asked of the other? Am I not too honorable a person to show not a wide distinction between the act of my own and that of that by his better no one owes? Am I not entitled to my own substance at the cost of that, by means of which human art and the of these, to whose counsels... but nothing healthful or exalting in the smooth conventions of society; I do not like the close air of saloons. I begin to suspect myself to be a prisoner, though treated with all this courtesy and luxury. I pay a destructive tax in my conformity.

The same insatiable criticism may be traced in the efforts for the reform of Education. The popular education has been taxed with a want of truth and nature. It was complained that an education to things was not given. We are students of words: we are shut up in schools, and colleges, and recitation-rooms, for ten or fifteen years, and come out at last with a bag of wind, a memory of words, and do not know a thing. We cannot use our hands, or our legs, or our eyes, or our arms. We do not know an edible root in the woods, we cannot tell our course by the stars, nor the hour of the day by the sun. It is well if we can swim and skate. We are afraid of a horse, of a cow, of a dog, of a snake, of a spider. The Roman rule was to teach a boy nothing that he could not learn standing. The old English rule was, ' All summer in the field, and all winter in the study.' And it seems as if a man should learn to plant, or to fish, or to hunt, that he might secure his

III

sufficience at all events, and not be painful to his friends and fellow-men. The lessons of science should be experimental also. The sight of a planet through a telescope is worth all the course on astronomy; the shock of the electric spark in the elbow, outvalues all the theories; the taste of the nitrous oxide, the firing of an artificial volcano, are better than volumes of chemistry.

One of the traits of the new spirit is the inquisition it fixed on our scholastic devotion to the dead languages. The ancient languages, with great beauty of structure, contain wonderful remains of genius, which draw, and always will draw, certain like-minded men, — Greek men, and Roman men, — in all countries, to their study; but by a wonderful drowsiness of usage they had exacted the study of all men. Once (say two centuries ago), Latin and Greek had a strict relation to all the science and culture there was in Europe, and the Mathematics had a momentary importance at some era of activity in physical science. These things became stereotyped as *education*, as the manner of men is. But the Good Spirit never cared for the colleges, and though all men and boys were now drilled in Latin, Greek and Mathematics, it had quite left these shells high and dry on the beach, and was now creating and feeding other matters at other ends of the world. But in a hundred high schools and colleges this warfare against common-sense still goes on. Four, or six, or ten years, the pupil is parsing Greek and Latin, and as soon as he leaves the University, as it is ludicrously styled, he shuts those books for the last time. Some thousands of young men are graduated at our colleges in this country every year, and the persons who, at forty years, still read Greek, can all be counted on your hand. I never met with ten. Four or five persons I have seen who read Plato.

But is not this absurd, that the whole liberal talent of this country should be directed in its best years on studies which lead to nothing? What was the consequence? Some intelligent persons said or thought, ' Is that Greek and Latin some spell to conjure with, and not words of reason? If the physician, the lawyer, the divine, never use it to come at their ends, I need never learn it to come at mine. Conjuring is gone out of fashion, and I will omit this conjugating, and go straight to affairs.' So they jumped the Greek and Latin, and read law, medicine, or sermons, without it. To the astonishment of all, the self-made men took even ground at once with the oldest of the regular graduates, and in a few months the most conservative circles of Boston and New York had quite forgotten who of their gownsmen was college-bred, and who was not.[1]

One tendency appears alike in the philosophical speculation and in the rudest democratical movements, through all the petulance and all the puerility, the wish, namely, to cast aside the superfluous and arrive at short methods; urged, as I suppose, by an intuition that the human spirit is equal to all emergencies, alone, and that man is more often injured than helped by the means he uses.

I conceive this gradual casting off of material aids, and the indication of growing trust in the private self-supplied powers of the individual, to be the affirmative principle of the recent philosophy, and that it is feeling its own profound truth and is reaching forward at this very hour to the happiest conclusions. I readily concede that in this, as in every period of intellectual activity, there has been a noise of denial and protest; much was to be resisted, much was to be got rid of by those who were reared in the old, before they could begin to affirm and to construct. Many a reformer perishes in his removal of rubbish; and that makes the offensiveness of the class. They are partial; they are not equal to the work they pretend. They lose their way; in the assault on the kingdom of darkness they expend all their energy on some accidental evil, and lose their sanity and power of benefit. It is of little moment that one or two or twenty errors of our social system be corrected, but of much that the man be in his senses.

The criticism and attack on institutions, which we have witnessed, has made one thing plain, that society gains nothing whilst a man, not himself renovated, attempts to renovate things around him : he has become tediously good in some particular but negligent or narrow in the rest; and hypocrisy and vanity are often the disgusting result.[1]

It is handsomer to remain in the establishment better than the establishment, and conduct that in the best manner, than to make a sally against evil by some single improvement, without supporting it by a total regeneration. Do not be so vain of your one objection. Do you think there is only one ? Alas ! my good friend, there is no part of society or of life better than any other part. All our things are right and wrong together. The wave of evil washes all our institutions alike. Do you complain of our Marriage? Our marriage is no worse than our education, our diet, our trade, our social customs. Do you complain of the laws of Property? It is a pedantry to give such importance to them. Can we not play the game of life with these counters, as well as with those? in the institution of property, as well as out of it? Let into it the new and renewing principle of love, and property will be universality. No one gives the impression of superiority to the institution, which he must give who will reform it. It makes no difference what you say, you must make me feel that you are aloof from it; by your natural and supernatural advantages do easily see to the end of it, — do see how man can do without it. Now all men are on one side. No man deserves to be heard against property. Only Love, only an Idea, is against property as we hold it.

I cannot afford to be irritable and captious, nor to waste all my time in attacks. If I should go out of church whenever I hear a false sentiment I could never stay there five minutes. But why come out? the street is as false as the church, and when I get to my house, or to my manners, or to my speech, I have not got away from the lie. When we see an eager assailant of one of these wrongs, a special reformer, we feel like asking him, What right have you, sir, to your one virtue? Is virtue piecemeal? This is a jewel amidst the rags of a beggar.

In another way the right will be vindicated. In the midst of abuses, in the heart of cities, in the aisles of false churches, alike in one place and in another, — wherever, namely, a just and heroic soul finds itself, there it will do what is next at hand, and by the new quality of character it shall put forth it shall abrogate that old condition, law, or school in which it stands, before the law of its own mind.

If partiality was one fault of the movement party, the other defect was their reliance on Association. Doubts such as those I have intimated drove many good persons to agitate the questions of social reform. But the revolt against the spirit of commerce, the spirit of aristocracy, and the inveterate abuses of cities, did not appear possible to individuals; and to do battle against numbers they armed themselves with numbers, and against concert they relied on new concert.

Following or advancing beyond the ideas of

St. Simon, of Fourier, and of Owen, three communities ' have already been formed in Massachusetts on kindred plans, and many more in the country at large. They aim to give every member a share in the manual labor, to give an equal reward to labor and to talent, and to unite a liberal culture with an education to labor. The scheme offers, by the economies of associated labor and expense, to make every member rich, on the same amount of property that, in separate families, would leave every member poor. These new associations are composed of men and women of superior talents and sentiments; yet it may easily be questioned whether such a community will draw, except in its beginnings, the able and the good; whether those who have energy will not prefer their chance of superiority and power in the world, to the humble certainties of the association; whether such a retreat does not promise to become an asylum to those who have tried and failed, rather than a field to the strong; and whether the members will not necessarily be fractions of men, because each finds that he cannot enter it without some compromise.' Friendship and association are very fine things, and a grand phalanx of the best of the human race, banded for some catholic object; yes, excellent; but remember that no society can ever be so large as one man. He, in his friendship, in his natural and momentary associations, doubles or multiplies himself; but in the hour in which he mortgages himself to two or ten or twenty, he dwarfs himself below the stature of one.

But the men of less faith could not thus believe, and to such, concert appears the sole specific of strength. I have failed, and you have failed, but perhaps together we shall not fail. Our housekeeping is not satisfactory to us, but perhaps a phalanx, a community, might be. Many of us have differed in opinion, and we could find no man who could make the truth plain, but possibly a college, or an ecclesiastical council, might. I have not been able either to persuade my brother or to prevail on myself to disuse the traffic or the potation of brandy, but perhaps a pledge of total abstinence might effectually restrain us. The candidate my party votes for is not to be trusted with a dollar, but he will be honest in the Senate, for we can bring public opinion to bear on him. Thus concert was the specific in all cases. But concert is neither better nor worse, neither more nor less potent, than individual force. All the men in the world cannot make a statue walk and speak, cannot make a drop of blood, or a blade of grass, any more than one man can. But let there be one man, let there be truth in two men, in ten men, then is concert for the first time possible ; because the force which moves the world is a new quality, and can never be furnished by adding whatever quantities of a different kind. What is the use of the concert of the false and the disunited ? There can be no concert in two, where there is no concert in one. When the individual is not *individual*, but is dual; when his thoughts look one way and his actions another; when his faith is traversed by his habits ; when his will, enlightened by reason, is warped by his sense ; when with one hand he rows and with the other backs water, what concert can be ?

I do not wonder at the interest these projects inspire. The world is awaking to the idea of union, and these experiments show what it is thinking of. It is and will be magic. Men will live and communicate, and plough, and reap, and govern, as by added ethereal power, when once they are united ; as in a celebrated experiment, by expiration and respiration exactly together, four persons lift a heavy man from the ground by the little finger only, and without sense of weight. But this union must be inward, and not one of covenants, and is to be reached by a reverse of the methods they use. The union is only perfect when all the uniters are isolated. It is the union of friends who live in different streets or towns. Each man, if he attempts to join himself to others, is on all sides cramped and diminished of his proportion ; and the stricter the union the smaller and the more pitiful he is. But leave him alone, to recognize in every hour and place the secret soul ; he will go up and down doing the works of a true member, and, to the astonishment of all, the work will be done with concert, though no man spoke. Government will be adamantine without any governor. The union must be ideal in actual individualism.[1]

I pass to the indication in some particulars of that faith in man, which the heart is preaching to us in these days, and which engages the more regard, from the consideration that the speculations of one generation are the history of the next following.

In alluding just now to our system of education, I spoke of the deadness of its details. But it is open to graver criticism than the palsy of its members : it is a system of despair. The disease with which the human mind now labors is want of faith. Men do not believe in a power of education. We do not think we can speak to divine sentiments in man, and we do not try. We renounce all high aims. We believe that the defects of so many perverse and so many frivolous people who make up society, are organic, and society is a hospital of incurables. A man of good sense but of little faith, whose compassion seemed to lead him to church as often as he went there, said to me that "he liked to have concerts, and fairs, and churches, and other public amusements go on." I am afraid the remark is too honest, and comes from the same origin as the maxim of the tyrant, "If you would rule the world quietly, you must keep it amused." I notice too that the ground on which eminent public servants urge the claims of popular education is fear; 'This country is filling up with thousands and millions of voters, and you must educate them to keep them from our throats.' We do not believe that any education, any system of philosophy, any influence of genius, will ever give depth of insight to a superficial mind. Having settled ourselves into this infidelity, our skill is expended to procure alleviations, diversion, opiates. We adorn the victim with manual skill, his tongue with languages, his body with inoffensive and comely manners. So have we cunningly hid the tragedy of limitation and inner death we cannot avert. Is it strange that society should be devoured by a secret melancholy which breaks through all its smiles and all its gayety and games?

But even one step farther our infidelity has gone. It appears that some doubt is felt by good and wise men whether really the happiness and probity of men is increased by the culture of the mind in those disciplines to which we give the name of education. Unhappily too the doubt comes from scholars, from persons who have tried these methods. In their experience the scholar was not raised by the sacred thoughts amongst which he dwelt, but used them to selfish ends. He was a profane person, and became a showman, turning his gifts to a marketable use, and not to his own sustenance and growth.[1] It was found that the intellect could be independently developed, that is, in separation from the man, as any single organ can be invigorated, and the result was monstrous. A canine appetite for knowledge was generated, which must still be fed but was never satisfied, and this knowledge, not being directed on action, never took the character of substantial, humane truth, blessing those whom it entered. It gave the scholar certain powers of expression, the power of speech, the power of poetry, of literary art, but it did not bring him to peace or to beneficence.

When the literary class betray a destitution of faith, it is not strange that society should be disheartened and sensualized by unbelief. What remedy? Life must be lived on a higher plane. We must go up to a higher platform, to which we are always invited to ascend; there, the whole aspect of things changes. I resist the scepticism of our education and of our educated men. I do not believe that the differences of opinion and character in men are organic. I do not recognize, beside the class of the good and the wise, a permanent class of sceptics, or a class of conservatives, or of malignants, or of materialists. I do not believe in two classes. You remember the story of the poor woman who importuned King Philip of Macedon to grant her justice, which Philip refused: the woman exclaimed, "I appeal:" the king, astonished, asked to whom she appealed: the woman replied, "From Philip drunk to Philip sober." The text will suit me very well. I believe not in two classes of men, but in man in two moods, in Philip drunk and Philip sober. I think, according to the good-hearted word of Plato, "Unwillingly the soul is deprived of truth." Iron conservative, miser, or thief, no man is but by a supposed necessity which he tolerates by shortness or torpidity of sight. The soul lets no man go without some visitations and holydays of a diviner presence. It would be easy to show, by a narrow scanning of any man's biography, that we are not so wedded to our paltry performances of every kind but that every man has at intervals the grace to scorn his performances, in comparing them with his belief of what he should do;—that he puts himself on the side of his enemies, listening gladly to what they say of him, and accusing himself of the same things.

What is it men love in Genius, but its infinite hope, which degrades all it has done? Genius counts all its miracles poor and short. Its own idea it never executed. The Iliad, the Hamlet, the Doric column, the Roman arch, the Gothic minster, the German anthem, when they are ended, the master casts behind him. How sinks the song in the waves of melody which the universe pours over his soul! Before that gracious Infinite out of which he drew these few strokes,

how mean they look, though the praises of the
world attend them. From the triumphs of his
art he turns with desire to this greater defeat.
Let those admire who will. With silent joy
he sees himself to be capable of a beauty that
eclipses all which his hands have done; all which
human hands have ever done.[1]

Well, we are all the children of genius, the
children of virtue, — and feel their inspirations
in our happier hours. Is not every man sometimes a radical in politics? Men are conservatives when they are least vigorous, or when
they are most luxurious. They are conservatives after dinner, or before taking their rest;
when they are sick, or aged. In the morning,
or when their intellect or their conscience has
been aroused; when they hear music, or when
they read poetry, they are radicals. In the circle
of the rankest tories that could be collected in
England, Old or New, let a powerful and stimulating intellect, a man of great heart and mind
act on them, and very quickly these frozen con-
servators will yield to the friendly influence,
these hopeless will begin to hope, these haters
will begin to love, these immovable statues will
begin to spin and revolve. I cannot help recall-
ing the fine anecdote which Warton relates of

Bishop Berkeley, when he was preparing to leave England with his plan of planting the gospel among the American savages. " Lord Bathurst told me that the members of the Scriblerus Club being met at his house at dinner, they agreed to rally Berkeley, who was also his guest, on his scheme at Bermudas. Berkeley, having listened to the many lively things they had to say, begged to be heard in his turn, and displayed his plan with such an astonishing and animating force of eloquence and enthusiasm that they were struck dumb, and, after some pause, rose up all together with earnestness, exclaiming, ' Let us set out with him immediately.' " Men in all ways are better than they seem. They like flattery for the moment, but they know the truth for their own. It is a foolish cowardice which keeps us from trusting them and speaking to them rude truth. They resent your honesty for an instant, they will thank you for it always. What is it we heartily wish of each other? Is it to be pleased and flattered? No, but to be convicted and exposed, to be shamed out of our nonsense of all kinds, and made men of, instead of ghosts and phantoms.' We are weary of gliding ghostlike through the world, which is itself so slight and unreal. We

III

crave a sense of reality, though it comes in strokes of pain. I explain so, — by this man-like love of truth, — those excesses and errors into which souls of great vigor, but not equal insight, often fall. They feel the poverty at the bottom of all the seeming affluence of the world. They know the speed with which they come straight through the thin masquerade, and conceive a disgust at the indigence of nature : [1] Rousseau, Mirabeau, Charles Fox, Napoleon, Byron, — and I could easily add names nearer home, of raging riders, who drive their steeds so hard, in the violence of living to forget its illusion : they would know the worst, and tread the floors of hell.[2] The heroes of ancient and modern fame, Cimon, Themistocles, Alcibiades, Alexander, Cæsar, have treated life and fortune as a game to be well and skilfully played, but the stake not to be so valued but that any time it could be held as a trifle light as air, and thrown up. Cæsar, just before the battle of Pharsalia, discourses with the Egyptian priest concerning the fountains of the Nile, and offers to quit the army, the empire, and Cleopatra, if he will show him those mysterious sources.[3]

The same magnanimity shows itself in our social relations, in the preference, namely, which each man gives to the society of superiors over that of his equals. All that a man has will he give for right relations with his mates. All that he has will he give for an erect demeanor in every company and on each occasion. He aims at such things as his neighbors prize, and gives his days and nights, his talents and his heart, to strike a good stroke, to acquit himself in all men's sight as a man. The consideration of an eminent citizen, of a noted merchant, of a man of mark in his profession; a naval and military honor, a general's commission, a marshal's baton, a ducal coronet, the laurel of poets, and, anyhow procured, the acknowledgment of eminent merit, — have this lustre for each candidate that they enable him to walk erect and unashamed in the presence of some persons before whom he felt himself inferior. Having raised himself to this rank, having established his equality with class after class of those with whom he would live well, he still finds certain others before whom he cannot possess himself, because they have somewhat fairer, somewhat grander, somewhat purer, which extorts homage of him. Is his ambition pure? then will his laurels and his possessions seem worthless: instead of avoiding these men who make his fine gold dim, he will cast all behind him and seek their society only, woo and embrace this his humiliation and mortification, until he shall know why his eye sinks, his voice is husky, and his brilliant talents are paralyzed in this presence. He is sure that the soul which gives the lie to all things will tell none. His constitution will not mislead him. If it cannot carry itself as it ought, high and unmatchable in the presence of any man; if the secret oracles whose whisper makes the sweetness and dignity of his life do here withdraw and accompany him no longer, — it is time to undervalue what he has valued, to dispossess himself of what he has acquired, and with Cæsar to take in his hand the army, the empire and Cleopatra, and say, " All these will I relinquish, if you will show me the fountains of the Nile." Dear to us are those who love us; the swift moments we spend with them are a compensation for a great deal of misery; they enlarge our life; — but dearer are those who reject us as unworthy, for they add another life: they build a heaven before us whereof we had not dreamed, and thereby supply to us new powers out of the recesses of the spirit, and urge us to new and unattempted performances.[1]

As every man at heart wishes the best and

not inferior society, wishes to be convicted of his
error and to come to himself, — so he wishes
that the same healing should not stop in his
thought, but should penetrate his will or active
power. The selfish man suffers more from his
selfishness than he from whom that selfishness
withholds some important benefit. What he
most wishes is to be lifted to some higher platform, that he may see beyond his present fear
the transalpine good, so that his fear, his coldness, his custom may be broken up like fragments of ice, melted and carried away in the
great stream of good will. Do you ask my aid?
I also wish to be a benefactor. I wish more to
be a benefactor and servant than you wish to be
served by me; and surely the greatest good fortune that could befall me is precisely to be so
moved by you that I should say, ' Take me and
all mine, and use me and mine freely to your
ends!' for I could not say it otherwise than
because a great enlargement had come to my
heart and mind, which made me superior to my
fortunes.' Here we are paralyzed with fear; we
hold on to our little properties, house and land,
office and money, for the bread which they have
in our experience yielded us, although we confess that our being does not flow through them.

We desire to be made great; we desire to be touched with that fire which shall command this ice to stream, and make our existence a benefit. If therefore we start objections to your project, O friend of the slave, or friend of the poor or of the race, understand well that it is because we wish to drive you to drive us into your measures. We wish to hear ourselves confuted. We are haunted with a belief that you have a secret which it would highliest advantage us to learn, and we would force you to impart it to us, though it should bring us to prison or to worse extremity.

Nothing shall warp me from the belief that every man is a lover of truth. There is no pure lie, no pure malignity in nature. The entertainment of the proposition of depravity is the last profligacy and profanation. There is no scepticism, no atheism but that. Could it be received into common belief, suicide would unpeople the planet. It has had a name to live in some dogmatic theology, but each man's innocence and his real liking of his neighbor have kept it a dead letter. I remember standing at the polls one day when the anger of the political contest gave a certain grimness to the faces of the independent electors, and a good man at my side,

looking on the people, remarked, " I am satisfied that the largest part of these men, on either
side, mean to vote right." ' I suppose considerate observers, looking at the masses of men in
their blameless and in their equivocal actions,
will assent, that in spite of selfishness and frivolity, the general purpose in the great number
of persons is fidelity. The reason why any one
refuses his assent to your opinion, or his aid to
your benevolent design, is in you : he refuses
to accept you as a bringer of truth, because
though you think you have it, he feels that
you have it not. You have not given him the
authentic sign.

. If it were worth while to run into details this
general doctrine of the latent but ever soliciting
Spirit, it would be easy to adduce illustration in
particulars of a man's equality to the Church,
of his equality to the State, and of his equality
to every other man. It is yet in all men's memory that, a few years ago, the liberal churches
complained that the Calvinistic church denied
to them the name of Christian. I think the
complaint was confession : a religious church
would not complain. A religious man, like
Behmen, Fox, or Swedenborg, is not irritated
by wanting the sanction of the Church, but

the Church feels the accusation of his presence and belief.

It only needs that a just man should walk in our streets to make it appear how pitiful and inartificial a contrivance is our legislation. The man whose part is taken and who does not wait for society in anything, has a power which society cannot choose but feel.¹ The familiar experiment called the hydrostatic paradox, in which a capillary column of water balances the ocean, is a symbol of the relation of one man to the whole family of men. The wise Dandamis, on hearing the lives of Socrates, Pythagoras and Diogenes read, "judged them to be great men every way, excepting that they were too much subjected to the reverence of the laws, which to second and authorize, true virtue must abate very much of its original vigor."²

And as a man is equal to the Church and equal to the State, so he is equal to every other man. The disparities of power in men are superficial; and all frank and searching conversation, in which a man lays himself open to his brother, apprises each of their radical unity. When two persons sit and converse in a thoroughly good understanding, the remark is sure to be made, See how we have disputed about

words! Let a clear, apprehensive mind, such as
every man knows among his friends, converse
with the most commanding poetic genius, I think
it would appear that there was no inequality such
as men fancy, between them; that a perfect understanding, a like receiving, a like perceiving,
abolished differences; and the poet would confess that his creative imagination gave him no
deep advantage, but only the superficial one that
he could express himself and the other could
not; that his advantage was a knack, which
might impose on indolent men but could not
impose on lovers of truth; for they know the
tax of talent, or what a price of greatness the
power of expression too often pays. I believe it
is the conviction of the purest men that the net
amount of man and man does not much vary.
Each is incomparably superior to his companion
in some faculty. His want of skill in other direc-
tions has added to his fitness for his own work.
Each seems to have some compensation yielded
to him by his infirmity, and every hinderance
operates as a concentration of his force.[1]

These and the like experiences intimate that
man stands in strict connection with a higher fact
never yet manifested. There is power over and
behind us, and we are the channels of its com-

munications. We seek to say thus and so, and over our head some spirit sits which contradicts what we say.' We would persuade our fellow to this or that; another self within our eyes dissuades him. That which we keep back, this reveals. In vain we compose our faces and our words; it holds uncontrollable communication with the enemy, and he answers civilly to us, but believes the spirit. We exclaim, 'There's a traitor in the house!' but at last it appears that he is the true man, and I am the traitor. This open channel to the highest life is the first and last reality, so subtle, so quiet, yet so tenacious, that although I have never expressed the truth, and although I have never heard the expression of it from any other, I know that the whole truth is here for me. What if I cannot answer your questions? I am not pained that I cannot frame a reply to the question, What is the operation we call Providence? There lies the unspoken thing, present, omnipresent. Every time we converse we seek to translate it into speech, but whether we hit or whether we miss, we have the fa⸻ discourse is an approximate answer:

that we do not

st it abides for

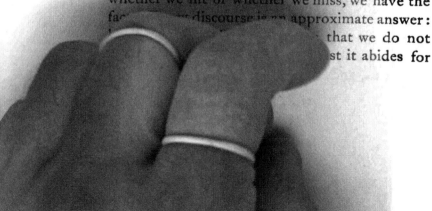

If the auguries of the prophesying heart shall
make themselves good in time, the man who
shall be born, whose advent men and events pre-
pare and foreshow, is one who shall enjoy his
connection with a higher life, with the man within
man ; shall destroy distrust by his trust, shall
use his native but forgotten methods, shall not
take counsel of flesh and blood, but shall rely
on the Law alive and beautiful which works over
our heads and under our feet. Pitiless, it avails
itself of our success when we obey it, and of our
ruin when we contravene it.[1] Men are all secret
believers in it, else the word justice would have
no meaning : they believe that the best is the
true ; that right is done at last ; or chaos would
come. It rewards actions after their nature, and
not after the design of the agent. 'Work,' it
saith to man, 'in every hour, paid or unpaid, see
only that thou work, and thou canst not escape
the reward : whether thy work be fine or coarse,
planting corn or writing epics, so only it be honest work, done to thine own approbation, it shall
earn a reward to the senses as well as to the
thought : no matter how often defeated, you are
born to victory. The reward of a thing well
done, is to have done it.'

As soon as a man is wonted to look beyond

surfaces, and to see how this high will prevails without an exception or an interval, he settles himself into serenity. He can already rely on the laws of gravity, that every stone will fall where it is due; the good globe is faithful, and carries us securely through the celestial spaces, anxious or resigned, we need not interfere to help it on: and he will learn one day the mild lesson they teach, that our own orbit is all our task, and we need not assist the administration of the universe. Do not be so impatient to set the town right concerning the unfounded pretensions and the false reputation of certain men of standing. They are laboring harder to set the town right concerning themselves, and will certainly succeed. Suppress for a few days your criticism on the insufficiency of this or that teacher or experimenter, and he will have demonstrated his insufficiency to all men's eyes.' In like manner, let a man fall into the divine circuits, and he is enlarged. Obedience to his genius is the only liberating influence. We wish to escape from subjection and a sense of inferiority, and we make self-denying ordinances, we drink water, we eat grass, we refuse the laws, we go to jail : it is all in vain; only by obedience to his genius, only by the freest activity in the way constitutional to him, does an angel seem to arise before a man and lead him by the hand out of all the wards of the prison.

That which befits us, embosomed in beauty and wonder as we are, is cheerfulness and courage, and the endeavor to realize our aspirations. The life of man is the true romance, which when it is valiantly conducted will yield the imagination a higher joy than any fiction. All around us what powers are wrapped up under the coarse mattings of custom, and all wonder prevented. It is so wonderful to our neurologists that a man can see without his eyes, that it does not occur to them that it is just as wonderful that he should see with them ; and that is ever the difference between the wise and the unwise: the latter wonders at what is unusual, the wise man wonders at the usual. Shall not the heart which has received so much, trust the Power by which it lives? May it not quit other leadings, and listen to the Soul that has guided it so gently and taught it so much, secure that the future will be worthy of the past ?

NOTES

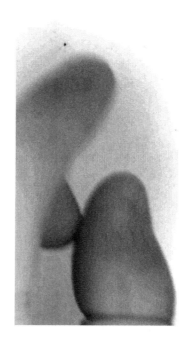

NOTES

THIS second book of Essays followed the first by a three
years' interval, allowing time for the rehearsal of the lectures, or rather the trial of them on assemblages of men and
women in country villages, and before more cultivated, if not
more critical, audiences in the city. During that time the matter
was often rearranged and extended, and always severely pruned.
The book was published by James Munroe & Co., of Boston, in 1844. The papers of the time show that it was better
received than either of its predecessors. The Rev. Dr. Hedge,
writing in the *Christian Examiner*, praising the *Essays*, though
troubled at some expressions with regard to Jesus, went so far
as to say that they "were destined to carry far into coming
time their lofty cheer and spirit-stirring notes of courage and
hope." Chapman, the English publisher, had written to Mr.
Emerson asking him to send some work not yet published, for
which he would try to get and maintain copyright, and allow
half profits to the author. So the book appeared in America
and England about the same time.

Carlyle wrote in November : "Your English volume of
Essays, as Chapman probably informs you by this Post, was
advertised yesterday, ' with a Preface from me.' That is hardly
accurate — that latter clause. My ' Preface ' consists only of a
certificate that the Book is correctly printed, and sent forth by
a Publisher of your appointment, whom therefore all readers
of yours ought to regard accordingly. Nothing more. There
proves, I believe, no visible real vestige of a copyright obtain-
able here. . . . I will say already of it, It is a *sermon* to
me, as all your other deliberate utterances are ; a real *word*,

which I feel to be such, — alas, almost or altogether the one such, in a world all full of jargons, hearsays, echoes, and vain noises, which cannot pass with me for *words*. This is a praise far beyond any ' literary ' one; literary praises are not worth repeating in comparison. For the rest, I have to object still (what you will call objecting against the Law of Nature) that we find you a Speaker indeed, but as it were a *Soliloquizer* on the eternal mountain-tops only, in vast solitudes where men and their affairs lie all hushed in a very dim remoteness; and only *the man* and the stars and the earth are visible, — whom, so fine a fellow seems he, we could perpetually punch into, and say, ' Why won't you come and help us then ? We have terrible need of one man like you down among us! It is cold and vacant up there ; nothing paintable but rainbows and emotions ; come down, and you shall do life-pictures, passions, facts, — which *transcend* all thought, and leave it stuttering and stammering ! ' To which he answers that he won't, can't, and does n't want to (as the Cockneys have it); and so I leave him, and say, ' You Western Gymnosophist! Well, we can afford one man for that too. But —!' — By the bye, I ought to say, the sentences are very *brief ;* and did not, in my *sheet* reading, always entirely cohere for me. Pure genuine Saxon; strong and simple; of a clearness, of a beauty — But they did not, sometimes, rightly stick to their foregoers and their followers; the paragraph not as a beaten *ingot,* but as a beautiful square *bag of duck-shot* held together by canvas! I will try them again, with the Book deliberately before me. There are also one or two utterances about ' Jesus,' ' immortality,' and so forth, which will produce wide-eyes here and there. I do not say it was wrong to utter them; a man obeys his own Dæmon in these cases as his supreme law.''

In Mr. Emerson's answer, freely acknowledging himself to be a poor transmitter of celestial law, his faith in the ideals and intelligence of his countrymen at large shines conspicuous. An audience of "middle class" hearers being attracted and held by such discourses was a thing incomprehensible to his English friends.

DECEMBER, 1844.

My knowledge of the defects of these things I write is all but sufficient to hinder me from writing at all. I am only a sort of lieutenant here in a deplorable absence of captains, and write the laws ill as thinking it a better homage than universal silence. You Londoners know little of the dignities and duties of country lyceums. But of what you say now and heretofore respecting the remoteness of my writing and thinking from real life, though I hear substantially the same criticism made by my countrymen, I do not know what it means. If I can at any time express the law and the ideal right, that should satisfy me without measuring the divergence from it of the last act of Congress. And though I sometimes accept a popular call, and preach on Temperance or the Abolition of Slavery, as lately on the 1st of August, I am sure to feel, before I have done with it, what an intrusion it is into another sphere, and so much loss of virtue in my own.

As to his call to speak on his favorite themes, he earlier wrote to a friend: —

"I am just announcing my new course of lectures [the matter later included in this volume], so far does the thirst of publishing my solitudes, and the need sometimes felt by me of a stated task — add even some small degree of superstition of a necessity to speak what one fancies people ought to hear — with other reasons, drive me."

Readers of the Essays should bear in mind that most of them were spoken man to man. The thoughts were received — so the speaker held — and reported as truly as he could, but what labor was spent on the form was in presenting them clearly and strongly in the plain English which is the language of the best poetry, and in illustrating them by anecdotes from the past and analogies of daily life and from advancing science. In the chapter " Emerson as Essayist," in Mr. John Albee's admirable *Remembrances of Emerson*, is a good account of the lecturer, his method and his audience.

THE POET

The poet in Emerson was in these years struggling through impediment to expression. *Nature* has been called more of a rhapsody than an essay. In his solitary walks by day and night, he listened for the song of the pine-tree and the music of the stars, and he placed an Æolian harp in his study window while he wrote. It was the poetic side of philosophy, history, science and divinity that interested him. Seeing the harmonies of the Universe, he naturally longed to show them in poetry, the fitting form. His note-books at this period are full of trials to do so, and several of his poems had already appeared in the *Dial*. He had given another lecture, " The Poet," between " The Conservative " and " The Transcendentalist " in the course in Boston in the winter of 1841–42. Only a few paragraphs of this appear in the present lecture, and a few more in " Poetry and Imagination " in *Letters and Social Aims*. But in a poem often referred to in these notes, which Mr. Emerson never finished, so it was only printed in the Appendix to the collection of his verse, the same thoughts and high estimate of the office of the Poet appear that occur in the published and unpublished essays on this theme.

The first motto is taken from this poem, where in improved form it is found in the latter lines of the first part: —

> But oh, to see his solar eyes
> Like meteors which chose their way
> And rived the dark like a new day, etc.

The second motto is taken from the " Ode to Beauty."

Page 4, note 1. In " Literary Ethics " in *Nature, Addresses and Lectures,* early in its second division, is an interesting passage showing how Emerson, when he came from his studies in classic poetry to the wild woods, found " all new and undescribed: " " Further inquiry will discover . . . that not these chanting poets themselves knew anything <u>sincere</u> of these handsome natures they so commended," etc.

Page 4, note 2. In the unpublished lecture " The Poet," alluded to in the introductory note, is this passage: " The sense of nature is inexhaustible. You think you know the meaning of these tropes of nature, and to-day you come into a new thought, and lo! all nature converts itself into a symbol of that, and you see it has been chanting that song like a cricket ever since the creation. . . . 'T was the moral of the river, the rock and the ocean. The river, the rock and the ocean say ' Guess again.' "

Page 4, note 3. The doctrine of the immanence of spirit — the universal mind — imaged in the doctrine of Heracleitus that Fire is the ultimate ground of the world.

Page 6, note 1. This whole paragraph is from the earlier lecture " The Poet." Adopting the not altogether pleasing

Page 8, note 2.

> Ever the words of the gods resound ;
> But the porches of man's ear
> Seldom in this low life's round
> Are unsealed, that he may hear.
>
> "My Garden," *Poems.*

Page 9, note 1. The allusion here is probably to Tennyson, who had not come to his full strength ; possibly to Mr. Emerson's unseen friend and correspondent in England, John Sterling, who died the year these essays were published.

Page 10, note 1. In a letter Mr. Emerson spoke of the priority of music to thought in young scholars, and referring to the college declamations and exhibitions, and certain poems, said, " What fools a few sounding sentences and verses made of me and my mates ! " To his children he often quoted these with amused affection.

Page 11, note 1. Dr. Holmes quotes this sentence as one " meant for the initiated, rather than for him who runs, to read," and thus comments: " Does this sound wild and extravagant ? What were the political ups and downs of the Hebrews ? what were the squabbles of the tribes with each other or with their neighbors compared to the birth of that poet to whom we owe the Psalms, — the sweet singer whose voice is still the dearest of all that ever sang to the heart of mankind ? " Mr. Emerson looked along the heights of history and saw mainly the men of faith and insight who moved the masses. In the unpublished lecture on the Poet referred to he says, " A man apparently foolish and helpless, with nothing magnetic in him, who is a churl in the drawing-room, an idiot in the legislature, — hides himself in his garret from the pride and pity of men, and writes a poem which . . . is at first

neglected, then kissed, — and it pushes all potentates from
their thrones, changes the course of affairs in a few years, and
actually wipes out the memory of that transient state of things
under which he suffered when he existed.'' On the reverse
of the sheet he noted a list of names of some '' Poets,'' in the
wider sense, as they came to mind, who have in their degree
had such influence : Plato, Aristophanes, Tyrtæus, Rouget
de Lisle, Rousseau, Machiavel, Voltaire, Tom Paine, Swift,
Luther, Rabelais, Mahomet, Mirabeau.

Page 13, note 1. His steady belief was that thought was
common property, and not to be *defended*, and that all good
teaching and poetry was affirmative, and by its merit made
denials unnecessary.

Page 13, note 2. Jamblichus, who lived in the fourth century B. C., was the pupil of Porphyry and the teacher of Proclus. He wrote on the Egyptian mysteries; also the Life
of Pythagoras. Mr. Emerson, alluding to him in the essay
'' Books '' in *Society and Solitude*, quotes the Emperor Julian's
saying of him, '' He was posterior to Plato in time, not in
genius.'' In a letter in 1842 he mentions that he is reading
Jamblichus's Life of Pythagoras.

Page 14, note 1. From *An Hymne in Honour of Beautie*,
Stanza xix.

Page 14, note 2. Writing to Miss Elizabeth Hoar from
Nantasket Beach in July, 1841, and telling of his reading,
after speaking of his delight in Plato's *Phædrus, Meno* and the
Banquet, he adds, '' I have also three volumes new to me of
Thomas Taylor's Translations. Proclus, Ocellus Lucanus,
and Pythagorean Fragments

Page talk with stage-
England roads,
enjoyed their racy

vernacular and picturesque brag. On his walks he fell in with pot-hunters and fishermen, wood-choppers and drovers, and liked to exchange a few words with them. "I always felt as if every man I met was my master," he said.

Page 16, note 2. This part of the essay is from the lecture "The Poet," which was written soon after the election of Harrison to the Presidency.

Journal, 1840. "The simplest things are always better than curiosities. The most imposing part of this Harrison celebration of the Fourth of July in Concord, as in Baltimore, was this ball, twelve or thirteen feet in diameter, which, as it mounts the little heights and slopes of the road, draws all eyes with a certain sublime movement, especially as the imagination is incessantly addressed with its political significance.[1] So the Log Cabin is a lucky watchword."

Page 18, note 1. This recalls the last lines of the little poem "Limits," printed in the Appendix to the *Poems*, in which man's ignorance of animal life and feeling is spoken of (as also in the end of "History" in *Essays, First Series*). There, speaking of the rat, Mr. Emerson says, —

> His wicked eye
> Is cruel to thy cruelty.

Page 19, note 1. In "A Letter" written at the time of the publication of these essays, — when the Fitchburg Railroad was just finished to Concord, — in the *Dial* (vol. iv.), also printed in *Natural History of Intellect*, Mr. Emerson, after his way, makes the best of its coming, thus: "To the railway we must say, — like the courageous lord-mayor at his first hunting, when told the hare was coming, — 'Let it come in

---

[1] "Keep the ball a-rolling" was the campaign watchword, with "Tippecanoe and Tyler too."

Heaven's name, I am not afraid on 't,'" and speaks of the unlooked-for social and political effects fast appearing.

Page 21, note 1. Much of this paragraph came from the earlier lecture of the same title, and it should be read with "Woodnotes," II., in the *Poems*, written about the same time. It also suggests Mr. Emerson's reading. Thomas Taylor said, giving "the substance of Porphyry's Life of Plotinus," that Plotinus applied himself to the canons concerning the stars, but not according to a very mathematical mode, like the calculation of eclipses or measuring the distance from the sun to the earth, etc. "For he considered employment of this kind as more the province of the mathematician than the profound and intellectual philosopher. The mathematical sciences are indeed the proper *means* of acquiring wisdom, but they ought never to be considered as its end. They are the bridge, as it were, between sense and intellect by which we may safely pass through the night of oblivion over the dark and stormy ocean of matter to the lucid regions of the intelligible world. And he who is desirous of returning to his true country will speedily pass over this bridge without making any needless delays in his passage."

Page 22, note 1. In the opening of the poem parallel with this essay, it is said of the Poet: —

> The things whereon he cast his eyes
> Could not the nations re-baptize,
> Nor Time's snows hide the names he set,
> Nor last posterity forget.

In the chapter "Language" in *Nature*, these thoughts of the origins of words are developed.

Page 22, note 2. The Evolution concisely stated.

Page 23, note 1. In his collection of "Fragments of Pin-

dar'' in the *Dial,* published this same year, Mr. Thoreau
quoted this passage from Ælius Aristides: '' Pindar used such
exaggeration [in praise of poetry] as to say that even the gods
themselves, when, at his marriage, Zeus asked them if they
wanted anything, ' asked him to make certain gods for them
who should celebrate these great works and all his creation
with speech and song.' ''

Page 24, note 1. For a poem written in Emerson's youth
on a sunrise seen by him from the hill opposite the Old
Manse, his grandfather's house, see '' Fragments on Nature ''
in the *Poems.*

Page 25, note 1.

> The gods talk in the breath of the woods,
> They talk in the shaken pine, etc.
>> '' The Poet,'' *Poems,* Appendix.

Page 26, note 1.

> Thee, gliding through the sea of form.
>> '' Ode to Beauty,'' *Poems.*

Page 28, note 1. It was his consolation that '' Evil was
only Good in the making.''

Page 29, note 1. '' He who sings the holy decrees of
the gods and pious heroes and the heaven of Jove, let him live
sparely, let herbs be his harmless food, and clear water from
a beechen cup give him a sober draught. Let his youth be
chaste and free from sin, his morals rigid and his name stain-
less. So lived Orpheus and Homer. For the poet is dedicated to the gods and is their priest.'' — Milton, *Elegia
Sexta,* lines 55–78, translated.

Page 30, note 1. Since the poet sees the permanent truth
symbolized by each transient appearance, this is another ver-

sion of the word of the Evangelist, "The truth shall make you free."

Page 31, note 1. These lines come from the Dedication of Chapman's Homer.

Page 31, note 2. This passage from "The Wif of Bathe's Tale" was a favorite of Mr. Emerson's : —

> Take fire, and bere it to the derkest hous
> Betwix this and the Mount of Caucasus,
> And let men shette the dores and go thenne,
> Yet wol the fire as faire lie and brenne
> As twenty thousand men might it behold;
> His office naturel ay wol it hold,
> Up peril of my lif, til that it die.

Page 32, note 1. Always eclectic in his reading, he wrote : —

> That book is good
> Which puts me in a working mood.
> Unless to thought be added will,
> Apollo is an imbecile.
> "Fragments on the Poet," *Poems,* Appendix.

Page 33, note 1.

> The heavens that now draw him
> With sweetness untold,
> Once found, — for new heavens
> He spurneth the old.
> "The Sphinx," *Poems.*

Much to this purpose is in the earlier lecture on "The Poet," as, "Swedenborg had this vice, that he nailed one sense to each image, — one and no more." And he speaks there of the face of Nature as "a sympathetic cipher or alphabet, and to exist that it may serve man with a language. . . . We say of man that he is grass, that he is a stream, a star, a lion, fire, a day ; . . . these names are comparatively unaffecting in our ears, hearing them, as we do, merely caught by ear from others, and spoken without thought, but the man who first called another man Puppy or Ass was a poet, and saw at the moment the identity of nature through the great difference of aspect, . . . he could hear him bark or bray with a bestial necessity under the false clothing of man."

Page 34, note 1. Perhaps the answer to "The Problem" in his *Poems*.

Page 37, note 1.

> All the forms are fugitive,
> But the substances survive.
> > "Woodnotes," II., *Poems*.

Page 39, note 1.

> One who having nectar drank
> Into blissful orgies sank;
> He takes no mark of night or day,
> He cannot go, he cannot stay,
> He would, yet would not, counsel keep,
> But, like a walker in his sleep
> With staring eye that seeth none,
> Ridiculously up and down
> Seeks how he may fitly tell
> The heart-o'erlading miracle.
> > "The Poet," *Poems*, Appendix.

Page 42, note 1. Compare in "The Poet" the passage: —

Beside him sat enduring love,
Upon him noble eyes did rest,
Which, for the Genius that there strove,
The follies bore that it invest.

EXPERIENCE

This essay was written at one of the critical epochs of Mr. Emerson's life. "The Angel troubled the pool." The old and the new were contending in him. His growth was not without pain. He bore "the yoke of conscience masterful," and this inheritance he fortunately could not shake off. But his sudden intellectual growth possibly made the yoke gall at times. He had cut loose from tradition and experienced the difficulties attendant on trying to live only according to each day's oracle. Life became experimental, and manifold experiments were suggested in that period of spiritual and social upheaval. He was severely tried in these years. In many places in his journals he gratefully recognizes his debt to the Puritan tradition of a virtuous ancestry and their inherited impulse. This carried him through the whirlpools or sloughs in which he saw many of the sons of the morning of that day sink. Grief came to him in heavy form — the death of his first-born child, of wonderful promise and charm. In this essay, which presents moods and aspects in an unusual degree of contrast, and of which he says, "I have set my heart on honesty in this chapter," he speaks of the speedy healing of this wound and his grieving at the slightness of the scar left. In his desire for utter freedom from hypocrisy, he makes an overstrong statement. But his health and faith and great power of detachment shortened and soothed his suffering.

He passed through this epoch of unrest bravely, and came soon into that serene strength and happiness which remained for life.

I find no record of this essay delivered as a lecture. A very small part of it was taken from " Being and Seeming " in the course on " Human Culture " in 1837–38.

The motto would seem to have been written after the essay. The " lords of life " are named a little more fully in a paragraph near its closing portion. This image of a passing of demigods in procession pleased Emerson's fancy, and he often used it. The last lines show him aware of the unrestful character of the piece, and in sure faith of a harmonious solution of the difficulties on a better day.

The dear, dangerous lords that rule our life

are spoken of in his poem " Musketaquid."

Page 45, note 1. In the procession of the " lords of life," Dream has been seen. In the paragraph near the end of the chapter, he is called Illusion. At the time when it was written, Mr. Emerson was becoming more acquainted with the ancient religion of India, in which Maya or Illusion bears such a part. The *Dial*, which he had lately edited, had quotations from the " Ethnical Scriptures," as they are there called, in several of its numbers.

Page 46, note 1. His own want of animal spirits, unfitting him in his opinion for action or society, but serenely received as driving him thence to solitary places to listen and report, is again and again dwelt upon by Mr. Emerson in his journals.

Page 46, note 2. In a letter written to John Sterling in the previous year, he had said: " Truly, I think it a false standard to estimate health, as the world does, by some fat man, instead of by our power to do our work. If I should lie by whenever people tell me I grow thin and puny, I should lose all my best days. Task these bad bodies and they will serve us and be just as well a year hence, if they grumble to-day."

Page 46, note 3. " Rhea having accompanied with Saturn by stealth, the Sun found them out, and pronounced a solemn curse against her, containing that she should not be delivered in any month or year; but Hermes afterwards making his court to the goddess, obtained her favor, in requital of which he went and played at dice with the Moon and won of her the seventieth part from each day, and out of all these made five new days, which he added to the three hundred and sixty other days of the year, and these the Egyptians . . . observe as the birthdays of their gods. Upon the first of these, as they say, Osiris was born, and a voice came into the world with him, saying, ' The Lord of all things is now born.' " — *Plutarch's Morals,* " Of Isis and Osiris."

Page 47, note 1. Three critical writers of the eighteenth century.

Page 48, note 1. The source of these lines cannot be found.

Page 48, note 2. Ruggiero Boscovich, an Italian, author of a system of natural philosophy, which regarded the senses as immediately cognizant, not of matter itself, but only of the attractive and repelling forces of particles.

Page 48, note 3. In the journal whence this passage is taken Nature speaks more loudly, — " the death of my sweet Boy." This was written at the same time with the second part of the Threnody beginning " The deep Heart answered, ' Weepest thou ? ' " two years after the first part, when time and thought had " reduced the calamity within the sphere."

Page 49, note 1. In the poem *The Curse of Kehama,* by Southey.

Page 50, note 1. "The young mortal enters the hall of the firmament. . . . On the instant, and incessantly, fall snow-storms of illusions." — *Conduct of Life*, "Illusions."

Page 50, note 2. His creed was always onward ; let your next act, and not your word, correct your past mistake.

Page 51, note 1. Mr. Emerson was always troubled that most of Mr. Alcott's hearers did not find the spot where the rays of his illumining thought focussed. Indeed, he admitted that, while Mr. Alcott's angle of vision was wider than that of other men, the rays did not always appear to come together: "There are defects in the lens and errors of refraction and position, etc., to be allowed for, . . . but 't is the best instrument I have ever met with."

Page 51, note 2. Dr. Gamaliel Bradford.

Page 52, note 1. The almost fatality of temperament was interesting to him, but it was an evening thought, and his steady faith disowned it, as in the next pages. "Hear what the morning says and believe that" was his counsel.

Page 53, note 1. The pseudo-science of Phrenology at this time attracted great attention in America. In a lecture in the course on New England in this same year, speaking of the restlessness of our people and their too ready acceptance of novelties, he said, "A hint like phrenology is exalted into a science to outwit the laws of nature and pierce to the courts of power and light by this dull trick."

Page 53, note 2. "The soul is its own witness." — *Laws of Menu*, printed among the "Ethnical Scriptures" in the *Dial*.

Page 55, note 1. The power of Effort, then accepted by few biologists, spiritualized.

Page 55, note 2. "Still, it moves." — Galileo's remark on rising from his knees when, by command of the Court of the Inquisition, he made retraction of his heretical teaching that the Earth was not stationary and central, but moved around the Sun.

Page 56, note 1. The answer to the child is the answer with which he often had to console himself when he could not meet the demands for special sympathy from his friends, or for enlistment in particular reform movements. " My reforms include, so will outlast, theirs," he said.

Page 58, note 1. To come down from the timeless cloudland of the philosophers who visited him, to talk with a solid farmer or honest laborer, gave Mr. Emerson great comfort. It is told of him by Mr. Albee that he left the discussion in the study, seeing through the window a man drive a load of wood into his yard, saying to his guests, " Excuse me. We have to attend to these things just as if they were real."

Page 58, note 2. He was glad that the Brook Farm enterprise should be tried, and honored the motives of the Community, but from the first saw that a man's own problem could not be solved by a company.

Page 59, note 1. A similar passage about " the American disease, a paralysis of the active faculties " of young men after leaving college, occurs among the *Papers from the Dial*, " A Letter," in *Natural History of Intellect.*

The quotation which occurs in both is probably from some of the sayings ascribed to Zoroaster.

Page 59, note 2. See the quatrain " Nature," *Poems.*

Page 61, note 1. Mr. Emerson's trust was rewarded by his experience. Looking for the best, even in humble people, he found it. His early resolve was to give only his best thoughts in his lectures : " Do not cease to utter them, and make them as pure of all dross as if thou wert to speak to sages and demi-gods, and be no whit ashamed if not one in the assembly should give sign of intelligence. Is it not pleasant to you — unexpected wisdom ? depth of sentiment in middle life ? persons that in the thick of the crowd are true kings and gentlemen without the harness and the envy of the throne ?"

Page 62, note 1. Mr. Emerson's "content in these low fields" of Concord, and life there, is told in "Musketaquid" in the *Poems.*

Page 64, note 1. Dr. Garnett,[1] Mr. Emerson's English biographer, seems a little troubled by this evidence of the period of unrest that .he was going through, and thus comments : " The essay on ' Experience ' seems at first a singular discourse for a preacher of righteousness. It must be regarded as an endeavour to atone for previous over-statements by a frank recognition of the unmoral aspects of the universe. . . . The essay is full of the apparent contradictions established by experience, but concludes that experience indefinitely protracted will reconcile all."

In " The Park " (*Poems*) the thought of this passage will be found.

Page 65, note 1. In this passage is a strange mixture of the " saving common-sense " of Mr. Emerson, and the Poet's attitude, sitting in the sun and minding his rhyme while

> Sad-eyed Fakirs swiftly say
> Endless dirges of decay,

and letting

> Theist, atheist, pantheist,
> Define and wrangle how they list.
>> " Saadi," *Poems.*

[1] *The Life of Emerson,* by Richard Garnett, LL.D. London, Walter Scott, 1888.

Page 66, note 1. Thoreau in his *Walden* humorously tells of his "half-witted and *one-and-a-half-witted* visitors" there.

Page 68, note 1. "Everything in the Universe goes by indirection. There are no straight lines."— *Journal.*

A very similar passage is found near the end of "Gifts" in this volume.

Page 68, note 2. See Luke xvii. 20.

Page 69, note 1.

> I am the doubter and the doubt.
> "Brahma," *Poems.*

"Not unto us, O Lord, not unto us, but to thy name be the praise!"

Page 70, note 1. Sir Everard Home, a Scottish surgeon and writer on Comparative Anatomy, supposed to have been mainly indebted for his knowledge to the manuscripts of his brother-in-law, John Hunter, which he burned.

Page 72, note 1. Antigone, in Sophocles's tragedy, reproached by Creon for burying her outlawed brother's body, says, "Nor did I think thy proclamation, since thou art a mortal, of force to outweigh the unwritten and secure laws of the gods, for these are not matters of now and yesterday, but always were, and no man knows whence they came."

Page 74, note 1. With regard to Mr. Emerson's utterances concerning the Immortality of the Soul and kindred subjects, Mr. John Albee says, in his *Remembrances,* "Emerson refused to dogmatize about what is necessarily obscure at present. So some thought the obscurity lay in him."

Page 75, note 1. The doctrine announced in the opening pages of "Circles" in the first book of *Essays,* suggesting also the poems "Uriel" and "Brahma."

Page 75, note 2. " The discovery we have made that *we* exist " would perhaps make the sentence clearer: the discovery of our lower self, warping the divine universal self.

Page 79, note 1. These pages were bravely written, in endeavor for utter honesty and freedom from cant. To " give the Devil his due," find the good leaven in apparent evil, which may surround and beset us, that is, our lower selves.

The intellect alone working at the problem arrives at that " sad self-knowledge " which

> Withering fell
> On the beauty of Uriel,

and which, as in the next pages, carries the soul up to bleak rocks where it needs faith to see that God inhabits.

Page 81, note 1. He could not deal with other people's facts in the sense of problems, but he always valued the facts, whether of the man of science, business, or farm, for what they meant to him. He warned people of the " disloyalty of mistaking other people's chivalries for their own." Yet he was patient in considering them.

Journal, 1841. " Bores are good too. They may help you to a good indignation, if not to a sympathy; to ' a mania better than temperance,' as Proclus would say. Long-Beard and Short-Beard, who came hither the other day with intent to make Artesian wells of us, taught me something."

Page 84, note 1. Adrasteia was a name of Nemesis or Destiny. " And there is a law of Destiny that the soul which attains any vision of truth in company with the god is preserved from harm until the next period, and if attaining always, is always unharmed." — The *Phædrus* of Plato, Jowett's Translation.

Page 86, note 1. In this essay is less of the ascension to

Page 90, note 1. This conversation seems to have been of Mr. Emerson's invention.

Iole, daughter of King Eurytus, was carried home captive by Hercules, after he had conquered and slain her father. Dejanira, his wife, jealous of Iole, tried to retain her husband's love by putting on him the tunic poisoned by the blood of the centaur Nessus, which she believed to be a love charm, whereby Hercules died. The story of Iole is told in the *Trachiniæ* of Sophocles.

Page 91, note 1. The foregoing passage refers to Webster, then the idol of New England.

Page 92, note 1. Compare his poem " Fate."

Deep in the man sits fast his fate, etc.

Page 93, note 1. At the time of his first marriage and during the few years of his ministry in Boston, Mr. Emerson and his young wife found a home in Chardon Street with his parishioner, Mr. Abel Adams, a merchant of integrity and success. All through his life Mr. Adams was a valued and helpful friend and adviser. This passage in the journal has his initials attached. In later years this place was filled by Mr. John Murray Forbes. Friendship and sympathy united the scholar and the man of large affairs. In " Social Aims " Mr. Emerson has given a portrait of this silent power for good in public and private affairs (but without naming Mr. Forbes) as an " American to be proud of."— *Letters and Social Aims.*

Page 94, note 1. Leonora, widow of Concini, Marquis d'Ancre (murdered in 1617 for exercising an almost usurping power over the young Louis XIII.), was accused and burned for having used the influence of a sorceress over the queen of Henry IV.

Page 96, note 1.

> Unit and Universe are round ;
> In vain produced, all rays return.
>
> "Uriel," *Poems.*

Page 96, note 2. In the lecture on "Politics," as first delivered, these sentences occur: "Character is the true theocracy. It will one day suffice for the government of the world."

Page 97, note 1. A verse from a rude Danish ballad, "Svend Vonved," was a favorite with Mr. Emerson:—

> Success shall be in thy courser tall,
> *Success in thyself, which is best of all,*
> Success in thy hand, success in thy foot,
> In struggle with man, in battle with brute.

Page 98, note 1. His friend Thoreau's speech, quoted in the "Biographical Sketch," pleased him: "Nothing is so much to be feared as fear. Atheism may comparatively be popular with God himself."

Page 100, note 1. This sentence, reading a little obscurely, shows the sign of a paper written for delivery. It was certainly helped by the emphatic delivery of the first word, which in the manuscript and first edition was repeated. Original men, conductors of the water of Life from its source, are those whom he values.

Page 101, note 1. The journal shows that the person alluded to is Mr. George Ripley, the head of the Brook Farm Community. The passage, written in April, 1840, there begins, "You might know beforehand that your friends will not succeed, since you have never been able to find the institution in the Institutor."

Page 102, note 1. A new life put into the sentence by the change from the first edition, where it read, "which sheds a splendor on the passing hour."

Page 103, note 1.

> When success exalts thy lot
> God for thy virtue lays a plot.
> "Prayer," *Poems*, Appendix.

Page 106, note 1. A few years later in England, Mr. Emerson gave a lecture on "Natural Aristocracy," "an attractive topic, . . . an interest of the human race, and, as I look on it, inevitable, sacred and to be found in every country and in every company of men, . . . true and not spurious pictures of excellence." This, with additional matter from later writings, was published by Mr. Cabot in *Lectures and Biographical Sketches* under the title "Aristocracy."

Page 107, note 1. Rev. Edward Taylor, of the Sailors' Bethel in Boston, between whom and Mr. Emerson were mutual regard and honor. He is also alluded to in the essays on "Greatness," "Eloquence," "The Preacher," and "Historic Notes of Life and Letters in Boston."

Page 107, note 2. When Mr. Alcott returned from England in 1842 with Messrs. Lane and Wright, two Englishmen interested in the same ideas, who came in high hope to realize them in a new and aspiring country, — a hope that met with failure in the Fruitlands attempted community, — Mr. Emerson wrote in his journal: "Alcott and Edward Taylor ["Father Taylor"] resemble each other in the incredibility of their statement of facts. One is the fool of his idea and the other of his fancy. When Alcott wrote from England that he was bringing home Wright and Lane, I wrote him a letter which I required him to show them, saying that they might safely trust his theories, but that they should put no trust whatever in his statement of facts. When they all arrived here, he and his victims, I asked them if he showed them that letter; they answered that he did: so I was clear.''

Page 109, note 1. This passage is quoted from "The Book of Shet the Prophet Zirtûsht" in the second volume of *The Desatir, or Sacred Writings of the Ancient Persian Prophets, together with the Ancient Persian Version and Commentary of the Fifth Sasan, carefully published by Mulla Firuz Bin Kaus.* Bombay, 1818.

As the book is exceedingly rare, I give the whole passage. "It is said that when the fame of the excellence of the nature of Zertûsht had spread all over the world, and when Isfendiar went around the world, erected fire-temples and raised domes over the fires, the wise men of Yunân selected a Sage named Tûtîânûsh, who at that time had the superiority in acquirements over them all, to go to Irân and to enquire of Zertûsht *concerning the real nature of things.* If he was puzzled and unable to answer, he could be no prophet, but if he returned an answer, he was a speaker of truth.'' (Here follows the passage quoted in the text.) "He then asked the day of the prophet's nativity. The prophet of God told it. He said, 'On such a day, and under such a fortunate star a deceiver cannot be born.' He next enquired into his diet and mode of life. The prophet of God explained the whole. The Sage said, 'His mode of life cannot suit an impostor.' The prophet of Yezdân then said to him, 'I have answered you the questions which you have put to me; now in return retain in your mind what the famed Yunâni Sage directed you to enquire of Zertûsht and disclose it not, but listen and hear what they ask; for God hath informed me of it and hath sent his word unto me to unfold it.' The Sage said, 'Speak.' Thereupon the prophet of Zertûsht repeated the . . . texts.''

Page 109, note 2. This is said in the *Timæus.*

Page 110, note 1. Mr. Emerson applies this saying of Milton to his venerated friend, Samuel Hoar, Esq., in the notice of him printed in *Lectures and Biographical Sketches.*

Page 112, note 1. Homer's *Odyssey*, Book V., 99.

Page 112, note 2. These lines are in the third division of " Initial, Dæmonic and Celestial Love " in the *Poems.*

Page 114, note 1. This might be supposed to refer to Mr. Emerson's disappointment that Carlyle could see nothing elevating and helpful in Mr. Alcott, and treated him rather rudely, but this passage occurs in the journal a year before that time. Nevertheless, it very likely refers to similar experiences in Boston. When some one later said, " Mr. Alcott is impracticable," Mr. Emerson answered, " Yes, impracticable as our thoughts are. You will reply that it will not do to say our thoughts are quite impracticable, — nor do I think that any man is quite impracticable. I do not feel at liberty to decline the thoughts or the men that go by, because they are not quite easy to deal with and conformable to the opinions of the Boston *Post.*"

MANNERS

A lecture with this name had been given by Mr. Emerson in the Boston course on " The Philosophy of History " in the winter of 1836–37.

This essay is the lecture in the course on " The Times " given at Tremont Temple in the winter of 1841–42. A year later, and before this essay was published, Mr. Emerson gave in New York five lectures on " New England," the third of which treated of " Manners and Customs of New England."

This subject, always attractive to Mr. Emerson and constantly recurring in his writings, he treats at length in "Behavior" in the volume *Conduct of Life*.

The present essay shows that, like most of the others, it was largely made up from notes taken at various times on manners, whether commanding or charming or merely conventional ; in some cases with a Montaigne-like frankness and tolerance. Readings both in scientific books and in romance contribute to the subject, and Mr. Emerson's humor crops out occasionally, as in "Circe's horned company."

The motto is taken from Ben Jonson's "Masques," the first four lines from a song by the Priest in "Love Freed from Ignorance and Folly;" the others from the song of Dædalus in "Pleasure reconciled to Virtue," beginning —

> O more and more ! this was so well
> As praise wants half his voice to tell.

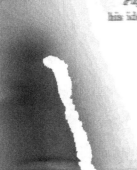

Page 120, note 1. Architecture, like sculpture, though he never had opportunity to study it, always interested Mr. Emerson. He was especially quick to notice any pretentiousness or sham. In "The Problem" it is in the architecture, not in the painting or sculpture, of Italy that he saw the Great Soul working through the hand of the passive master.

Page 121, note 1. This idea is presented in the first pages of "Heroism" in *Essays, First Series*.

Page 122, note 1. He took great pleasure in the passage in Chaucer's "Wife of Bathe's Tale" that treats of Gentilesse, and it is printed under that title in *Parnassus*, the collection of poetry edited by him.

Page 122, note 2. Sadi, or Saab, as Mr. Emerson named his ideal poet, loved humble cottages and honors near, —

Nor loved he less
Stately lords in palaces,
Princely women hard to please,
Fenced by form and ceremony,
Decked by courtly rites and dress
And etiquette of gentilesse.

" Fragments on The Poet," *Poems*, Appendix.

Page 123, note 1. These ideas are set out more fully in the lecture " Aristocracy," [1] better called (as it was at first, to avoid any misunderstanding in England as to what was meant) " Natural Aristocracy." He there asks, Why this invincible respect for war, that in the triumphs of our commercial civilization we can never quite smother the trumpet and the drum ? and answers, Why, but because courage never loses its high price ? Why, but because we wish to see those to whom existence is most adorned and attractive foremost to peril it for their object, and ready to answer for their actions with their life ?

Page 123, note 2. Mr. Emerson might well make this exclamation in those days of " The Newness."

Page 124, note 1. In allusions to himself in his journals, Mr. Emerson often speaks of his hopeless lack of animal spirits as unfitting him for general society and for action, and in " Terminus," the poem of his old age, he speaks of it, but with serene acceptance.

Page 125, note 1. Two Persian monarchs of the name of Sapor, of the dynasty of the Sassanidæ, conquered the Roman emperors in battle in the third and fourth centuries A. D.

In the previous sentence the real gentleman is spoken of as good company for pirates and academicians. Mr. Emerson

[1] *Lectures and Biographical Sketches.*

always took pleasure in the story told by Plutarch, that when the young Cæsar was the captive of the pirates he made them listen to his rhetorical compositions, at the same time freely telling them that when he was ransomed he should crucify them, which promise he fulfilled.

Page 126, note 1. Among Mr. Emerson's friends in whom the philosophic mind and habit·prevailed, Thoreau especially is brought to mind by this sentence. He was something of a Diogenes, but with no sourness, and more human; though almost all his days were spent in peaceful Concord, there was much of the heroic Epaminondas in his temper. Though unlike Socrates in having a poetic rather than a dialectic taste, it is surprising how much of the description in the Symposium of Plato as given by Alcibiades of Socrates, when they were tent-mates in the campaign in Potidæa, suggests Thoreau.

Page 127, note 1. Most of the above paragraph is taken from a lecture on "Prudence" in the course on "Human Culture" in 1838. It there goes on as follows: "Thus we understand exceeding well in America the charm of what is best in English manners, and, as we by age, cultivation and leisure refine and ripen, come to set a high value on that species of breeding, which foreigners, from a more sanguine temperament, and we too, from our democratic wantonness, usually blame in the English — the mild, exact decorum, the cool recognition of all and any facts by a steadiness of temper which hates all starts, screams, faintings, sneezings, laughter and all violence of any kind. The English, and we also, are a commercial people, great readers of newspapers and journals and books, and are therefore familiar with all the variety of tragic, comic, political tidings from all parts of the world, and are not to be thrown off their balance by any accident near by,

like villagers whom the overturn of a coach, or a robbery, or
a dog with a kettle sets agape, and furnishes with gossip for a
week.''

Page 129, note 1.

> The lord is the peasant that was,
> The peasant the lord that shall be;
> The lord is hay, the peasant grass,
> One dry, and one the living tree.

> .   .   .   .   .   .

> What prizes the town and the tower?
> Only what the pine-tree yields;
> Sinew that subdued the fields, etc.
> > '' Woodnotes,'' II., *Poems.*

Page 130, note 1. Journal, 1841. '' It is not a *word*
that ' I am a gentleman and the king is no more,' but is a
fact expressed in every passage between the king and a gentleman.''

Page 132, note 1. The strength and dignity of calmness
he held as essential to man as modesty to woman. In one of
his earlier poetic fragments he said: —

> Composure
> Is the pudency of man.

Page 132, note 2. This allowance by the world of some
latitude in virtue to men who are real masters is even more
strongly expressed in '' Aristocracy'' in *Lectures and Biographical Sketches.*

Page 133, note 1. The henchman of McIvor in Scott's
Waverley thus expresses his wish that the young English officer
could see the chief at the head of his clan.

Page 134, note 1. Mr. Emerson's feeling on calling on

his manly neighbor, Edmund Hosmer, who did the necessary ploughing and planting for him, is expressed in Oriental form in the verses in the Appendix to the *Poems* : —

> Said Saadi, " When I stood before
> Hassan the camel-driver's door," etc.

This neighbor is the Farmer described in Mr. Emerson's " Agriculture in Massachusetts," a paper written for the *Dial*, but now included in the volume *Natural History of Intellect*.

Page 137, note 1. He perhaps had in mind here the expression, in which he took pleasure, of Jean Paul Richter with regard to the Greek statues: " The repose, not of weariness but of perfection, looks from their eyes and rests upon their lips."

Page 137, note 2. Compare " Give All to Love " and the last passage in " The Celestial Love " in the *Poems*.

Page 138, note 1. " Recall," as expressing something that we all should ever have in mind, was an improvement made by Mr. Emerson on " signify " of the first edition.

Page 139, note 1. The essay on " The Superlative," in *Lectures and Biographical Sketches*, warns Americans in an amusing way of a besetting national foible.

Page 139, note 2. This reminder of the exact sense from the derivation of a common word is an instance of Mr. Emerson's habitual consideration of his words.

Page 140, note 1. This is an expression of Heracleitus quoted by Plutarch in his *Morals* in the essay " Of Eating of Flesh." The passage as translated there is, " The wisest soul is like a dry light." [1] Its meaning might be, — unobscured by the fogs of passion and circumstance; but Professor John

---

[1] Professor W. W. Goodwin, in his edition of the *Morals*, thus refers : " See Mullach, *Fragm. Philos.* p. 325 (No. 73)."

H. Wright, of Harvard University, says that the original expression of Heracleitus was corrupted in transmission; that the word which he used signified rather *nearest to Fire*, his first principle. Αὔη ψυχὴ σοφωτάτη καὶ ἀρίστη, ' The dry soul is wisest and best.' — Heracleitus, *On Nature*.

Page 140, note 2. " The ignoring eye " here is autobiographical, the expression describing Mr. Emerson's own habit at awkward or disagreeable chances in daily life.

Page 143, note 1. In the journal of 1842 is noted " Profound meaning of *Good-will makes insight.*"

Page 144, note 1. Circe and her company of lions, or horned beasts, recalls a remark which I heard Mr. Emerson make about a zealous lady of wide sympathies whom he valued more for her virtues than for her judgment. Some one said at his table, when Mr. Emerson did not seem to think highly of some traveller who was spoken of, " But Miss X says that he is a very remarkable man ! " " O, Miss X," — said Mr. Emerson, " she has always a whole stud of Phœnixes in charge."

Page 145, note 1. I have been unable to find any source of this epitaph, though much search has been made for it, yet hardly believe that it was composed by Mr. Emerson.

Page 146, note 1. Ruy Diaz de Bivar in the eleventh century, the *preux chevalier* of Spain, in the struggle against the Moors, was celebrated in ancient chronicles, romances and ballads. Southey from these materials composed his noble *Chronicle of the Cid.* Mr. Emerson liked to read passages from this to his children. Many of the ballads about the Cid are translated by Lockhart in *Spanish Ballads.*

Page 147, note 1. Keats, *Hyperion.*

Page 150, note 1. Mr. Emerson early took exactly this ground and always held to it. It was not for man to say what

III

woman should or should not do. What the sense and virtue of the sex demanded should of course come to them. He spoke to this purpose many times. One of his addresses on this theme is printed in *Miscellanies*.

Page 152, note 1. Dr. Holmes said of the foregoing passage that Emerson "speaks of woman in language that seems to pant for rhythm and rhyme."

Page 153, note 1. This consoling prescription of country life for the hurts of disappointed social ambition recalls his verses in "Musketaquid," though his troubles were not these: —

> All my hurts
> My garden spade can heal. A woodland walk, ·
> A quest of river-grapes, a mocking thrush,
> A wild-rose, or rock-loving columbine,
> Salve my worst wounds.

Page 153, note 2. The ascension to a high plane, which characterizes the end of the essays, here appears in showing love which is open to all as the basis of true gentility, — at which gentility so-called is a rude attempt. Mr. Emerson often repeated Wordsworth's lines: —

> O what is honour? 'T is the finest sense
> Of justice which the human mind can frame,
> Intent each lurking frailty to disclaim,
> And guard the way of life from all offence,
> Suffered or done.

Page 154, note 1. In previous notes it has been mentioned that Osman was the name given by Emerson to the ideal man, subject to the same conditions as himself.

Page 155, note 1. This fable is original.

GIFTS

This short essay was one of Mr. Emerson's contributions to the *Dial*.

In the widest sense he held that there was no such thing as giving. The Over-soul common to all, the community of nature, rendered it impossible. Moreover, what belongs to the individual will come to him ; what does not cannot be given. " Direct giving is agreeable to the early belief of men ; direct giving of material or metaphysical aid. . . . The boy believes there is a teacher who can sell him wisdom. Churches believe in imputed merit. But in strictness we are not much cognizant of direct serving. Man is endogenous. . . . Gift is contrary to the law of the Universe. Serving others is serving us. . . . Indirect service is left." — " Uses of Great Men," *Representative Men*. And elsewhere, " When each comes forth from his mother's womb, the gate of gifts closes behind him."

But in the domestic and usual sense he was a giver and receiver. And yet so fine was his sense both of honor and of fitness that it was hard for him to receive, and not always easy for him to choose a gift for another that should have a bloom of symbolism upon it.

In the family the old-time New England custom of New Year's presents was never supplanted by the modern Christmas-tree. To his last days, when his grandchildren were around him, Mr. Emerson gave New Year's morning to this ceremony, and obeyed the rule of writing a poem to be read before each present was opened. Over these verses he often sat out the old year, and took great pleasure next morning in hearing the young people's efforts, though most humble about his own. "The Maiden Song of the Æolian Harp" accompanied that characteristic gift to his daughter and her husband. As far as time and taste allowed him, he selected his presents for his family, but, even from them, it was a little hard for him to receive.

Great gifts went out from him to those to whom he thought them due, but on this subject his lips were closed.

Page 160, note 1. Fruits always pleased him, — his other senses more than that of taste, however, — his pears and plums seemed such a triumph achieved in evolution out of hard seed-cases, hips and haws. Van Mons (a Dutch pomologist mentioned in his copy of Downing's book on fruit-culture) was a saint he honored because of his doctrine and practice of "Amelioration." Care of his orchard and especially the harvesting of its small crop of pears, which perfumed his study, was the only farm-work of his later years.

Page 161, note 1. A saying of Landor's was often quoted by Mr. Emerson : "The highest price you can pay for a thing is to ask for it." The Nemesis of regret, or a least misgiving, would in a sensitive mind show the price to have been too high.

Page 161, note 2. John Thoreau, who died in his youth, Henry's older brother, was a lover of Nature and of children. He gave Mr. Emerson an instance of giving according to one's character. The latter recorded in his journal: "Long ago I wrote of Gifts and neglected a capital example. John Thoreau, Jr., one day put a blue-bird's box on my barn, — fifteen years ago, it must be, — and there it still is with every summer a melodious family in it adorning the place and singing its praises. There's a gift for you which cost the giver no money, but nothing which he bought could have been as good.

" I think of another quite inestimable : John Thoreau knew how much I should value a head of little Waldo, then five years old. He came to me and offered to take him to a daguerreotypist who was then in town, and he, Thoreau, would see it well done. He did it and brought me the daguerre, which I thankfully paid for. A few months after, my boy died, and I have since to thank John Thoreau for that wise and gentle piece of friendship.''

The happy thought of other friends, of an investment for him in beauty and comfort at compound interest, he recorded within two years after he made his home in Concord : " May 2, 1837. Day before yesterday Dr. Hobbs, Dr. Adams and Mr. Ripley [1] sent me from Waltham thirty-one trees which I have planted by my home. What shall I render to my benefactors ? " These pines and chestnuts still shelter and adorn his house.

Page 162, note 1. Epimetheus thus counsels his brother Prometheus : —

οὐδ' Ἐπιμηθεὺς
ἐφράσαθ' ὥς οἱ ἔειπε Προμηθεὺς μήποτε, δῶρον
δέξασθαι πὰρ Ζηνὸς Ὀλυμπίου ἀλλ' ἀποπέμπειν
ἐξοπίσω μή πού τι κακὸν γένηται.

Hesiod, *Works and Days*, 85–88.

Page 162, note 2. In Mr. Emerson's copy of Cotton's translation of Montaigne, which book, as a boy, he read with delight and " felt as if I myself had written this book in some former life, so sincerely it spoke my thoughts,'' the following passage is marked : —

" Oh, how am I obliged to almighty God, who has been pleased that I should immediately receive all I have from his bounty, and particularly reserved all my obligation to him-

---

[1] Rev. Samuel Ripley, his uncle, and two other friends in Waltham.

self ! How instantly do I beg of his holy compassion that
may never owe a real thanks to any one. O happy liberty i
which I have thus far lived ! May it continue with me t
the last. I endeavour to have no need of any one. *In m
omnis est spes mihi.*"

Page 163, note 1. A new and strange experience and tri
came to Mr. Emerson when in his age his house was nearl
destroyed by fire. A common impulse moved his friends, nea
and far, to seize the opportunity to show their love or reverence
for him by restoring it, and sending him abroad for refreshment
meantime. Something of the struggle in Mr. Emerson's mind,
and more of the emotion which he felt, is shown in the corre-
spondence with Dr. Le Baron Russell and Judge Hoar, the
friends to whom the contributors committed the pleading of
their case. ·This is printed in the Appendix to Mr. Cabot's
Memoir, from which I extract a few sentences. The ingenious Judge, the ambassador, relates how ' "I told him by
way of prelude that some of his friends had made him a
treasurer of an association who wished him to go to England
and examine Warwick Castle and other noted houses that had
been recently injured by fire, in order to get the best ideas
possible for restoration, and then apply them to a house which
the association was formed to restore in this neighborhood.

"When he understood the thing . . . he seemed very
deeply moved. He said that he had been allowed so far in
life to stand on his own feet, and that he hardly knew what
to say, — that the kindness of his friends was very great. . . .
But he must see the list of contributors. . . .

"I am glad that Mr. Emerson, who is feeble and ill, can
learn what a debt of obligation his friends feel to him."

When he made up his mind to accept his friends'
kindness he wrote: "Thank them for me whenever you meet

them, and say to them that I am not wood or stone if I have not yet trusted myself to go to each one of them directly." And when he was allowed to see the list of his benefactors he wrote: " It cannot be read with dry eyes or pronounced with articulate voice. Names of dear and noble friends; names also of high respect with me, but on which I had no known claims; names, too, that carried me back many years, as they were of friends of friends of mine more than of me, and thus I seemed to be drawing on the virtues of the departed."

Page 165, note 1. There were certain persons whose Oriental temperament seemed to him to bestow on them a right to exercise their genius for gifts, perhaps as valid as that of the Puritan to maintain his independence of favors.

NATURE

In June, 1840, Mr. Emerson wrote in his journal: " I think I must do these eyes of mine the justice to write a new chapter on Nature. This delight we all take in every show of night or day or field or forest or sea or city, down to the lowest particulars, is not without sequel, though we be as yet only wishers and gazers, not at all knowing what we want. We are predominated, here as elsewhere, by an upper wisdom, and resemble those great discoverers who are haunted for years, sometimes from infancy, with a passion for the fact, or class of facts, in which the secret lies which they are destined to unlock, and they let it not go until the blessing is won. So these sunsets and starlights, these swamps and rocks, these bird-notes and animal forms off which we cannot get our eyes and ears, but hover still, as moths round a lamp, are no doubt a Sanscrit cipher covering the whole religious history of the universe, and presently we shall read it off into action and character. The pastures are full of ghosts for me, the morning woods full of angels.

. . . .

"No inventory is complete. . . . The Select-men assess me no tax for my use of the woods, where I find first-sight, second-sight and insight.

"The asters and eupatoriums are maturing their leaves and buds, the gerardia is getting ready its profuse flowers, warning me that my book should be ended before their capsules are filled with seed."

In the course given in Boston in the winter immediately before the publication of the second series of Essays, one of the lectures was called *Relation to Nature*. The manuscript of this was not preserved, but certain stray leaves seem to indicate that they were what remained when that lecture was prepared for publication as an essay. The oration delivered at Waterville College, *The Method of Nature*, in 1841, drew much of its matter from the same journals which furnished that for the present essay.

When Mr. Emerson was writing his first book *Nature*, between 1833 and 1836, his mind was in a state of ferment; he was beginning a new life. He walked with faith into this beautiful but strange temple to receive the oracle. Now, softened by home life, after reverent and happy communion with Nature for nearly ten years, he is in serener mood. The essay reflects this. For the assault on this problem the forces are not arrayed in due order, as in the earlier work. With an opening pæan on the cheering or consoling beauty of passive nature, he passes to the consideration of living Nature, the struggle and the *becoming*, which man, by the Universal Mind, understands in part. He cannot quite solve Nature's riddle, nor was it meant that he should. She will hint at a new meaning daily, and to new men continue to give new meanings.

This sentence and verse from the journal might serve as a second motto : " Go to the forest if God has made thee a poet, and make thy life clean and fragrant as thy office."

> True Brahmin, in the morning meadows wet,
> Expound the Vedas and the violet.

Page 169, note 1. The passage in the journal has a freshness that makes it worth copying.

" Oct. 30th, 1841. On this wonderful day when Heaven and earth seem to glow with magnificence, and all the wealth of all the elements is put under contribution to make the world fine, as if Nature would indulge her offspring, it seemed ungrateful to hide in the house. Are there not dull days enough in the year for you to write and read in, that you should waste this glittering season when Florida and Cuba seem to have left their seats and come to visit us with all their shining hours, and almost we expect to see the jasmine and cactus burst from the ground instead of these last gentians and asters which have loitered to attend this latter glory of the year? All insects are out, all birds come forth, the very cattle that lie on the ground seem to have great thoughts, and Egypt and India look from their eyes."

Page 172, note 1.

> And the countless leaves of the pine are strings
> Tuned to the lay the wood-god sings.
> > "Woodnotes," II., *Poems.*

Page 173, note 1. Journal, June, 1841. " The good river-God has taken the form of my valiant Henry Thoreau here,

and introduced me to the riches of his shadowy, starlit, moon-
lit stream, a lovely new world lying as close, and yet as
unknown, to this vulgar, trite one of streets and shops as death
to life, or poetry to prose. Through one field we went to the
boat, and then left all time, all science, all history behind us
and entered into nature with one stroke of the paddle. Take
care, good friend! I said, as I looked West into the sunset
overhead and underneath, and he, with his face towards me,
rowed towards it, — take care : you know not what you do,
dipping your wooden oar into this enchanted liquid, painted
with all reds and purples and yellows, which glows under and
behind you."

Page 173, note 2.

> Stars taunt us with their mystery.
> > "The World-Soul," *Poems.*

Page 175, note 1. The memory of this horn, heard when
in his youth he visited the White Mountains, always remained
a joy when recalled to mind. It is alluded to in "The
Scholar" in *Lectures and Biographical Sketches,* where the
note of a bugle scatters in an instant the negative views which
the poet, in a low hour, is accepting.

Page 175, note 2.

> Enchanters ! enchantresses !
> Your gold makes you seem wise ;
> The morning mist within your grounds
> More proudly rolls, more softly lies.
> > "The Park," *Poems.*

Page 176, note 1. I am indebted to Dr. Ralph Barton
Perry, of Harvard University, for the following information.
These terms were probably first used by Averroës, the Ara-

bian commentator on Aristotle ; later, Nicolas Cusanus, Giordano Bruno and Spinoza employed the same distinction. It is used by pantheistic philosophers to distinguish the universe in its ultimate, unitary significance from the universe as aggregate of objects. In Aristotelian terms *natura naturans* would be *form* and *activity*, and *natura naturata* would be *matter*.

Page 178, note 1. A favorite image which occurs in " The Two Rivers " and in the last verse of " Peter's Field " in the *Poems*.

Page 179, note 1. The attraction of the pseudo-sciences for low minds is dwelt upon in " Demonology," *Lectures and Biographical Sketches*.

Page 180, note 1. Emerson's reading, whether of the doctrines of the Flowing and the Identity in the ancient philosophers, of immanence and emanence in the Neo-Platonists, of *natura naturans* in the Schoolmen, of the nebular hypothesis of the astronomers, of Evolution by the paleontologists and biologists, — was all confirmed and laid. before his eyes by his study of nature and man.

Page 181, note 1. Compare his poem " Xenophanes."

Page 181, note 2.

> And the poor grass will plot and plan
> What it will do when it is man.
> " Bacchus," *Poems.* ·

These doctrines of the struggle for existence, with the survival of the fittest, had not then attracted the attention which Darwin and Spencer gave them a few years later.

Page 183, note 1. Dr. Paul Richer, of Paris, in his recent admirable *Introduction to the Study of Artistic Anatomy,* calls attention to the fact that all the greatest *savants* have had something of the artist or poet in their minds ; that is, that they had *Intuition*, and *then*, with all care and conscience, made the necessary experiments to establish their discovery on a scientific foundation.

Page 184, note 1. By leaving out the hyphen Mr. Emerson skilfully makes " common sense " here signify his " Universal Mind."

This passage and the succeeding ten pages first appeared under the title " Tantalus " in the last number but one of the *Dial* (January, 1844). Its name signified the unsatisfied thirst which man must feel in studying the Universe. He writes: " Tantalus is but another name for you and me." In his " Ode to Beauty " he wrote : —

> I drank at thy fountain
> False waters of thirst.

Page 184, note 2.

> But Nature whistled with all her winds,
> Did as she pleased and went her way.
> " Fragments on Nature," *Poems*, Appendix.

Page 186, note 1. Similar affectionate paintings of the child appear in " Domestic Life " in *Society and Solitude,* and in "Courage " in *Natural History of Intellect.*

Page 188, note 1. In Mr. Emerson's journals, about the time of his parting with his church, are many references to George Fox, the founder of the Society of Friends, in whose life he was greatly interested. Later he found much that appealed to him in the works of Jacob Boehme, the mystic, born a peasant shoemaker of Silesia in the sixteenth century. James Naylor was a humble English religious enthusiast, persecuted for his supposed blasphemous views in the time of the Commonwealth.

Page 192, note 1. This image is carried out in the early poem "The Forerunners."

Page 193, note 1. In "Tantalus" this passage follows: "So is it with these wondrous skies and hills and forests. What splendid distances, what recesses of ineffable pomp and loveliness in this sunset. But who can go where they are or lay his hand or plant his foot thereon? Off they fall from the round world forever and ever; glory is not for hands to handle."

Page 193, note 2.

> Daily the bending skies solicit man, etc.
> "The Adirondacs," *Poems.*

Page 194, note 1. Here we have the image of "the passive Master" in the poem "The Problem."

This is the end of "Tantalus" in the *Dial*, but the following words are omitted here that there occur after "soul of the workman streams through us:" — "that a paradise of love and power lies close beside us, where the Eternal Architect broods on his thought and projects the world from his bosom."

Page 195, note 1. In the last years of Mr. Emerson's life the little blue self-heal crept into the grass before his study window.

Page 195, note 2. This bit of scientific information Dr. Holmes found a little too popular, and classed it under the heading *On-ditologie.*

Page 196, note 1.

> Wonderful verse of the gods,
> Of one import, of varied tone;
> They chant the bliss of their abodes
> To man imprisoned in his own.
> "My Garden," *Poems.*

POLITICS

This essay was based on a lecture in the Boston course of 1839–40 on " The Present Age." The lecture on " Politics" followed " Literature" and preceded " Reforms" and " Religion." Much new matter was added in the essay. Some passages that were omitted it seemed well to give in these notes. In this essay one sees Emerson fearlessly apply his doctrine of the Universal Mind, or the *common* sense of man, to politics, and find therein good hope for democracy. And his faith in evolution encourages a fearless optimism when at last in the nineteenth Christian century he has found one man — it does not appear whether himself or another — " to whom no weight of adverse experience will make it for a moment impossible that thousands of human beings might exercise towards each other the grandest and simplest sentiments, as well as a knot of friends, or a pair of lovers."

The motto is an example of the earlier poems of Emerson's second period, when, perhaps influenced by the Bardic fragments, he felt that the strength of the thought would be lost in too much attention to melodious expression. His " Merlin" says of the bard: —

> He shall not his brain encumber
> With the coil of rhythm and number,
> But, leaving rule and pale forethought,
> He shall aye climb
> For his rhyme.

With severe condensation, in the twenty-six short lines, none too melodious, of the motto, we have Merlin from old Cymrian forests bearing witness, and the Man of Destiny of the early nineteenth century proving by his overthrow, that like begets only like. The precedent of the mystic building of Thebes to the god-inspired harping of Amphion is cited to show that the divine must enter into all that shall have strength. Then the Muses from Helicon and the personified virtues from Europe of the Renaissance cross the Atlantic to find, in a country where a Lincoln may follow the example of Cincinnatus, a promise of a better republic than that of Plato.

Page 199, note 1. In those days of eager plans for social reforms, and gallant forlorn-hope attacks on slavery, Mr. Emerson had steadily to keep before his eyes, and present to others, that the larger included the less, and that one must not spend all one's energy on the transient.

Page 200, note 1. This simile of ropes to be twisted out of sand came from the old treatises on the black arts. Such an attempt is described in Scott's ballad "Lord Soulis."

Page 200, note 2. The late Professor James B. Thayer, of the Harvard Law School, wrote in 1876 to Mr. Emerson's daughter: "I was almost startled yesterday in our Law Library on opening an English treatise on 'The Law of Carriers,' by J. H. Balfour Browne (1873), to see this on the title-page, and Mr. Emerson's name under it: 'Our statute is a currency,'" etc., giving the whole passage.

In the original lecture this passage occurs: "Out of a thousand errors, oppositions, compromises, springs ever the actual statute-book which regulates to-day the economy of the Commonwealth."

Page 201, note 1. He lived to see the apparent fulfilment of these words in the issue of the War of the Rebellion.

Page 205, note 1. He quotes often the Latin proverb of which I cannot learn the source, — *Res nolunt diu male administrari.*

Page 205, note 2. This paragraph from the lecture was omitted here : —

"The philosopher, who is never to stop at the outside or appearance of things, will find more to justify his faith in the harmony of politics with the constitution of man, than the mere statute-book can furnish him. There is more history to a nation than can be gathered from its code. Its code is only the high-water mark showing how high the last tide rose, but at this moment perhaps the waters rise higher still, only they have not yet notched their place by a line of pebbles, shells and seaweed. Observe that the law is always the last and never the first step. One person, a few persons, an increasing minority do the thing ; defend it ; irresistibly urge it ; until finally, against all reluctance, roaring opposition, it becomes the law of the land. The thing goes before, — the form comes after. The elements of power, namely, persons and property, must and will have their just sway."

Page 206, note 1. "Away with this hurrah of masses. . . . In old Egypt it was established law that the vote of a prophet be reckoned equal to a hundred hands. . . . Pairing off ! As if one man who votes wrong, going away, could excuse you, who mean to vote right, for going away ; or as if your presence did not tell in more ways than in your vote. Suppose the three hundred heroes at Thermopylæ had paired off with three hundred Persians. Would it have been all the same to Greece and to history ?" — "Considerations by the Way," *Conduct of Life.*

Page 207, note 1. From this point the lecture ended differently, as given below.

"It seems to follow from these doctrines that nothing is less important than the laws or forms of government. Power belongs to persons and to property. Property is merely the

obedience of nature to human labor and follows of course the
moral quality of the persons who create and hold it. With
the progress of any society, with the cultivation of individuals,
the existing forms become every day of less consequence.
Every addition of good sense that a citizen acquires destroys
so much of his opposition to the laws of nature and the well-
being of society, and of course brings the power of his property on the side of justice. Knowledge transfers the censor-
ship from the State House to the reason of every citizen, and
compels every man to mount guard over himself, and puts
shame and remorse for sergeants and maces. And we find in
all times and countries every great man does, in all his nature,
point at and imply the existence and well-being of all the
orders and institutions of a state. He is full of reverence.
He is by inclination (how far soever in position) the defender
of the grammar-school, the almshouse, the holy day, the
church, the priest, the judge, the legislator, the executive
arm. Throughout his being is he loyal, even when by circumstance arrayed in opposition to the actual order of things.
Such was Socrates, St. Paul, Luther, Milton, Burke.

" The education of every man is bringing him ever to postpone his private to the universal good, to comport himself,
that is, in his proper person, as a state, and of course whilst
the whole community around him are doing the like, the persons who hold public offices become mere clerks of business,
in no sense the sovereigns of the people.

" It were very much to be wished that these laws drawn
from the nature of things could become a part of the popular philosophy, that at least all endeavors for the reform of
education or the reform of political opinion might be made
where only they can have any avail, in the speculative views
of the individual, for it was justly said by Bacon that the spec-

III

ulative opinions of men in general between the age of thirty
and forty were the only sure source of political prophecy.
The philosophy of property, if explored in its foundations,
would open new mines of practical wisdom, which would in
the event change the face of the world; would destroy the
whole magazine of dissimulation, for so many ages reckoned
the Capital art of Government. It would purge that rottenness
which has defamed the whole Science until *politic* has come
to mean cunning; would show the pretenders in that science
that they were their own dupes; would show that the cunningest man cannot cheat nature or do any wrong without
suffering the same. It would go deep into ethics and touch
all the relations of man. It would teach the subtle and inex-
tricable compensation that attaches to property. Everything
God hath made hath two faces. Every cent in a dollar covers
its worth, and also covers its evil. The man who covets the
wealth of London should know that whilst each pound and
penny represents so much commodity, so much corn and wine
and cloth, of necessity it also represents so much mould or
sourness and moth as belongs to these commodities: if so much
property, then so much risk; if so much power, then so
much danger; if so much revenue, then so much tax. When
his honest labor and enterprise attract to him a great estate,
then his exertions stand over against his gains to make him
whole. But could his wish without his honest labor transfer
out of another's vaults a million pounds sterling into his own
chest, so would also, against his wish, just so massive an ill
will and fear concentrate its black rays on him in darkness
that might be felt. All property must and will pay its tax. If
it come not by fair means, then it comes by foul. The wise
man who sees the unerring compensations which worked
themselves out in the world, will pay the state its full dividend
on his estate, if not for love of right, then for fear of harm.

" And as in respect to property so also in respect to persons it takes an ounce to balance an ounce; the fair house of Seem is never an equivalent for the house of Be. Nor can the loudest Pretension supply the place of the smallest piece of Performance. A just view of human nature would convince men of that truth (how hard to learn) that it is the man makes the place. Alfred, Washington, Lafayette, appear half divine to the people followed in their office by a nation's eye. Ambitious but pitiful persons see them and think it is the place alone that makes them great, and that if they sat in the same chairs they would be as much admired. All means are used to this end; all sorts of shame accumulated; and by and by perhaps they sit in the high seat only to make subtleness and pitifulness quite bare to the view of all men.

" In our own times, without satire, this mistake is so common that all society and government seems to be making believe, when we see such ignorant persons with a grave countenance taking their places as legislators and statesmen. This could not be, but that at intervals throughout society there are real men intermixed, whose natural basis is broad enough to sustain the paper men in common times, as the carpenter puts one iron rod in his banister to five or six wooden ones. But inexorable time, which brings opportunity once to every man, brings also to every man the hour of trial to prove him whether he is genuine, or whether he is counterfeit.

" The last ages have been characterized in history by the immense creation of property. The population of the globe, by the nations of western Europe in whom the superiority of intellect and organization seems to reside, has set at work so many skilful hands that great wealth is added. Now no dollar of property is created without some direct communication with nature, and of course some acquisition of knowledge and

practical power. The creation of all this property, and that by millions, not by a few, involves necessarily so much education of the minds of the proprietors. With power always comes the consciousness of power, and therefore indomitable millions have demanded forms of government more suited to the facts. Throughout Europe, throughout America, the struggle exists between those who claim new forms at all hazards, and those who prefer the old forms to the hazard of change. Of course on the whole is a steady progress of innovation. In London, they write on the fences, ' Of what use are the Lords ? ' In Spain and in Portugal, the liberal monarchists can scarce hold out against the mob. The South American States are too unsettled than that an ordinary memory can keep the run of the powers that be.

" The era seems marked in many countries by the separation of real power from its forms, and the continual interference of the popular opinion between the executive and its will. A levity before unknown follows. The word ' Revolution ' is stripped of its terrors, and they may have many in a year. They say in Paris, There will be no revolution to-day, for it rains.

" The struggle is envenomed by the great admixture of ignorance and selfishness on both sides which always depraves human affairs, and also prevents the war from being one purely of ideas. The innovators are led not by the best, but by the boldest, and often by the worst, who drive their private trade on, take advantage of the march of the principle. The conservatives make up for weakness by wiles and oppose indiscriminately the good and evil measures of their antagonists. Meantime Party, that bellowing hound that barks or fawns, that defamer and bargainer and unreasoning self-lover, distorts all facts and blinds all eyes. Party counts popularity success. Its whole aim ever is *to get the hurrah on our side.* It infects from the bar-room and ward-caucus up, all the veins of the state, stealing even into literature and religion; and in our age every Party has written history for itself as Gibbon, Lingard, Brodie, Hume, Hallam, Mitford.

" Meantime if we rise above the hubbub of parties, and the uncovered selfishness of many of the actors, we shall see that humanity is always the gainer, that the production of property has been the education of the producers, that the creation of so many new households and so many forcible and propertied citizens, has been the creation of lovers of order, knowledge and peace, and hating war. Trade and war are always antagonists. The progress of trade has been the death of war, universally. In these days nations have stretched out the hand to each other. In our times, it is said for the first time, has the word ' International ' been compounded. Some progress has been made by national compact in hindering offences against all the world as piracy and kidnapping. Mediation is made to supersede armies and navies. The projects with which the minds of philanthropists teem, are themselves a sure mark of progress. The black colony at Liberia, the proposition of the congress of nations to arbitrate controversies arising between two states, and so to prevent war or at least aid the right cause by the moral force of a decision, these are projects the bare starting of which in any practicable shape, proves civilization and Christianity. The mutual helpfulness of nations and the sympathy of all in the projects of each and the continual approximation by means of mechanical improvements seem to point at stricter union and simpler legislation, at a legislation more purely official, such as shall not hold out such bribes to vanity and avarice.

" The philosopher must console himself amidst the harsh discord of what is called politics by the reflection that its errors, like the errors of the planets, are periodic; that a firm bound is set by counterchecks in man to every excess, that the discipline which the events of every day administer to every man, tend always to make him a better citizen, and to make him independent of the mutations of parties and states."

Page 208, note 1. As the inventor by a mechanical device shows man's previous stupid waste of energy, and the man of science shows by his heresies the errors of the church's teaching, so Mr. Emerson held good men to their duty of protest against unjust law. Six years later the passage of the Fugitive Slave Law brought this question home to every brave man of the North, and this is what Mr. Emerson said to his Concord neighbors of the duty of the hour : —

"The last year has forced us all into politics. There is infamy in the air. I wake in the morning with a painful sensation which I carry about all day, and which, when traced home, is the odious remembrance of that ignominy which has fallen on Massachusetts. I have lived all my life in this State and never had any experience of personal inconvenience from the laws until now. They never came near me to my discomfort before. *But the Act of Congress of September 18th, 1850, is a law which every one of you will break on the earliest occasion, — a law which no man can obey, or abet the obeying, without loss of self-respect and forfeiture of the name of a gentleman.*"

Page 215, note 1. Mr. Cabot, in the Appendix F to his Memoir, giving an account of the lecture "Politics," printed the following passage as omitted in the essay. I cannot find it in the manuscript, and suppose it may have dropped out : —

"The State and Church guard their purlieus with jealous decorum. I sometimes wonder where their books find readers among mere mortals, who must sometimes laugh, and are liable to the infirmity of sleep. Yet politics rest on real foundations and cannot be treated with levity. But the foundation is not numbers or force, but character. Men do not see that all force comes from this, and that the disuse of force is the education of men to do without it. Character is the true theocracy. It will one day suffice for the government of the world. Absolutely speaking, I can only work for myself. The fight of Leonidas, the hemlock of Socrates, the cross of Christ, is not personal sacrifice for others, but fulfils a high necessity of his proper character: the benefit to others is merely contingent."

Page 215, note 2. In dealing with his children after they began to grow up, Mr. Emerson held to his theory. He did not command or forbid, but laid principles and facts before us and left the case in our hands, — a helpful confidence.

Page 215, note 3. His townsman, Squire Hoar, was an exception. "When I talked with him one day of some inequality of taxes in the town, he said it was his practice to pay whatever was demanded; for, though he might think the taxation large and very unequally proportioned, yet he thought the money might as well go in this way as any other." — "Samuel Hoar," *Lectures and Biographical Sketches.*

Page 216, note 1. When the question arose what epitaph to put upon the stone over Emerson's grave, a young man who had often been his guest wrote suggesting that much of the foregoing paragraph would be fitting, beginning "The wise man . . . needs no library," etc.

Page 217, note 1.

> His instant thought a poet spoke,
> And filled the age his fame ;
> An inch of ground the lightning strook,
> But lit the sky with flame.

"Fragments on the Poet," *Poems,* Appendix.

Page 220, note 1. In an address prefixed to the first number of the *Massachusetts Quarterly*, in 1848, Mr. Emerson said : " We believe politics to be nowise accidental or exceptional, but subject to the same laws with trees, earths and acids."

Page 221, note 1. In the first edition the wording was " full of fate," instead of " full of faith."

NOMINALIST AND REALIST

What Emerson said in writing of Plato [1] might, with little change, be said of himself and of his fairness in considering the " famous dispute of the Nominalists and Realists: " —

" The unity of Asia and the detail of Europe . . . he came to join, and by contact to enhance the energy of each. . . . In short, a balanced soul was born, perceptive of the two elements. . . . If he loved abstract truth, he saved himself by propounding the most popular of all principles, the absolute good, which rules rulers and judges the judge. If he made transcendental distinctions, he fortified himself by drawing all his illustrations from sources disdained by orators and polite conversers; . . . from pitchers and soup-ladles, . . . the shops of potters, horse-doctors, butchers, and fish-mongers. He cannot forgive in himself a partiality, but is resolved that the two poles of thought shall appear in his statement."

The wise men of the East and the Greek philosophers, and poets everywhere, spoke to Emerson, and in them he joyfully recognized his instinctive belief in the Soul-Universal, and in living Law. On the other hand, he was born into the hard and brilliant daylight of America in the youth of the nineteenth

[1] *Representative Men.*

century. While by sympathy a Realist, he admired the courage and performance of the Nominalist, *if only he would take the next step.*

This essay does not appear to have been given as a lecture. Even in the short motto Mr. Emerson recognizes both the ideal archetype and the happiness and privilege of the individual.

Page 225, note 1. In his Ode the hold which Beauty has upon him is less for what she has shown him than as a

Lavish, lavish Promiser.

Page 226, note 1. This is true in the body also, and notably in the face. Mr. Emerson's head furnishes a marked example. The sculptors who made good portraits of him — Daniel Chester French, whose fine bust represents him in his serene age, and Sidney H. Morse, who made an excellent statuette bust of him in his prime — recognized this. In the work of both the face has a very different expression according to the side looked at, one representing Emerson the thinker and speaker, the other Emerson among his friends.

Page 230, note 1. He foresaw truly. Four years later in England he found good men and customs and results, but falling far short of the ideal English men and institutions. Yet he chose rather to look at and give them credit for their best tendencies. And in America, six years later, Webster, an idol of his youth, turned his back on the ideals that he had stood for in the minds of the best New England, yet for a time was supported by Northern people.

Page 231, note 1. This contest occupied the Church and the universities from the end of the ninth century down; the Realists, with the motto *Universalia ante rem* (or *in re*), supporting revelation of law to the mind, but, as churchmen rather than philosophers, less broadly than the ancients. The Nominalists studied man and nature in the individual, "proved all things," and generalized later, — *Universalia post rem,* — and were the party of criticism and advance. The Reformation and modern science drew their strength from this class.

Page 231, note 2. Comparing this sentence with what he has said elsewhere, it is clear that he would have dwelt a little on the words "have been." Mr. Emerson's almost invariable rule in writing was, Never italicize.

Page 232, note 1. Compare "Aristocracy," *Lectures and Biographical Sketches.*

Page 233, note 1. Journal, 1839. "Plutarch fits me better than Southey or Scott, therefore I say, there is no age to good writing. Could I write as I would, I suppose the piece would be no nearer to Boston in 1839 than to Athens in the fiftieth Olympiad. Good thought, however expressed, saith to us, 'Come out of time; come to me in the Eternal.'"

Page 233, note 2. Mr. Emerson had no ear for music, unless for a ballad sung with expression, and by a woman. The wild music of nature and the wind singing in the Æolian harp in his window spoke to him, as scientific music did not. Yet he was interested in it, and occasionally liked to go to a concert.

Page 235, note 1. When all the competing reforms and theories were urged on him, instead of accepting or rejecting, he considered them calmly, and his practice was, like his Humble-bee, to —

Leave the chaff and take the wheat.

Page 236, note 1.

> Saw the endless rack of the firmament,
> And the sailing moon where the cloud was rent,
> And through man and woman and sea and star
> Saw the dance of Nature forward and far.
>
> "The Poet," Poems, Appendix.

Page 236, note 2. His reconciliation of two views here considered.

Page 238, note 1. Alphonso X., King of Castile [1] in the thirteenth century, a monarch of wonderful literary, legal and scientific achievement, whose criticism of Nature's ways was versified by Emerson among his early poems. He is reported to have said that, had God consulted him in the making of the world, he would have made it differently. Nature's wholesome influence in bringing us down to earth after our flights is symbolized by hellebore at the bottom of her draught, because the ancients found hellebore quieted the insane. It is said that the philosophers drank hellebore to clear their brains before intellectual labor. Whether this was true *helleborus* or *veratrum,* still used as a heart-sedative, is uncertain.

Page 240, note 1. Evolution is thus condensed into an answer to the Sphinx's question, —

> The fate of the man-child,
> The meaning of man ?

Page 240, note 2. Three communities then recently established.

Page 241, note 1. From "The Paint-King," by Washington Allston. " Plato had no external biography. If he had lover, wife, or children, we hear nothing of them. He ground

---

[1] See *A History of Spain,* by Ulick Ralph Burke, M. A.

them all into paint." This simile in *Representative Men*
Mr. Emerson no doubt owed to the line he quotes above.

Page 242, note 1. Compare the lines in the " Fragment
on Life " in the Appendix to the *Poems* beginning —

You shall not love me for what daily spends.

Page 242, note 2. As Nature presents different facets and
man sees the beauty of one at a time, so as a writer Emerson
reported on one aspect at a time. Hence his remarks in " Self-
Reliance" on a foolish consistency.

Page 247, note 1. This is a harsh statement of the loose-
ness with which a growing man should hold his beliefs of the
day. In this very connection an instance can be given of how
bravely sincere Mr. Emerson was. While temporarily preaching in East Lexington, he introduced into his discourse leaves
from a sermon written a few years before while he was a Boston minister. In delivering it, he suddenly stopped and quietly
said to his hearers, " The sentence which I have just read I do
not now believe," turned the page, and went on.

Page 248, note 1. These were the good Englishmen that
Mr. Alcott brought home with him, and who joined in the
Fruitlands experiment. Though they came in spite of Mr.
Emerson's warning, they weighed rather heavily upon his
mind, but they were not of his kind.

NEW ENGLAND REFORMERS

The Society which met at Amory Hall from 1841 to
1848 was the Church of the Disciples, of which Rev. James
Freeman Clarke was the minister.

In the period of the Awakening in New England those

who felt its influence wished to join others with them in helpful movements, and zealously urged organization; but the schemes which they felt to be of first importance varied with the individual temperament or need, and the individual was to take counsel of no man. Persons reputed high-minded and generous were eagerly assailed by competing advocates of measures for the regeneration of man, varying much in their wisdom, and usually woefully partial. Mr. Emerson stood rather for the Individual than for organization, believing that the universal or common mind of men would take care of the latter. His hospitality to thought, however, and the belief that he had means and influence, drew all the reformers to his door, sure that he would see that they brought the one thing needful, and join in proclaiming this newest and best gospel. Already in 1840 he had spoken on "Reforms" in the course on *The Present Age*, and in the following year had said a good word for "Man the Reformer" before the Boston Mercantile Library Association.

This essay shows well his character. Although for years his time and sympathy, his patience and his power, had been over-freely drawn upon by the wise and the foolish, he honored and defended such wisdom and courage, or even trace of it, as each brought. Many of these pilgrims were unpresentable, rude and tedious ; few had any eyes and heart for Nature, and almost all were without any sense of humor. But Mr. Emerson's high hope for man, if only some leaven of the Spirit were in him, made him gracious and forbearing to the "monotones," and welcome the wise and brave. So he treats his subject hopefully, and even the absurdities with good humor and a characteristically light hand.

Mr. George W. Cooke,[1] speaking of the charge made

1 *Ralph Waldo Emerson, his Life, Writings, and Philosophy.* Boston, J. R. Osgood & Co., 1881.

against Mr. Emerson of neglect and undervaluing of special reforms, says: "He would aim at the very centre of all vice and defect, dry up that fountain, and then all the lesser evils would cease. His method may be wrong, but it is the method of every great moral and religious teacher that the world has known."

Yet Mr. Emerson was a little troubled at his want of sympathy, and asks, after these strange and noisy conventions were over, "And where were the men of genius whilst these coarse missionaries were making odious the high doctrines of temperance, love and the life of nature which they had first broached in solemn hymns? Alas, . . . I saw them each taking himself in charge to keep himself silent nor plague the world longer with the harsh counsel of reform, drugging and quieting, how he best could, the nerves that were once harp-strings on which every sun-beam played music."

The motto did not appear in the first edition. Its last lines recall a fragment of verse printed in the Appendix to the *Poems* : —

> The archangel Hope
> Looks to the azure cope,
> Waits through dark ages for the morn,
> Defeated day by day, but unto victory born.

Page 251, note 1. The " Chardon Street Convention " was called by the " Friends of Universal Progress " early in 1840 and lasted three days. It was followed by two more the same year. In the *Dial* an amusing account of this occasion, seen through Mr. Emerson's eyes, was published by him. It is printed in *Lectures and Biographical Sketches.*

Page 252, note 1. Mrs. Emerson, with her ready interest in domestic chemistry, which she learned from her brother

Dr. Charles T. Jackson, no doubt supplied this good argument.

Page 252, note 2. The Fruitlands Community was handicapped in getting its support from its lean acres by its theories. Cattle must not be enslaved; animal manure was abhorrent; all cultivation must be done by man-power when time could be spared from contemplation and high discussion; insects must not be murdered. Meat, fish, poultry, milk, cheese, butter, honey, eggs, as food, and wool and feathers as clothing or bedding, were unlawful, because obtained by wrongs done to the animal creation; leavened bread and fermented drinks were poisonous; cane-sugar, molasses, rice, and spice, and cotton for clothing, were products of slave-labor. Such grain and fruits as could be raised without manure, and wild nuts and berries and maple sugar, must furnish the food, and linen the raiment, for these good but over-refining people. Necessity, which knows no law, prevented their carrying these rules quite to extremes.

Page 253, note 1. The Antinomians, who troubled the early days of the New England colony, held that, as the elect cannot fall from grace nor forfeit the divine favor, any wicked actions which they may commit are not really sinful, and consequently they have no need to confess their sins or to break them off by repentance.

Page 254, note 1. This parable, written in Mr. Emerson's journal, was suggested by the views advanced by his visitors : "You ask, O Theanor, said Amphitryon, that I should go forth from this palace with my wife and children, and that you and your family may enter and possess it. The same request in substance has been often made to me before by numbers of persons. Now I also think that I and my wife ought to go forth from the house and work all day in the fields, and lie at night under some thicket, but I am waiting where I am only until some god shall point out to me which among all these applicants, yourself or some other, is the rightful claimant.''

Page 255, note 1. In the previous year Thoreau, Alcott, and Lane (his English friend) had been arrested for refusal on conscientious grounds to pay their taxes. Mr. Sanborn in his Memoir of Alcott quotes from a letter of Thoreau to Emerson the following testimony of the officer of the law as to the grounds of refusal: '' When Staples (the deputy-sheriff) came . . . my sister Helen asked him what he thought Mr. Alcott meant, — what his idea was, — and he answered, 'I vum, I believe it was nothing but principle, for I never heard a man talk honester.' ''

. *Page 256, note 1.* The *Non-Resistant* newspaper was started in Boston five years before this time. Its editors were William Lloyd Garrison, Edmund Quincy, and Mrs. Maria Chapman.

Page 256, note 2. Among the active and interesting *doctrinaires* that thronged the ways in those days was Edward Palmer, who wrote a book to show that money was the root of evil and urged the abolishment of property, each person to serve others by exercising his own gift. On the title-page he added to his name the words '' who has nothing to do with money,'' and for a time held stoutly to this abstinence.

Mr. Cabot in his Memoir (pp. 415, 416) quotes, among other writings of Mr. Emerson's upon money, the following: '' We may very well and honestly have theoretical and practical objections to it; if they are fatal to the use of money and barter, let us disuse them; if they are less grave than the inconvenience of abolishing traffic, let us not pretend to have done with it whilst we eat and drink and wear and breathe it.''

Page 260, note 1. The spirit of the times was working in the schools. Five years earlier, as a result of a memorial of the American Institute of Instruction, headed by George Barrell Emerson, the Massachusetts legislature laid aside other business to consider how the then wretched schools of the Commonwealth could be improved, and chose Horace Mann, then president of the Senate, the secretary of the new Board of Education. His zeal and extreme devotion in these very days was regenerating the schools. It is remarkable to find in this essay suggestions for object-teaching and field-work, and some election in studies, and criticism of the mediæval rating of the classics, — ideas which hardly took root in the schools and colleges until twenty-five years later. Yet Mr. Emerson prized the classics: it was neglect of their beauty in too much gerund-grinding that disgusted him.

Page 261, note 1. With entire faith in the power of the better to quietly displace the worse, if opposition were not aroused, he prized an earnest priest more than a coarse or narrow denier. Once after a conversation at which a radical had explained that the death of Jesus might have been simulated and planned beforehand for effect on the people, and he thereafter kept in hiding, Mrs. Emerson said to her husband, " Should you have liked to have the children hear that ? " " No," he answered, " it is odious to have lilies pulled up and skunk-cabbages planted in their places."

Page 264, note 1. The communities at Brook Farm in West Roxbury (see " Historic Notes of Life and Letters in New England," *Lectures and Biographical Sketches*), at Hopedale in Worcester County, founded by the Rev. Adin Ballou, and probably that at Northampton, as the Fruitlands experiment, had already failed.

These communities are often alluded to in the *Dial*, espe-

III

cially Brook Farm. Interesting accounts of them by members may be found in Hawthorne's writings, and in the volumes of the *Atlantic, Century,* and *Overland Monthly* magazines.

Page 264, note 2. Mr. Emerson's doubts were justified. Speaking of the material of these communities, he said: "These reformers were of a new class. Instead of the fiery souls of the Puritans, bent on hanging the Quaker, burning the witch, and banishing the Romanist, these were gentle souls with peaceful and even genial dispositions, casting sheep's eyes even on Fourier and his houris."

Page 267, note 1. A part of this page was taken from the lecture on "Politics," to the teaching of which it is akin.

Page 269, note 1. This distinction between talent and genius is made by him in many places.

Page 272, note 1.

> The heavens that now draw him
> With sweetness untold,
> Once found, — for new heavens
> He spurneth the old.
>
> "The Sphinx," *Poems.*

Page 273, note 1.

> I serve you not, if you I follow
> Shadow-like o'er hill and hollow, etc.
>
> "Étienne de la Boéce," *Poems.*

Page 274, note 1. Mr. Emerson dealt with this mood in the poems "Alphonso of Castile" and "Blight."

Page 274, note 2. This phrase comes from a fragment of Pindar, in the older English version of Plutarch's *Morals,* rendered, "Tread the floors of Hell with necessities as hard as iron." Professor Goodwin's translation gives it, "We are bound to the floors," etc. — *Consolation to Apollonius.*

Page 274, note 3.

Postquam epulis Bacchoque modum lassata voluptas
Imposuit, longis Cæsar producere noctem
Inchoat adloquiis summaque in sede iacentem
Linigerum placidis conpellat Achorea dictis:
' O sacris devote senex, quodque arguit ætas,
Non neclecte deis, Phariæ primordia gentis
Terrarumque situs volgique edissere mores
Et ritus formasque deum; quodcunque vetustis
Insculptum est adytis, profer noscique volentes
Prode deos.   Si Cecropium sua sacra Platona
Maiores docuere tui, quis dignior umquam
Hoc fuit auditu, mundique capacior hospes ?
Fama quidem generi Pharias me duxit ad urbes,
Sed tamen et vestri; media inter prœlia semper
Stellarum cœlique plagis superisque vacavi,
Nec meus Eudoxi vincetur fastibus annus.
Sed cum tanta meo vivat sub pectore virtus
Tantus amor veri, nihil est, quod noscere malim
Quam fluvii causas per sæcula tanta latentis
Ignotumque caput; spes sit mihi certa videndi
Niliacos fontes: bellum civile relinquam.'

Lucan, *De Bello Civili*, Lib. X.

Page 276, note 1. Here is the reaction from the intoxication of persons which is told of in the poems " The Park "
and " Manners."

Page 277, note 1. The material aid which Mr. Emerson
gave unasked to supply the manifest need of some of his spirit-
ually-minded guests, he held slight in comparison with the
stimulus to thought which he often found in their society.
The labourer was worthy of his hire.

Page 279, note 1. This was his philosophic farmer-neighbor, Mr. Edmund Hosmer.

Page 280, note 1. In one of his addresses to students Mr. Emerson said, "The relation of men of thought to society is always the same ; they refuse that necessity of mediocre men, to take sides. They keep their own equilibrium. The sun's path is never parallel to the equator."

Page 280, note 2. See Montaigne's Essays, Book III., chapter i., *On Utility and Honesty.*

Plutarch relates that Alexander the Great sent Onesecritus, a disciple of Diogenes, to the Indian sages who lived a retired life, to desire them to come to him. Some of them were haughty, but Dandamis behaved with civility. "When Onesecritus had given him an account of Pythagoras, Socrates and Diogenes, he said, ' They appear to have been men of genius, but to have lived with too passive a regard for the laws.' Others say Dandamis entered into no discourse with the messenger, but only asked ' Why Alexander had taken so long a journey.' "

Page 281, note 1. Rev. Dr. Hale in his *Ralph Waldo Emerson* relates that, when a youth in whom they both were interested took high honors at a Cambridge exhibition, he addressed Mr. Emerson, expecting delighted sympathy in the young man's triumph. "Yes," was the answer, "I did not know he was so fine a fellow. And now if something will fall out amiss — if he should be unpopular with his class, or his father should fail in business, or if some other misfortune can befall him — all will be well." Dr. Hale adds : "I was green enough to be inwardly indignant at what seemed to me the cynicism of the philosopher. But I did not know that when he was eight years old his father had died, and that to the penury . . . of those early days — to his mother's de-

termination that the boy should be bred at Harvard College, to
the careful struggles by which each penny was made to work
the miracles of the broken bread by the Sea of Galilee — he
owed . . . much of the vigor, the rigor and the manhood of
his life.''

Page 282, note 1. Mr. Emerson took especial delight in
the noble passage to this purpose, in Scott's *Lord of the Isles,*
where the Abbot in vain tries to lay his ban upon Robert
Bruce : —

> De Bruce ! I rose with purpose dread
> To speak my curse upon thy head,
> And give thee, as an outcast, o'er
> To him who burns to shed thy gore :
> But, like the Midianite of old,
> Who stood on Zophim, heaven controlled,
> I feel within mine aged breast
> A power that will not be repressed.
>
> .   .   .   .
>
> De Bruce, thy sacrilegious blow
> Hath at God's altar slain thy foe ; —
> O'ermastered yet by high behest,
> I bless thee, and thou shalt be blest !

Page 283, note 1. Compare the lines in the *Poems,* —

> And conscious Law is king of kings.
>
> > "Woodnotes," II.

> The patient Dæmon sits
>   With roses and a shroud ;
> He hath his way and deals his gifts, —
>   But ours is not allowed.
>
> > "The World-Soul."

Page 284, note 1.   " Let a man's social aims be proportioned to his means and power. 1 do not pity the misery of a man underplaced ; that will right itself presently ; but I pity the man overplaced.   A certain quantity of power belongs to a certain quantity of faculty.   Whoever wants more power than is the legitimate attraction of his faculty, is a politician, and must pay for that excess; must truckle for it." — " Aristocracy," *Lectures and Biographical Sketches.*

The Riverside Press

Electrotyped and printed by H. O. Houghton & Co.
Cambridge, Mass, U. S. A.

www.ingramcontent.com/pod-product-compliance
Lightning Source LLC
LaVergne TN
LVHW012206040326
832903LV00003B/146